Shadows of the Dark

Shadows of the Dark

John Zaffis and Brian McIntyre

iUniverse, Inc.

New York Lincoln Shanghai

Shadows of the Dark

iUniverse, Inc.

For information address:
iUniverse, Inc.
2021 Pine Lake Road, Suite 100
Lincoln, NE 68512
www.iuniverse.com

ISBN: 0-595-32509-2

Printed in the United States of America

To my wife Cheryl, for putting up with me in my pursuit of ghosts and haunted homes for so many years, especially with people calling all hours of the night seeking help. To my daughters Erin and Aime'e, for their belief and support in me. To my son Chris, who I know someday will be getting into the work. I never realized how much you paid attention to all the things with which I got involved until that day you were asked to speak about my work. I heard some of your answers. I asked you how you knew all that, and you said to me, "Dad did you think I was sitting there, watching TV all that time? It was more interesting listening to you on the phone with some of the people, and I realized that they can't all be nuts." This is just my way of saying that all of you are my world, and without my wife and kids I have nothing.

This book is also dedicated to the memory of my mom and dad, Babe and John Zaffis. God only knows how much I miss you two every day of my life, and I know all the pain is gone now. I know you are with God, and I know that someday we will all be together, just like the old days. To my uncle Ed Warren Boy, without spending so much time with you over the years and learning so much about the paranormal, I do not think I would understand the work the way I do today, and I will always be thankful for that. Finally, my special thanks to Brian McIntyre for his patience and knack for sifting through my notes, my tapes, and my mind to piece together my life and work to put it into a book

John Zaffis

At the time this book was published Brian McIntyre had worked on over 125 cases and had assisted in 19 exorcisms with John Zaffis. He would like to offer his heartfelt appreciation to Brendan Keenan for his help with editing this book.

Contents

Preface

Demonic infestation, in one form or another, is not the rare phenomena it once was. In the last thirty-five or forty years, it has become a veritable plague in this country, if not around the world. That it is a reality—malignant spirits not only haunt places but harass people and invade and control their bodies—is the least thing to be learned from the author of this book. I have known John Zaffis for all of twenty-five years, and in my capacity as an exorcist have found him to be as sober and capable an investigator of the occult as one could ask for. Not readily inclined to believe every allegation of the preternatural, or paranormal, he has yet to present me with a case that I have not found genuine—not that I have succeeded with all of them!

It will be asked, who are the evil spirits, the devils or demons, of whom we speak? They are none other than the fallen angels of whom we read in The Apocalypse, or book of Revelation, of St. John the Apostle. "And there was a great battle in heaven, Michael and his angels fought with the dragon, and the dragon fought and his angels. And they prevailed not, neither was their place found any more in heaven. And that great dragon was cast out, that old serpent, who is called the devil and Satan, who seduces the whole world; and he was cast unto the earth, and his angels were thrown down with him" (Revelation 12:7–9). Of this same invisible horde, St. Paul tells us, "Our wrestling is not against flesh and blood; but against the principalities and powers, against the rulers of the world of this darkness, against the spirits of wickedness in the high places" (Ephesians 6:12).

Why the temporary epidemic of demonic infestation—the various forms which you will here read? Leaving aside the root cause (as I see it) in the religious upheaval of our day—this is one that the II Vatican Council precipitated—the immediate or proximate cause of this spiritual plague is involvement in the occult. Witchcraft is the religion of the day. "All these things I will give you, if falling down you will adore me!" (Matthew 4:9) To those who will deal with him by even ordinary superstitious practices, even unwittingly, the Devil promises knowledge and power beyond the natural, power beyond that which has been divinely appointed to man in exchange that the demon (or demons) may have power over them beyond his or their own allotted limits. Not that demonic obsession or possession is infallibly the penalty of witchcraft, or that it is found only in the case of those who practice or dabble in it. Many are simply its victims—victims of hexes or curses. May John Zaffis' timely work serve to warn the first and alert the rest. "The Lord is my refuge" (Psalm 93:22).

—Bishop Robert McKenna, O.P.

Foreword

Perhaps the most difficult thing to accept about supernatural experiences, or those of preternatural origin, is the reality factor. Are these experiences or occurrences actually real? The answer, in my experience as a psychic researcher, is quite clear—an answer that many would rather not accept. The answer is absolutely yes! Skeptics, researchers, and the sufferers of the assaults of severe hauntings do not want to even believe such occurrences are a possibility, but such situations, which can be menacing, are rather commonplace.

Deep thought on the origin of such peril obviously brings few clear-cut answers. Instead more questions arise. On the other hand how can a serious researcher deny such evidence as biting, punching, moving objects, horrific noises and visions, disgusting and revolting odors, and countless other occurrences. There are cases we refer to as human spirit, others which affect those of psychic ability, and those which can only be classified as inhuman. As a researcher my job is to gather evidence to identify the source of these problems and provide the proper closure to these extreme case studies.

This book deals with the more outrageous and frightening cases that have come into my hands over the past thirty years. Most of the cases herein are of preternatural origin, meaning that they have occurred outside of the natural existence as we know it, but on a level that is strictly devious and diabolical. Negative intelligences that orchestrate such activities are often thought to be mythical or that which is constructed by an unstable mind. Instead we see a level of consciousness that does indeed plague many people, families, or specific dwellings. The term *demonology* is often assigned to this particular area of study. *Demonology* is the general study of the hierarchy of evil, negative intelligences, and their direct attributes, missions, personalities, rankings, powers, and direct interferences in human lives. This field of research has been pushed to the backburner of conventional thought, but it will never be dismissed because it is a real area of study, regardless of how subtle these energies may be.

Today, those studying psychic research are essentially working against two distinct blockades: the inhuman intelligences themselves and those who are unwilling to believe that such spirits exist. I know these spirits exist. I have witnessed their wrath on individuals and families, their terror at the expense of human beings, like you the reader. I hope that the true examples reflected within this text will give you insight into an area few tread, many refuse to believe or just want no part of. This is the true story of perhaps the world's greatest mystery—the relatively unknown reality that exists in regards to spirit and the struggle many endure in the process of finding out that such "things" are real.

John Zaffis

Interview with a Psychic Researcher

Interview with a Psychic Researcher
(Interview conducted by Brian McIntyre with questions answered by John Zaffis)

The following information was taken from many of the tapes in which I spoke with John Zaffis about the field of psychic research, the study of demonology, and many other forms of belief that have often been stigmatized and hidden in the fringe of society. This chapter is meant to inherently discuss some of the theories, types of situations, the actual physical phenomena, dangers, and underlying themes that one encounters in this avant-garde territory of study. I have had the unique opportunity to work on many of the cases that Zaffis obtains from his organization, the Paranormal Research Society of New England, as well as cases that he has handled for his aunt and uncle, Ed and Lorraine Warren, who head the New England Society for Psychic Research. Zaffis has shown me first-hand many of the types of situations that are out there. As of the writing of this book, not only have I been exposed to the element of human spirit, but also to the demonic realm of evil. What he speaks about is not a concoction of myth and an avid imagination, but instead a reality that many will face in their lifetime. Many human beings will have experiences of a psychic nature, whereas others may not. The reality, regardless of whether these experiences are universal, is that ghosts exist. There are travesties caused by demonic entities. There is another side to life that often goes unrecognized, but it is still present.

I understand Ed and Lorraine Warren, your aunt and uncle, had a great impact on your decision to become a psychic researcher. How exactly did your interest take hold?

"My grandmother, Ed's mom, had lived with my family, and I used to look forward to Ed and Lorraine stopping over to visit my grandmother. I couldn't wait to hear the stories they had about their work. I'd sit there, very quietly, intrigued by the stories they had to tell. At that time, he did not get into anything too heavy or severe at that point because I was too young at the time, and in addition, my mom, Ed's sister, was extremely petrified of anything pertaining to the supernatural. As years went by I heard him speak more and more about the different cases he and Lorraine had been on. "Ed and Lorraine Warren are considered by many to be the foremost authorities on the matter of ghosts, demonic possession, and psychic research. They have investigated thousands of cases and have been involved in the field for over fifty years. They worked on the Amityville Horror case, as well as many other prominent cases. "When I was about sixteen, I became very interested in the subject matter. At this time in my life, something very special happened to me: something I have subsequently never forgotten and never will forget. At this time, an apparition appeared to me at the foot of my bed. It formed and just stood there looking at me. The form was transparent, allowing me to actually see right through it. It was full figured, and I could tell that it was a male whose head was shaking back and forth as if to say 'no.' Honestly, it scared the living daylights out of me, and I ran downstairs to tell my mother. I was telling her about it when she asked me if the presence said anything. I replied that it was shaking its head back and forth. My mother looked at me with an intense, serious look, saying that my grandfather always used to do that, and she guaranteed that it was him who had appeared to me. My mother never quite got over that situation because there was no way for me to know that he did that particular nod all the time, which was very characteristic of him. Shortly after that, my grandmother passed on. Perhaps he was coming back to get her; who knows? It was after this experience that I started to think that ghosts indeed did exist, and there had to be more to the world in which we know. I thought that there really had to be something to it all, and I began to do a great deal of reading and researching, digging deeper into the subject, getting my hands onto anything that I could that appeared to be a true representation of the matter.

"Through all this I began to speak to Ed more extensively, and I would beg him to death to be able to start going on cases, but Ed and Lorraine had a rule that no one under the age of 18 would be allowed to go on any of the cases regardless of how light in nature they were. I understood what they meant, and, on top of it all, I was family—that gave me a double whammy getting involved with the research end of it all. Ed knew for a fact that he would have to deal with my mom if anything happened.

"So, anyhow, after that I began to check out some of the different haunted locations to see if there was anything to it all. The very first haunted place I ever went to was the Phelps Mansion in Stratford, Connecticut. This was when I was about sixteen or seventeen. At this point in time, the mansion was abandoned. The property had changed hands several times, and the last occupants of the home were in actuality not a family. Instead, a nursing home occupied the large premises. Many of the nurses were experiencing many types of phenomena until the mansion was hit by a major fire and was initially closed down. At that site, people saw apparitions, were touched, felt cold spots, and encountered many other interesting occurrences. From then on, it was abandoned, too ruined to be restored.

"I still remember two of my buddies and I decided we wanted to go and check out the haunted house and see what was really going on with it. All the doors and windows were broken, and we went into big hallway at the foot of the main staircase. To this day, I don't know if there was someone on the second floor or what exactly it really was, but I heard a bunch of strange noises. The noises were real and physical, causing my heart to pound and my fight-or-flight reaction to kick in. The three of us headed right out the front door and ran as fast as we possibly could to get away from there. To this day, I don't know if there was something unexplainable occurring there, but I sure heard noises. It fueled me to search on to try to make sense of this uncertain world of hauntings. Anyway, that was really my first haunted house experience. It took place in the early 1970s and was the first time I went into an area rumored to be haunted.

"Over the next few years, until I was eighteen, I would poke around and do a lot of reading. When I was actually eighteen, I spoke with Ed and told him that since now I am legal, that I would like to start going on cases. He looked at me with a very serious look on his face and he and Lorraine looked at each other. He said, 'Ok, come on kid, we're going to go downstairs and talk for a bit.' We went downstairs into his Halloween room, and we discussed the true nature of the *Work*, a term we use to refer to psychic research. I remember following him down the stairs, curious about what he was going to tell me. At the time, I really did not have any idea how in depth and absorbed one becomes once they enter the Work. I thought busting ghosts was simple—go in, talk to the people, and leave. I did not understand how far a person must go to help people who are having a terrible haunting.

"'I want you to realize something; once you've been touched by the supernatural and once you get involved, your life will never be the same,' Ed said to me.

"Little did I know at the time what he really meant. Years later, now I know. As we were sitting there, I looked at him and said, 'Yeah, I'm not too concerned or worried about it.' Ed looked at me and said, 'I am. There is one thing you better always remember. You are my nephew and my blood. People will seek you out and they will always look for you, especially on the other side when you get involved with the Work,' said Ed. 'Each step along the way you will cross farther and farther over the threshold, falling deeper into this Work. You will not go unblemished either, John. There are repercussions for your involvement. You will be targeted by forces that you do not yet understand for your involvement in cases. You've never experienced the demonic, but if you decide to pursue this Work you will. The risks are there and ready to grab hold of you. You'll be tempted every way possible to bring about the possibility of your own destruction. Your life will be far from normal. The Devil will try to divide and conquer and will do so by cloaking himself in secrecy. I've seen this all firsthand and have been put to the test and will as long as I live. Once you dive deep into this Work, you really cannot turn back. They remember who you are and will seek retaliation for treading into their world.'

"'Forces that few know about are there whether you choose to believe it or not, John. You need to expect the unexpected and will never be able to turn your back. It is all too easy to be *set up* by those who seek to ruin you.'

"He just sat there, looking at me, continuing to talk about the different aspects of the Work, trying to give me an overview of the reality of not only ghosts, but the cunning forces reflected in the background of all religions that are often unheard of. Honestly, I absorbed what he said, but at this time, I did not have the knowledge or experience to fully and deeply accept what he was saying.

"Well, he was right. Over the years I have been put to the test. There have been instances where the other side has tried to break me and tempt me, but through faith, you combat these temptations and stay strong. Even to this day, occasionally some type of case will arise that seems legit, but is nothing more than a 'setup,' as my uncle referred to it.

"A case in New York not so long ago reflected this. I was called in to investigate the claims a mother made about her son's new apartment. He had recently moved out and was having terrible nightmares, seeing shadowy figures in the apartment, hearing voices, and although a nonbeliever, he was deeply afraid of what had been happening to him at this point. He had confided in his mother, and she sought out help.

"However, this case was not so cut and dry. When I got to the home, I was immediately confronted by one of the roommates who asked if I was Ed Warren. When she entered the room, my ears started buzzing like crazy. After leaving the case and speaking with another researcher, he also picked up on something when this individual entered the room. I, of course, told her that I was not my uncle. The woman was disappointed and just smirked, her deep-set eyes staring at me like they were on fire. She was very defensive and was altogether sinister. She wanted to be interviewed on tape, so I allowed her the opportunity to speak. What ended up happening is that she directly challenged me.

"She basically came out and stated that she practiced black magic and used candles to invoke spirits. She even insinuated that after being married at a young age by blood, her brother had taken the life of someone as a sacrifice to his god. Her challenging persisted, and after a short while, the situation was becoming altogether uncomfortable. I knew why I was brought there and I left.

"Not all confrontations like this are so physical. Even involvement in a particular case can cause daunting and forbidding dealings to happen in your own home. Researching does not allow you to look at cases from an outside point of view. You are directly involved and can feel the repercussions at some times within your years involved with the Work.

"After dealing with my uncle in our discussion, it was then I went on my first investigation. It was then I got involved with and experienced the negative aspects of the Work, getting into the demonology end of it all.

"Did I really believe the devils, demons, imps, and all that really existed? No. I didn't believe it at all. I didn't think any of it was for real, but the more I became involved with cases and the more I became witness to it over the years, seeing actual exorcisms and assisting in them, that I realized it was all a reality.

"I do not perform exorcisms. I believe this has to come from the clergy, regardless of religious belief. I am a very analytical person and feel that it is absolutely necessary for the exorcist to be pure in belief and a person with a strong belief from deep within to perform an actual exorcism. I've seen a lot of priests and ministers over the years fall victim to the demonic because they were not pure of faith. You will see them come and go when exorcists get involved with such negative aspects of the world.

"I remember getting involved with my first case. It was not a public case, but a private one. The case pertained to a young woman that was being tormented. She was physically attacked where actual bites and scratches would appear on her. We had set up camp in the house overnight to be able to document some of the phenomena that had been taking place. Well, this young girl would start hollering, and we would run right into the room. You could actually see scratches where she could not get her hands to reach and there would be exactly three marks. In this Work, three is a number associated with the demonic. (Footnote: Three is seen as the traditional hour of Jesus' death, and is an insult by the Devil and his hierarchy to the Trinity.) There were also bite marks on the client, resembling bite marks like that of teeth. This really opened my eyes to some of the types of things that could take place.

"Over the years I have been involved with exorcisms from all different types of faiths and nationalities. It is really a bizarre and unique world that most people have not been touched by.

"When someone tells me that they do not believe in the supernatural or anything pertaining to the supernatural has not directly occurred to them, I always say 'I hope it remains that way, because once you are touched by or involved in the supernatural, your life will never be the same.'"

"The first case I went on with my aunt and uncle affected me to the point that I knew exactly what happened and I was witness to the occurrences, but I did not still believe 100 percent at that point. I was still trying to look for something logical. Was there something around that she was using to make the scratch marks, maybe, but the bite marks, no. Those bites could not have been duplicated the way they were done and there was no one else in the area when this transpired.

"It opened my eyes up to the fact that I did give it thought for several days afterward. If these things could really happen and there are such things as demonic influences, I was ever more convinced that there had to be a Higher Power, or there has to be a God. With me, when you look at something, there is black and white, there's Yin and Yang, there are always two sides to everything. If there is a negative here, has to be a positive.

"In the beginning of all this, I was eighteen years old, young and unaware that anything could have existed on a spiritual level. Sure, I was taught in school that God existed, that spirit was real, but I never really accepted any of it at all. These types of experiences started to make me realize that there is definitely a Higher Being, which I refer to as God. People use many terms to identify this Supreme Being, and I accept that. As time went on over the years, being directly involved with a multitude of cases, witnessing people being hurt, people going through the devastations that they would directly experience, especially at the infestation point.

"At this point is when a person will actually have things start to occur within their own homes. Knockings, banging, and the flickering of lights on and off are just some of the phenomena one might experience at this point. One of the key factors, and I've seen it over the years with several different cases that I have been a part of, is the fact that someone will hear a knock on the front door or perhaps the back door. Or perhaps it will be on a window and the initial response will be to open that door or window. Believe it or not, this actually grants permission for the entity to enter. You will, on the other hand, not see a full-bodied devil, demon, or ghost enter, but access was indeed granted, as future events will reveal. I can't even count how many people over the years have relayed this exact experience to me. They actually physically went to answer the door, but to their surprise, there was no one or nothing there at all which could be seen. As soon as I hear that, I know the door was actually opened for something to enter not only their homes, but also their lives. It sounds like something right out of a horror movie, but believe me when I tell you that it actually happens.

"Dealing directly with the Warrens for so many years on countless cases was the best education I could have received. There is only so much you can learn from books. Experiencing phenomena firsthand and being involved with a case from beginning to end is the best possible education you can receive in this field of study. You get to see the family, experience the phenomena, evaluate the situation, document what is going on, and try to obtain closure. Ed and Lorraine have had some of the most fascinating cases that one can comprehend. Attending these cases, I got a chance to live out the Work.

"Driving home from a case with them was a great tool as well. Ed would look over at me and ask what I thought about the case, the people involved, all the logistics, and the circumstances. It was a time for me to give my interpretations and be corrected if necessary. At this point, I was able to also ask questions and get answers, which I did not understand at that particular time. My aunt and uncle are the best at what they do, plain and simple. I could not have had better teachers than them. They are very straightforward and I could ask them anything and get a straight answer. Their quizzes were meant to help me, and they did.

"Another fascinating aspect in dealing with the Warrens was the schooling I got from Lorraine. She is clairvoyant and used her gift of discernment on the very cases her and Ed would investigate. Typically on a case, I would sit with Ed in the company of the family and listen to the interview. Lorraine would go about the house to discern. She would be crucial in many circumstances. She would pick up on the type of spirit that was there, what level it was, or she would often pick up on if someone had spirit around or attached to them. Other times, she would pick up on an object that tied in to the case. I got to speak with her constantly over cups of coffee on how she did this and how important it was to the very cases they worked on.

"In regards to Ed, I have spent innumerable hours one on one with him in his office, being directly tutored in the area of demonology. I was taught the different levels of the demonic, their functions, what they can do, what they respond to, and about cases they have come up in. Ed would teach me what to look for, what precautions to take, and how to identify and classify what I came across.

"Ultimately, the two of them have exposed me to the psychological end of it all, the dealing with the people, conducting the interviews, interpreting and picking up on their emotions. They have also taught me the ropes on classification and what is what in the field. They filled my formative years in the Work with so much knowledge—knowledge that was key then and will be all the days of my life in this field. There is so much to learn, and it is impossible to learn everything about the occult sciences. One can become very knowledgeable, but is always a student of the unknown.

*Is there a direct connection in the field of psychic research pertaining to one's faith and how it is incorporated in the work?

"I was never a strong Catholic beforehand at all. I grew up in the 1970s and we questioned everything, and I mean everything. We questioned the Devil, we questioned God, and we questioned our parents and society. There was not anything that my generation did not seem to question. When looking at the big picture, just like all the others, I would ask myself many questions: If there is a God, why does he let unspeakable situations happen to ordinary people? Why would He let things enter into their lives to hurt or torment them? Well, it is not God. God gave us free will and with that free will, a lot of people give permission for these entities to enter. That is something I have learned and truly and wholeheartedly believe. When such circumstances occur, it is more times than not the result of one's very own free will. God allows these things to exist, but it is by free will that they are negative. Everything is created positively, but corruption based on free will may cause that positive to cross over to the negative.

"My religious values as far as being a Roman Catholic hit home deeply after being involved with the Work for a few years. It was a foundation for the realization that there is a true God, a Supreme Being that does indeed watch out for us. I do not try to convert anyone, and am far from a religious hothead. I will work with any religion that embraces the positive side of life. I do encourage those experiencing some of the darker hauntings to seek out religion, but to do so within their own belief systems that makes them comfortable.

"It is a continuous battlefield, once you get involved with the work and research and trying to get people help. The Devil will constantly challenge you on all different levels. Just when you least expect it, it could strike and strike hard. You have to remember; those like me that are involved in the work are a constant threat to the Devil and his plans. They (the demonic hierarchy) are trying to do the deeds and win the souls of the victims and we are trying to help the victims understand that.

"Oftentimes I can tell you a couple of days ahead of time when a case is coming up. Totally bizarre types of situations will occur where something can be related or tied in with a case. You will usually be involved with three cases, especially when it is a demonic case. These cases will usually be similar and will take place in three different locations with the same type of phenomena happening. You will pick up on things as you go along and they will intensify.

"With me in the beginning, one of the key factors with knowing that something was there was that I would always be tapped on the top of my head, and things would intensify from there on. What I mean by intensify is that it preys upon the things it knows you are afraid of, or that which bothers you. One of the things I absolutely hated more than anything was anybody or anything touching me. When something touches you and you turn around and there is not an actual person standing there, no hands or anything to physically see, it can really shake you up.

"On an investigation several years ago, there were nine other researchers besides myself in attendance. The case involved an elderly woman who claimed unseen forces were attacking her sexually within her home. We sat in her bedroom waiting to see if anything would happen or if anyone would pick up on anything. There were cameras and audio surveillance set up to try to obtain some type of evidence. During the investigation, I felt two very strong hands wrap around me toward the front of my body, gripping my sides very tightly. Let me tell you, I jumped right out of that bed, practically flying across the room and exactly at that time, two light bulbs popped instantaneously. The temperature drop was recognized by all present. There were nine witnesses to all of this. The experience definitely shook me up and made me think even deeper into the realm of the supernatural and the preternatural. It was hard to accept that I was physically touched. At the time, it is so real, but at the same time seems so unnatural. As time went on with being exposed to more and more cases, touching became a sensation that I personally experienced on a more frequent basis. When something is around you and you are being touched, it is quite normal to be bothered or get frustrated or annoyed. It picks up on this. When you get excited, you are throwing off energy that acts as the catalyst to give it strength to manifest.

"The most common experience that I have encountered within my own home is 'tappings.' Also, I'll have the lights turning on and off. One particular experience that has reoccurred and still bothers me to this very day is when I am speaking to an individual who needs help, problems with the telephone will occur. Audible grunting and growling will emanate, making it hard to hear what the person on the other end of the line has to say. I know this type of situation to be of a higher level. Over the years, it has happened seven times. When the grunts or noises start, I never say anything to the person that I'm talking to, seeing how exactly they will react to the situation. In such a type of situation, I have found that most of the time, these people who are being troubled do not even realize that they are doing this or that what is around them is portraying such disturbing sounds on the telephone.

"I've had the situation where I've felt something, some type of presence around me. I can only describe it as a whirlwind. There would be something physically spinning around me in my own home. I have also had situations where there was actual hard pounding sensation occurring in my home. It was not only loud, but also just as physical as if you took your hand and started to smash the wall. When these types of poundings occur, it is usually around the time that an important event will be taking place, such as an exorcism. It is almost normal for physical phenomena to kick up a day or two before an exorcism. Usually the more complex and horrible the case, the more intense the phenomena becomes. The demonic will do anything to frighten, to warn, indicating to back off a given situation.

"Car problems also occur when dealing with the demonic. The car might die completely outright or the gauging will go completely out of whack. Another interesting car experience is when the radio changed on its own, going to a station number that tied in directly with the case with a specific song that tied in directly to the case.

"There was one case that I was working on and beforehand there was nothing apparent wrong with my car. It was recently serviced and I had four people with me. The case was about an hour from my home, and I'm not quite sure how the car made it there that day. It was about two and a half hours before we even made it there. The car would constantly stall, idle, buckle, and die. It would always start back up though. We were on our way to an exorcism to help assist the clergy. I specifically asked the priest after the rite to bless the car because I had a feeling that whatever was going wrong with the car was related to the case and the forces regarding the case. He ended up blessing the car and from then on we had no problems all the way home with the car, no problems whatsoever.

"Another specific scenario I have encountered over my years of investigating is a tremendous amount of people who are interested deeply in the Work. I picked up through trial and error that one must be extremely careful when choosing who they work with in this Work. There are those people who are pure of heart, who have a genuine interest in the field and want to help those who are encountering problems, but there are also those who are on the other side. These people are also interested in getting into the Work, but for totally separate reasons, reasons often to intensify or worsen the scenario. It really is a double-edged sword that you can encounter in the Work. When going on cases, meeting people related to the cases, and virtually anyone in any type of contact with the client, you just really don't know the motive at hand. In working with individuals you can certainly pick up on their motives and why they want to be involved with cases pertaining to the supernatural and the preternatural over a period of time. Is the interest to go into the home, collect data, help the people involved understand,

and bring closure to the case, or is the motive to help the situation intensify, to provoke and bring forth the negative that is already occurring in the home or around the person or persons? It is absolutely and undoubtedly a tough battle to decipher who is who in the Work. Over the years, I have seen those on both sides and I do find this quite disturbing. My goal is to help, not to hurt. These individuals only complicate what needs to be done when it comes to families in dire need of help.

"Keeping an eye on researchers when your ultimate goal is to help the victim or victims makes it hard on everyone. When people enter the Work, they may know what their motive is, while others may not. Why they are attracted to the Work and what their motives are remain crucial. It is tough to tell what motives lie just beneath the surface. They could fall victim or set themselves up for some real trouble.

"The field of psychic research has many temptations. The Devil will ultimately lie to you, things will be offered to you, and many cannot deal with this temptation. Once you get a taste for what is out there and the power and energy that exists, one may cross over to what I refer to as the other side, embracing a darker reality, when possibly the initial motives were actually positive. This is why it is not only essential, but crucial to have a strong belief system and a deep-rooted faith in some positive aspect, whether it be Roman Catholicism, Buddhism, the Presbyterian sect, Judaism, or what ever denomination one may choose. Any practice which embraces the positive is key in battling that which lies on the negative aspects of the Work. Not having a means to keep you level will end up ultimately being your demise. Cases of earthbound spirit are different than when you directly deal on occasion with an energy far more sinister and deviant. One cannot battle the demonic on their own, but only with the help of a high being that reflects the opposite of this negative force. They, being the demonic, fear God, not humans.

Once someone has crossed over and embraced evil, it makes it difficult to turn back and unwind what has been instilled. We all have free will, and it is by our own choice that we decide our own fate and direction. Different types of people will choose different paths. Sometimes these paths prove to be the one better left completely alone. Some even get into the field with the right intentions, but the subsequent temptation and the attractiveness of the power offered by the negative can convert some to adopt that which is unholy. Instead of resuming the fight for the positive, these researchers ultimately fall victim and rely on the dark side for their satisfaction in life. I cannot stress enough the fact that free will is the key.

People have the capability to make their own choices and can sink or stay afloat based on their decisions.

"A similar situation is when an individual wants to escape the torment of what has crept up in their lives, but has a hard time doing so because of confusion, a lack of knowledge, or the like. This seems to be true of those who have been dedicated at birth to the Devil. They were the victims of ritual abuse and were raised with these satanic beliefs instilled in them. Often, these people are trying to break the cycle of which is familiar to them, but cannot seem to integrate back into the normal scheme of life. They were obviously scarred from what had occurred in their formative years. The first step is to rid them of the demonic force that has physically crept into their lives, and then get them into the positive and into counseling to deal with what has happened."

*What is the difference between psychic research and parapsychology?

"In regards to parapsychologists, their main function is to go into a given situation and document the activity as it occurs. They (parapsychologists), as a serious area of study, often have a great deal of equipment and with these devices try to calculate changes in the environment which can be monitored. Often they will document changes in temperature or fields regarding static electricity. These findings will be regarded in relation to nature and fields pertaining to the known and understood natural elements. The scientific end of such phenomena does not acknowledge the fact that there is often an intelligence behind the phenomena.

"For example, in accounts where people pick up on information that they do not have access to, parapsychology or the scientific end of the spectrum will automatically assume that this information must be being fed to this individual by some means. There must be some reasonable explanation for this pertinent information being conveyed in their (the parapsychologists) eyes. They do not allow for the unknown or misunderstood to even be a factor.

"I obviously try to instate scientific means whenever necessary, but I go in as a psychic researcher and a paranormal investigator. I also have studied the end of the spectrum pertaining to demonology very in depth. My several years in the field have exposed me to all different aspects and the Work tends to embrace them all. When science can be incorporated, it is incorporated. If the case pertains to the demonic, then there are other methods that fit those particular guidelines. Each case is unique, and there is often not one clear-cut way to decipher what is occurring.

"From my perspective, I go into a case looking to gather evidence to decipher what is actually occurring at the site. By ruling out the logical, you can then start to place your focus on supernatural means. It is not unheard of for me to go outside and look for tree branches scraping the house, or to find a normal cause, like an animal that has made its way into the walls. It is obvious that more often than not, these people are so frightened and confused that they are on edge. The phenomena to some are just overwhelming. If it is electrical or an animal, the fix is easy. I still have solved their problem. However, most of the time when I undertake a case, it is the real deal. I often receive cases from reliable sources or directly from the clergy. Other times I get a call directly from the family, who are usually normal, hardworking, sane individuals who really have a supernatural problem they need to end or at least understand. In this field of research, you seldom get a call about something positive. Sure, there are those experiences that are positive, beautiful, or enlightening. I love hearing stories about a positive experience, but this rarely happens. I am brought in because there is a need. I need to prove what is there and explain it fully. If it needs to be terminated, I need to be positive that what is there is preternatural in origin so the clergy may intervene.

"What makes me carry on is a legitimate excuse—it is in my blood. Just as I believe a curse can be passed on from generation to generation, I feel that this has been passed on to me from my uncle, Ed Warren. I have the same types of instincts and enthusiasm he has had all these years. I will go to any possible extent to help families who so desperately need a resolution to the emotional agony they are enduring from hateful, external agents. Any way in which I can help to ease their burden, I will undertake. That's what has been passed down to me—the desire, that urge to help those who are plagued with the preternatural. It absolutely fuels me to know that at the end of a week, or the closing of a case, that I have directly affected someone or multiple people by bringing about some type of help by means of understanding or closure to their case. It may be through the clergy or on some type of professional level. Perhaps the case was not supernatural at all, but instead psychiatric. If this is the situation, I will get them the psychological help they need. Perhaps they need some type of counseling after dealing with such a horrible haunting. Once again, I will get them the help they need after the aftermath of an intense situation.

"There have been points within my years of investigating that I have tried to leave the Work. Many times this job will start to affect your personal life and it was at these points I decided to call it quits. As always, for some reason, I am drawn back into the game. In the past, I have stepped down, avoiding those I know involved in the Work and anything that ties in directly to investigating. Then, all of a sudden, some type of case will arise that I feel I need to get involved in. There is no way for me to turn my back on what has been brought to my attention. A phone call or an e-mail will spark my interest or appeal to my sensitivity, and in return, I know that person really needs help. When situations like this come around, I cannot turn my back on that individual. I'm willing to work with anybody who sincerely wants help with his or her dilemma.

"On a similar level, over the years I have also become involved with seminars, lectures, and the courses involved in teaching the field of research. Every year, there seems to be some type of event that requires me to get involved with a hands-on approach, sharing much of my knowledge and the unique experiences that I have had. This is only a small part of the journey, but nonetheless is an intricate part of the field because of the spark of interest or buzz it creates. It is through situations like this that I know that this whole field is something that will not just disappear out of my life."

*Are there points where you feel fear and on what levels is this felt? What concerns or irks you about the field you have undertaken?

"I still get scared. Just because I have seen quite a bit in my several years of investigating does not mean that I am fearless. There is so much out there that when the day comes that I no longer fear anything, that it would definitely be time for me to get out of the field. There is always a fear factor when dealing with anything demonic. The Devil is a very strong entity that works in virtually any way to bring about a negative outcome. You can be blindsided at the blink of an eye and not realize what is occurring. You can be attacked at anytime for your involvement with any given case. There is a price to pay for helping those plagued by evil. At times, it will seem unbearable and that there is no way to counteract what is happening to you. This, however, is not the case. It is through your will to carry on, your positive attitude, and most importantly, your faith in a Higher Being. Although the demonic may grip many and seem like it has the upper hand, God has more strength without a doubt.

"I fear more than anything that those in my personal life will be directly affected for my choice to become involved with such a field. They did not choose to undertake such a profession. Instead, it was my choice, and I therefore do not want them to be affected for my choices. It was my free will, not theirs, to undertake the caseload brought upon me. If something affects my wife or my children and I know it to be related to the supernatural realm, this factor is quite bothersome to me. This fear factor not only can make you vulnerable to attack, but can affect you all your days if not counteracted. By realizing the possibility of such an occurrence, you can better recognize when an attack is actually taking place. In this Work, there will be times that you are scared, confused, and just want out.

Things may fall apart on the home front for no known reason, perhaps your sleeping patterns will be altered, or some presence will make itself known in your home. You take home the emotional burden of cases and even sometimes part of the problem that will try to warn you to back off or remove yourself from a given case. In these situations, you need to be more levelheaded than ever and need to incorporate your faith."

*What types of groups are out there today and how do they fit into the realm of investigating legit phenomena?

"I think that nowadays, there are so many different organizations out there that many misconceptions can and may surface. There are many groups out there that are initiated just to "ghost hunt." This tells me that they are interested in visiting haunted locations and are searching for that which we refer to as human spirit. Often they will be searching for physical evidence, like photographs and video or sometimes tape recordings known as electronic voice phenomenon (EVP). These particular groups primarily seem to want to avoid anything on the demonic level or the preternatural level. These particular groups, in my findings, in some instances may come across some real negative spirit phenomena. When this type of contact is made, many of these groups will put aside their interest and seek the help of those who are familiar with this particular type of activity. On the other hand, there are those ghost hunting groups that do not believe in any negative spirits whatsoever, such as that which lies within the categorization of the demonic. These individuals or groups will get involved with people who are anxiously seeking resolve due to fright and will try all kinds of ridiculous home remedies based on mere superstition. Their so-called 'tricks of the trade' will be instated to help the spirit cross over, but it must be remembered that in some of these rare cases, the entity will be that of the demonic. It is then these researchers will open themselves up and risk the possibility of problems because of their connection and practices pertaining to a case. Also, provoking the situation may intensify occurrences for the family, an obvious unwanted result.

"This is not to say that all ghost hunting groups are unfamiliar or lack some type of knowledge, but with all the different groups arising with no real credentials, the risk is definitely there. People are just not prepared to encounter some of the entities that lurk out there. If they cross paths with them and are not fully prepared, they may suffer the consequences. Even those who have studied the demonic and have seen such cases firsthand are always at risk. Those who have never studied devils and demons, or those who reject the notion of their existence run a high risk of repercussions for the interaction with entities on such a level.

"When dealing with the negative, there needs to be some substance behind you. How can you deal with such negative influence without having a positive to counteract that which you are standing against? It does not seem to matter what a person's belief system is, or what religion they take part in throughout their lives. As long as it encompasses the positive, they will have some type of protection to assist them in their journey. If they don't have the faith, then they have little protection to act as a tool in the field."

*Are case numbers increasing in recent years?

"I think statistically that cases have been increasing in number and intensity over the past five years or so. I usually do not go a week without having at least two or three cases brought to my attention. On a heavy week, I might receive as many as ten or fifteen cases from both the phone and from incoming e-mail. Although they all do not require a full-scale investigation, some may need referrals due to their geographic location. Others, I may give suggestions or a theory as to what is happening based on the testimony I receive. Others are fraudulent and do not need any other assistance. When something seems rather legitimate and I am in constant contact with that individual, I will usually arrange for a time for us to meet and conduct an in-person, on-film interview. There is no real way of knowing unless you go into the home and experience it for yourself. All the books in the world cannot even compare to witnessing a physical attack, being touched, seeing objects move, or materializations.

"It seems that today, in regards to practices, both those which are misconstrued, misunderstood, and those which are downright negative and invoke the negative, the spiritual arts are more open for those who want to use them. Today, no one is going to burn you at the stake for your beliefs. It is easier to practice and gain materials for conjuring or practice. People are definitely experimenting more these days. The use of the Ouija board, experimentation with the runes, using tarot cards and other types of communication methods with the spirit world are pretty frequent. Most of the time, nothing will happen, but on some occasions, a door will be opened. It seems strange that many of the people who use these devices don't even really believe anything negative could happen, because they do not fully believe what they are doing. It is more like an experiment to many of those who play with these items. They will get really involved or experiment for just a short while, then stop using means of conjuration all together. Most of the time, nothing will happen, but some cases prove to be just the opposite. Some time down the road these individuals might start to have a problem. Phenomena kick up in their home and they can't explain it at all. Looking back, there is a direct reason for what is happening at this point in time.

"Over the years I have dealt directly with many people who will stress that they indeed did not play with the Ouija board. Later on, the truth comes out that they did experiment with the board, or sometimes it is some other means of experimentation. People often seemed embarrassed for some reason to admit that they have tried what most people probably have tried themselves. Human nature will lead us to many things, including a curiosity for the mystical. Most people have either taken part in or tried a Ouija board as a child, or maybe have confided in psychics. Everyone has his or her own story of some type of experimentation.

"Usually later in the interview, the person will state that perhaps when they were young they used a Ouija board or some other device with a friend. Oftentimes, they will even admit that some type of contact was made. If contact was indeed made, it is a pretty accurate indicator that a door was opened and entry could have been gained by some type of entity.

"In the spirit world, there are no time constraints. It may take weeks, months, or years for the entity to come through after a door has been opened. I see this in cases all the time. An individual could have performed some type of mystical practice twenty years ago when they were just a teenager. Years later, seemingly out of nowhere, activity occurs and intensifies. In some of these situations, there seems to be no other explanation. Eventually, what they did in the past catches up with them, and it is at that point in time their struggle to overcome this adversary becomes apparent.

"This opponent waits for just the right time to hit and what better time to hit than when every aspect of your life is utterly happy and seemingly complete. You could be married with a few children. You reside in a beautiful home and have a satisfying job. Then virtually out of nowhere, a slow but progressive energy surrounds you and starts to break down all that you have accomplished. This is not to say all downfalls in the human experience are due to the demonic. These cases are full of often-frightening phenomena that separate them from just a downfall in normal circumstances pertaining to life. Perhaps it hits because you are happy and it feels the need to revoke that happiness, or perhaps it is because when all is well your guard is at its most vulnerable point. No matter how you look at it, you are under attack. Perhaps the marriage collapses suddenly, their job falls apart before their very eyes, and all aspects within their lives are affected. Lurking just around the corner waiting is an oppressive force few but still many must face.

"I cannot even recall how many times people start a conversation with me starting out, 'John, don't think I'm crazy, but....' After some time, people realize they are having problems which extend outside of basic human explanation, and know they need help to expose, understand, and alleviate the situation.

"Over the years, being involved with many different researchers and organizations, I have seen a multitude of sessions where contact was indeed made. There have been situations where channelers have actually channeled something through their own body, releasing information that was pertinent to the case. The only problem I have is that the Devil will fool, preying on that which is familiar to you. You cannot assume with the spirit world that you are communicating with what apparently is coming through. Oftentimes, by lying and deceit, an entity will try to gain access by preying upon your weaknesses. That which comes forth is not always what it claims to be.

"Many end up dabbling with items such as a Ouija board and will establish communication with the spirit world. The person will swear that they are talking to a deceased relative or a human spirit. The fact is you just don't know what you are making contact with, and this is where the problem lies. It could be a low-level demonic entity preying upon you, just trying to gain access. You may think you have a deceased friend, brother, sister, or some other loved one, but you never know who it is. I can say that I have never really met anyone who has had an enlightening experience through such a device as the Ouija board. They possibly made contact with something, but nothing positive.

"There are countless amounts of cases I have been involved with over the years involving those who used a Ouija board on a regular basis because contact had indeed been made. After a few weeks, months, or even years, all hell broke loose, and problems were beyond comprehension. The end result was that the people had opened the door, given recognition, and let their guard down. Now, something dark and sinister plagues them. It happens time and time again.

"In regards to those who practice on the negative side, those who practice the black arts and the like, there is certainly an ever-growing population of such practitioners.

"Often I will get involved with people who have no desire to be involved with negative practices. In the past, they were heavily involved with Satanism, Santeria, Voodoo, and basically any imaginable practice out there. The problem is many of them have dedicated themselves to a darker being, and by removing themselves from the practices, they are reneging on what they initially promised to the conjured deity. For instance, rituals may have been performed for love, money, a beautiful man or woman, or revenge. Often, this force comes to collect or gains entry to an individual's life for some reason linked to the past.

"People will rely on the spirit world for assistance. They always have and always will. The interesting thing is that people will rely on the spirit world for help, but do not tend to fully believe or understand the reality of this realm. It is quite contradictory to rely on the spiritual realm for assistance in matters, and then when it backfires, deny its existence totally. The reality eventually fits into place, but is ultimately hard to accept. In these rare circumstances, people will have these deities or entities around them, and will begin to experience, often-times, very frightening phenomena—an all-out barrage of activity which does not make any logical sense, when in reality, it all makes total sense. A past action may link the occurrences taking place right now to them. Oftentimes, these victims will even realize what is going on, but understandably have an extremely difficult time accepting the fact that their lives are now fully invaded by an often unseen force. They might even get a researcher involved to verify what they believe to be in actuality: a very true circumstance.

"Unfortunately, in the very extreme, hard-core cases, the researchers are not even notified or called in until the situation has become progressively worse. By the time I am usually notified, there has been a dramatic turn in the case. Often, there have been recurrent nightmares, sleepless nights, and even physical attacks by these beings by the time I get involved. Most people obviously do not plan on a supernatural problem when they get their lives going, but some actually wander down this road of no return-a road which can lead the individual or individuals through months, years, and even decades of confusion and torment. Some cases are not resolved and others have their degree of activity lessened. Also, those having problems must make sure that if a case is resolved, they do not let the being or beings regain entry by continuing to dabble with occult activities.

"Oftentimes, the occult world is like a revolving door in which activity will cease and pick back up, prying back into the lives of people who have had past experiences. Many people who I have worked with that are adults and are having supernatural experiences had experiences as children.

"To walk down this road is a rarity which most men and women will probably never face on a real concrete level. For some though, it is a reality. It is not a psychological problem or a hallucination, but instead an experience which has existed for as long as time itself. The force has invaded their personal lives and does not want to go. Often, it will be there dormant, kicking back up every once in awhile, making itself all too well known to that individual."

*Today witchcraft, the old religion, is misunderstood and has a growing number of followers who adopt so many different paths

associated with the practice. How do you feel about witchcraft in the modern age?

"Wicca is a very old religion, one that actually predates Christianity. The basic principles are very harmless and ultimately positive. The Wiccan believes in Mother Nature by worshipping the elements pertaining to life: earth, wind, fire, and water. Common beliefs are channeling these energies for a positive result, not harming fellow humans by calling upon deities for negative results. By using these life forces they believe that they gain wisdom from living and a direct consciousness about their role in the universe. They learn about health and well-being as dated back to its origins, probably as far back as Paleolithic times. Wicca, if kept in a strict sense, would be quite harmless and would certainly encompass the positive. The problem is that many do not know the roots of witchcraft or do not adhere to the understood Wiccan principles. Instead, they adopt practices and surround themselves with the negative, trying to manipulate negative energies and call on negative deities for harmful outcomes and selfish desires.

"Commonly there is the belief that there is a thin line between white magic and black magic—a right-hand and a left-hand path, a good side and a darker side. Often, the initial intent was positive, but the temptation and the power led them to become very negative in regards to practices.

"Practices and rituals have basically remained the same, and have been somewhat preserved over time. Each practitioner may have his or her own twist, but common threads, such as the solstice and the full moon, remain a common link. The full moon represents a period of a great deal of energy, which the practitioners may use for positive or negative effects. The same runs true of the new moon. There actually is a three-day period both before and after when these believers try to accomplish what is required by their beliefs.

"Today, there is an abundance of material available in any bookstore, especially as a result of the New Age movement. People will buy a book and not really know what credibility the written work might have or what credentials the author has. That piece of writing could potentially represent a total perversion of Wicca.

"The more common name for these negative rituals is black magic, or black witchcraft. Black magic really, when you think of it, is man's extremely perverse desires being incorporated with the use of an external agent. That agent is the very deity that the black magician calls upon to have his selfish desires put into existence. The quest for money, power, sex, and any other desire is the root of the art. To gain everything in this life the magician will invoke these energies to fulfill his or her evil desires."

Who is Satan? What exactly is Satanism? Does this practice exist today or is it a mere myth? Explain the arcane lore of demonology and what it really is.

"Satan, in the perspective of religion, based on Christianity, was God's right-hand man. Satan was second only to God and had reign over all the angels. However, this was not enough for him. He wanted much more. He wanted to be God. The Devil is seen as the commander—in chief of the fallen angels who led himself and his dominions to be banished from knowing God forever due to their quest to be God from their deep-rooted sense of pride. It was through their own free will, the ability to choose right and wrong, that these creatures, which were created by God, fell from their purity. Satan, although banished from heaven, has retained his powers, as well as his angels, and seeks the ruin of man by preying on man's free will to choose. They want man to choose the wrong path and fall to the same fate that they endure presently and will endure in the future.

"Satan's demise was a result of his choice. Christianity concurs with the idea that through our own free will, we have the ability to choose between knowing God and not knowing Him by falling into sin and the acceptance of the doctrine of demons. Through the trials and tribulations caused by temptation, a battle reigns on. This battle is on an ostentatious and grandiose scale.

"Just like anything else there are many different levels when you look at those who are involved with Satanism. Many are just fooling around with it on an individual basis or with a few others around them, while others take it to another level and are far more organized. Their plan is far deeper; they worship Satan as their supreme master.

"Satanism is altogether different than merely involving one's self with matters of the unknown world or experimentation, or that which is not yet fully understood in regards to spiritual matters. Satanism is an outright approval and acceptance of Satan as the god of this world. Swearing allegiance to this evil one and separating one's self from God are what mark this practice as different from other occult practices. This is not mere dabbling, but an outright blasphemous act to separate one's self totally from God.

"By crossing to this way of life, those who practice Satanism are trying to fulfill their earthly desires, eliminating what scripture teaches in order to live the selfish desires of the flesh that they so intently pursue.

"Satanism is nothing new. It has been around since the beginning of man. Satan has always been seeking the ruin of souls and wants man to follow him. In a more modern perspective, popular Satanism stems from a man born in 1930 who many see as the forefather of contemporary Satanism, the man responsible for bringing the practice into popular culture. This man is Anton Szandor LaVey.

"LaVey wrote *The Satanic Bible* and other titles that have been adopted by modern Satanists as their doctrine or part of their main influence. LaVey was the founder of the Church of Satan in the mid-1960s and used it as a way for him and his followers to celebrate life by enjoying the desires that Christian religions frowned upon. LaVey and his followers saw Satan as a primordial source of indulgence and a representative of sins; sins being those actions that lead to the gratification of humanness. Many members of such groups will take part in one way or another in rituals aiming to fulfill their fleshly needs and swear allegiance to the "dark one." Some people renounce their baptism and swear themselves over to Satan. Others will indulge in the drugs and the sexual aspect of the belief system, and others sometimes take it to the ultimate extreme. They will take a life, either animal or human, for their act of worship to Satan. Ultimately, there are different levels of Satanism.

"Statistics do not really show any hard evidence of organized satanic groups in this country. Their existence is undeniable, but the exact number of those involved or how many organized satanic churches exist are unknown. Estimates show that there are possibly several hundred practicing groups of organized Satanists in operation throughout the United States, but exact numbers really are unknown. Other voodoo-based practices also embrace some of the negativity that the Satanists relish in. Satanism, when you really get down to it, is only one defining term in a sea of potentially harmful occult practices.

"I personally do not call myself a demonologist after over twenty-eight years in the field. I think the term is used very loosely nowadays, and many investigators term themselves with this label although they are not really demonologists. If you study the demonic, fallen angels, the underworld pertaining to Satan and his legion, then you could be termed this title, but the term has become overused and less credible over the years. Also, there would be the categorization of demonologists in the field today, some practicing the negative side and others working to help people on the positive. One might study demonology to encompass the darkness, while others will study and categorize to help those who are suffering at the hands of the demonic.

"By categorization of the legions, I mean that there are different levels of power when referring to the demonic realm. In cases that deal directly with this realm, the most common is the low-level activity. There is fear and mental oppression. Objects can be moved and physical altercations may occur with unseen menaces. As you go up the scale, the phenomena, and ultimately the strategy, intensifies. The knocking and rappings evolve into an all-out barrage of scratching and biting, the dematerialization of objects, interference in the dream state, and all-out fear on the part of the victim. Where the lower level occurs are the actions of the soldiers, the demons. Their main goal is to possess those who they torment, to cause mental, spiritual, and physical damage. They seek to torture and to menace human beings because humans are created in the image and likeness of God and still have free will, which they have already blemished indefinitely from potentiality for themselves. Their enormous pride, which caused their rebellion, causes their jealousy of the human. Their pride was not to know God, but instead to be God.

"The demonic have three attributes which stand out, proving their sophistication and reality as tangible beings. They are capable of thought, feeling, and action. They possess intellect. They know that they are doomed for their rebellion. Demons display emotion. When confronted, they fear Jesus Christ and bow down in His name. During an exorcism, they will weaken and fold when His name is used. They also possess anger, hate, and disgust toward human beings. They also have free will because they continue to rebel and try to hold on to individuals when they infest, oppress, and possess. They will even bow down, fear, and retreat in some instances when God is concerned, which shows their ability to know and comprehend.

"The demonic strives to violate one particular aspect of the world-our humanness or our essence. This is our very intricate self, ultimately the soul or life force that it so eagerly desires to taint. Since their intelligence and powers remain, even though they have been stripped of their link to the Almighty (God), they will do all they can to pervert and alter the path to eternal goodness. They are ultimately the flip side of righteousness, their powers reflecting a rather perverse nature. Their falsity is a recognizable attribute separating them from the positive and marking them the keepers of the fall. They seek the ruin of souls by means of outright temptation. They cannot make us fall, but prey upon our weaknesses so we, using our own free will, might follow their goal of separating as many humans as possible from God. They will seek to dehumanize human beings, lowering us to the point where all hope is lost.

"The more planned and concise the phenomena, the better the chance a devil has moved in. Devils are more progressive, and theologically speaking, are thought to command the demons. They will move in, take over, and finish the job that the demon cannot quite finish. They move larger objects, levitate not only objects, but also people, and have the ability to manipulate religious objects. Also, where devils are concerned, materializations of disgusting objects, such as bile-like fluids and other ghastly and nauseating substances, are always a possibility. Their powers transcend the demons, and you have a real problem if a devil or devils have stepped in.

"Demonology encompasses many attributes of the spiritual realm by studying, classifying, identifying, and helping to banish these forces, which often go unrecognized by the human race. It sounds like a horror movie, but is part of the very doctrine that religious people encompass, whether they fully believe or not. Demons and the hierarchy of the demonic are real, tangible beings.

*Is there a particular case or event that was a real turning point for you, an event that ultimately changed your life in regards to psychic research?

"I have been on so many cases over the years and witnessed many strange occurrences. I have seen many people direly affected by cases. I have witnessed the interaction of many different denominations of all religions and have seen people's lives literally ripped from them. There is an instance which forever changed my outlook not only in the area of psychic research, but life in general. It was an experience that has only occurred once in my twenty-eight years in the field, and I hope will never occur again. Will it occur again? No one knows for sure. There is certainly the possibility for it to happen, but I obviously cannot say for sure.

"Several years ago a landmark case erupted in Connecticut. The case was brought to the attention of the Warrens after a frightening encounter with the demonic, which convinced one woman and her niece that the eldest son really was not crazy. The story was revealed in the book *In A Dark Place* by Ed and Lorraine Warren and Al and Carmen Snedeker with Ray Garton. This was truly the story of one family's absolute nightmare based on eyewitness accounts of the family, researchers, and the clergy.

"The family had moved into a home that was converted from a funeral parlor to residential housing. The eldest son complained of being bothered by a force that resided in the home. He was very ill with Hodgkin's disease at the time, and his family thought that his stories were all part of the reaction from his treatments. The other children began to witness many of the terrible apparitions, and were shunned by the parents and scolded for their revelations. It was assumed the eldest son had influenced his brothers and sister. However, after he was removed from the home for psychiatric help, all kinds of phenomena occurred. Everyone experienced the wrath of the force in the home.

"I remember one of my first nights in that home. Honestly, I remember every night in that home. It was truly one of the worst cases I have ever encountered. It is one of those frightening cases in which seemingly everyone who stepped foot in that house had some type of experience that they would never forget.

"I remember hearing the chain pulley rattling. Under Al and Carmen's bedroom was the hoist that was used to bring the bodies up from the basement. You could actually audibly hear the chain rattling, but it had a muffled quality to it. Both myself and another researcher would hustle downstairs, only to find nothing. We leaned a large piece of wooden paneling against the pulley, but after returning upstairs the rattling would reoccur.

"This house was running rampant with activity. Every night, something was going on. It was a nine-week ordeal that was the definition of terror itself. Just sleeping in that house was enough to make you uncomfortable. The uncertainty of what might happen wore on your nerves. Those hot summer nights were shadowed with the fact that a negative intelligence existed in that house at all times.

"One night, there was screaming from upstairs. Immediately, I headed to the bedroom where Carmen's niece Tammy was being physically assaulted. This poor girl was a wreck. She had been assaulted before and these attacks were not only frightening but also degrading in a sexual nature. I remember when it calmed down a bit, she was still being touched. You could actually see her nightgown being moved and tugged on. As everyone joined in prayer, the assault slowly began to die down.

"This is one of those situations where all those involved experience the phenomena on a physical level. It is not an overactive imagination or mass hallucination. It was real. To experience such occurrences is to witness the essence of dread. It was so bad that everyone actually slept on mattresses in the living room so no one would be separated, just in case the demonic decided to strike while someone was alone. One night, however, I got the most intense experience I have yet to have.

"I sat by myself, relaxing, waiting to see if anything was going to happen that particular night. I was reviewing the notes from that day. Researchers were stationed at the home twenty-four hours a day to document everything. So far it had been rather uneventful. The room became unnaturally cold, absolutely frigid. Isolated from the others in the home, I knew something was going to happen, but not to the extreme that it did. I never thought what happened that night could really happen and it will be forever etched in my mind.

"I called out to the others, but no one responded. I knew something was going to happen, that some type of manifestation was going to take place, but what exactly? I got up, waiting for something to happen, but there was nothing. I turned and faced the opposite direction. At the top of the stairs, a physical form took shape. It was verbally responding and took on a full form. It kept saying over and over, 'You know what they did, you know what they did to us.' Within seconds, the reptilian-like body descended down the stairs toward me. It was not a complete full-formed being, but had features that were easily recognizable. As it came toward me, its murky colors were much stronger and directly behind it were quick, fluttering movements.

"Needless to say, it was not long after that I left the premises, grabbing my keys within seconds. It would be three days before I would return to the house. During those three days, I withdrew from the Work and all those who were associated with it. I really did not think I was going to ever return to that case or any case again, but I did.

"It is something that has only happened once, but will never be erased from my mind. The picture is as crisp as it was yesterday. Without a doubt, I had encountered a full-formed demonic entity. Sitting back after all this time makes me realize that there is a diabolical intelligence out there, and I was actually witness to it firsthand. I have seen what the demonic can do over the years, over many cases, but this was the first and so far the only time I had physically seen the menace in the actual form of a being.

"After that encounter I really had to think deeply about myself and how I related to the Work. Was it something that I needed to encompass in my life? Should I just turn my back on everyone and leave it all behind me? I thought about it, but one thing remained in my mind: if I gave up, the demonic would win. They do not want people to help those who are affected by their wrath. Retiring from it all would mark my own defeat. I knew there were those out there who truly needed help and I realized that I could not retire from the Work at any cost.

"There are other instances in general which stand out, a common thread in the Work which has happened countless times over the years. My uncle, Ed Warren, stated that, 'the Devil's greatest tactic is to divide and conquer;' especially significant in a field where unity is so crucial. I am not blaming basic human problems, arguments, or misconceptions on the evil encountered on cases, but there are times when this seems to be the only real answer. If conflict did not arise, if there were no issues with the clergy or the researchers, and if everyone saw eye to eye, it would be easier to combat these forces of evil. By dividing, the common main goal of bringing closure to a case is much more difficult. By division, it takes longer to bring closure to the victims or interrupts the flow needed to gather evidence, and proves the existence of some force and identifies exactly what it is inhabiting the premises.

"Also, infiltration is all too real and is very detrimental to the field. If a researcher crosses over, if you become too close to the families, or if you get drawn to some particular aspect of a case, you can become very vulnerable. Vulnerability is very dangerous because these entities will feed off of your weaknesses and use them to break you down mentally, spiritually, and any other way wear you down to your weakest point, making you incapable to deal with the case.

"It is rare, but not uncommon, for the demonic to try to tempt one by that which is appealing. This Work will show you much of the power that is out there and many of the secrets that are best left that way. If you are weak with your faith, you may suffer greatly. This power to cross over and dabble because of the power of the negative is a constant struggle, and it is only by free will many give up and cross over. I have seen it several times and it seems to occur with new researchers and the seasoned researchers as well. Ultimately, the threat is always present and is there several times throughout one's researching career.

"The demonic will also affect your mood in other ways, such as interrupting your sleep patterns. A lack of sleep will run you down mentally and physically. This is another factor in many heavy-duty cases where you might get woken up at three o'clock in the morning repeatedly. Three is a number that arises on many demonic cases. It is seen as an insult to the Trinity of the Christian tradition and is also recognized as the traditional hour of Jesus' death. Since the demonic represents the opposite of all which is holy and pure, it often chooses three o'clock in the morning, the opposite of Jesus' three o'clock in the afternoon hour of death. The number three also arises in many other aspects of cases as well as the Christian theology.

"Another really moving experience I had occurred back in the 1980s when I was over in England and Scotland with Ed and Lorraine, exploring many of the haunted sites. I am usually pretty bad when it comes to tour groups. Usually, I will end up wandering off on my own to explore the different areas. We arrived at Eilean Donan Castle to check out the place that is rumored to be very haunted. It has been said that in the earlier part of the fourteenth century, Robert the Bruce, in severe conflict with many of the clan chiefs and being sought after by the English, was given a safe haven in Eilean Donan Castle by John MacKenzie, II of Kintail. We wandered about the place, and I happened to find a secluded area down below in the castle. As I became more and more secluded and became more alone, an experience that I will never forget occurred. I could hear the clanking of metal swords and the hoofs of horses moving about. Similar reports are mentioned in such areas, but it is not until you experience yourself that you truly believe. I kept questioning myself, but the sounds were very real. Slowly and hesitantly, I headed back to the car where Ed and Lorraine were waiting for me. Lorraine turned to me and said, 'so you had an experience down there, didn't you, John?'

"I was dumbfounded, and evidently she could tell by my expressions that something had happened to me. That experience was positive for me and is one of the more moving experiences I have had."

*Over the years, approximately how many cases have you worked on, and what types of clientele do you tend to assist?

"Over the past twenty-eight years, I have worked on more than 7,000 cases throughout the United States, Canada, England, and Scotland. As far as the types of people I have assisted, they include a diverse and large spectrum. I have been called in by business owners, nurses, retirees, schoolteachers, doctors, law enforcement agents, and any other type of occupation you can think of out there in society. With so many cases over the years, you meet so many different people from all different religious, ethnic, and economic backgrounds. You physically go into all kinds of homes and establishments and deal with all types of personalities.

"Something that still amazes me to this day is working directly with a person or people who go through a complete turnaround in regards to spirituality. So many people in the Work or those who are having problems in their homes tend to believe, but not fully, in aspects of spirituality. Many disregard any type of spiritual beliefs altogether. After dealing with something that can only be defined as spirit activity, many walk away with a new respect or develop a belief system that beforehand, was weak, or lacking altogether. Even those in the scientific field who are often the most skeptical, or are nonbelievers in God and the deceased still living on, and intelligent beings behind the madness, are affected by exposure to such activity. I personally have seen scientifically driven people change their beliefs and take part in religion or actually acknowledge the presence of intelligence in the spirit world because of experiences they have directly had. Once you witness, once you see for yourself some of the scenarios that are out there, it is hard to reject the notion that the spirit world exists.

"A more recent case was brought to the attention of the Catholic clergy. I was called and attended the exorcism. A young man, whose health had dwindled to the point where there was no hope, was literally on his last leg. He was jobless for well over a year and everything that could have gone wrong did just that. He was an absolute mess and medical doctors could not identify the source of his deteriorating health, neither could clinical psychologists find a mental disorder to blame for all his mishaps. In the hospital, an exorcism was performed on him and after several weeks, he was back on his feet, had a steady job, and had almost fully recuperated. It is situations like this that prove to the investigator that there is more than meets the eye to many of the cases that are brought about. There was no hope for this man. After the rite of exorcism was performed, his life got better right away. Not many people make any substantial money in the field. You run into dangerous situations. There is stress, a lack of sleep, and endless criticism by nonbelievers. Exposing yourself to such problems would make no sense at all. The reason why serious researchers stay involved is because the cases are very real and the fact remains that there are those out there who are under attack. They need the help they deserve and that is why I stay in the Work."

*Exorcisms are seen as a myth or a misdiagnosed psychiatric problem. Have you seen cases of pure possession in your career as a researcher? Also, what exactly occurs at an exorcism?

"What you need to realize is that exorcisms are very real and do occur everywhere in the world. They are often shrouded in secrecy, but they do occur. Don't get me wrong, there are sects out there and people out there who claim certain cases are genuine but are mistaken, but the fact is that there are, without a doubt, real cases of diabolical possession.

"As far as my personal dealings with the rite of exorcism, I have assisted on over 65 genuine cases of possession over my years of research. This number, in comparison to my years in the field and the number of cases I have worked on, shows just how rare pure possession is. I have seen exorcisms performed by many different sects such as Catholics, Traditionalists, and even Buddhists.

"It is not uncommon after working on a case in which possession is absolutely the reason to experience phenomena at the rite of exorcism. Often, the exorcism will be fairly mellow, but usually in about seven out of every ten exorcisms, something will occur. People in my presence have revealed aspects of personal lives of those present that they could not have known, they may exhibit strength beyond that which would be normal for a human, they may speak in languages that they could not know. Also, smells, either putrid or appealing, may become apparent during an exorcism, as well as tappings or wrappings on the walls. Often, popping noises may emerge at the cessation of the rite, or the smell of ozone, similar to that after a thunderstorm. The possessed person may bite or scratch, or exhibit fits of rage. Often, the eyes of the possessed person will not blink for extended periods of time. Often at an exorcism, there is a feeling of absolute trepidation. There is usually an indication to those present that there is an entity around. Those assisting often feel a presence. Next, the demon will tend to hide behind the personality of the possessed person to avoid eviction from the person. Diversions will be created to interrupt the rite, and noises as well as voices and physical mayhem may occur. The desired outcome is, of course, the expulsion of the demon or demons from the person's body.

"Many ask about possession and how it actually takes place. Different people have different beliefs on the subject. I believe that most cases represent transient possession. Transient possession marks the ability of the possessing entity or entities to come in and out of the individual as it pleases. The individual is not always under possession, but instead goes through random bouts of possession. I believe that when the entity enters, it does so by means of the solar plexus. Pure possession is quite different than transient possession, because with pure possession that entity will reside with that individual at all times.

"A major problem that arises in people that have gone through such bouts of possession is that is an exorcism is successful, but the weeks, months, or years to come might be marked by an ever-present feeling of emptiness. This is absolutely true because there is a void; there is something missing. What once inhabited the person has been banished. I often encourage those who were marked as possessed and who go through such issues to fill that void with something positive, such as a belief system which adopts that which is good and wholesome. They need to fill this void or else they might unconsciously or consciously let the being or beings reenter, causing the whole cycle to start again. In such instances, I will try to follow up as much as possible with such individuals and try to notify the clergy to set up some type of counseling to help intercede in their dilemma. Exorcism may mark the hopeful banishment, but the force will remain at bay, trying to gain reentry.

"People may become possessed by a variety of means. Many cases have a similar link between them, but similar to how law enforcement cases have different twists and circumstances, so do cases in psychic research. Each case has its own facts that make it a unique case. We all have free will—the ability to choose. This door leading to possession can be opened either willingly or unwillingly. Often, trickery will come into play in which the possessing force will sneak its way in by lying and deceitfulness, such as when a means of contact is used such as a Ouija board. The talking board will prey on your weaknesses and desires to gain entry into your life. By letting your guard down, you can leave yourself open for a possible struggle with something very sinister. Others will open the door willingly for means of interaction or to have some desired outcome fulfilled.

"Others are what we refer to as soul victims. These individuals are sometimes the pure of heart. Many of the pious clergy throughout history report temptations or actual physical challenges by the demonic. This is not a symbolic struggle they are reflecting in regards to their faith, but for some an actual problem with real-life manifestations of evil making themselves known to try to tempt and deceive. The desired outcome of the wicked being is to destroy the faith that is so important to that member of the faithful.

"What motives do the entities have for possessing an individual? There are several reasons that are apparent over years of recorded religious history. When the demonic presence enters a person, the goal is ultimate control over that individual. By the infestation stage, the demonic starts to creep in bit by bit to start the initial breakdown of the individual. By the time oppression is in full effect, the demonic is closing in fast, waiting for the right moment to possess. By influencing thoughts, frightening the person by outward manifestations, and interrupting sleep patterns consistently, the soon-to-be-possessed person is so weak, scared, confused, and tired of the barrage of phenomena that they may give up and put their guard down. The demonic always seems to follow such patterns and rarely will skip any stages in between the onset of possession. This pattern ensures that the possibility of possession will be at its strongest, unless the person being plagued gives outright permission for the deities to possess. This process of breaking down the person usually takes several months, but in some instances may take a shorter or longer period of time, depending on the circumstances that tie in with the case.

"The main goal of possession is to acquire the soul of that person who becomes possessed. The demonic will gain entry to that individual and will try to bring on death, often by suicide. These demonic soldiers run amuck and try to recruit as many as they can, bringing individuals to their side, the side that is the polar opposite of the positive.

"You do not have to believe in the demonic to be affected by the force. Several of the cases I have researched involve people who have no religious beliefs or background. The demonic exists, plain and simple. Just because someone denies existence of demons does not mean that they are not there. They can prey upon anyone, regardless of societal status, religion, age, or any other factors. The demonic does not gain a foothold on everyone, but of those individuals who have experienced the demonic, there are people from all different origins.

"I find it hard to understand why those who are experiencing a negative haunting cannot accept the fact that there is a positive side, a flip side to the situation. After their experiences, they are convinced that the negative is a reality, but will not adopt a positive to counteract the situation. In such hauntings, adopting a positive belief system is the key to minimize the negativity of the oppressing entities. This is a force you cannot command to leave or physically remove from your home. The force needs to be counteracted with its antithesis-a positive belief system, no matter what religion that might be. It does not appear to be relevant in regards to what sect you belong to, as it is to simply have some type of faith behind you. Adopting the positive ensures that you have some type of weapon to help your fight.

"There is another interesting twist regarding the possessed and those who witness such diabolical phenomena. Very rarely does one go unmoved by such a situation. Many gain a new respect or become deeply religious after their experiences. There are also those who fall victim and adopt the darker side, enveloped by its appeal. You need to remember that the power of the darker realm is so strong and tempting that many cannot resist it, and as a result, accept the other side. One must remember that no matter how hard it seems or how appealing the other side is, the positive is far stronger and superior and will outweigh the negative.

"Today, modern man tends to reject the notion that evil exists. Major religions have put forth the idea that the existence of a hierarchy of hell is nothing more than medieval folklore. Man and his desires are often seen as the driving evil force. It is our own selfish desires that cause evil to arise. This is true in a sense. Much of what occurs is caused by man. There is, however, without a doubt, a deeper explanation for some of the evil that is seen in the world. When I entered the field almost thirty years ago, I never really believed in the demonic, devils, and other preternatural aspects of the world. Through experience, this possibility has become a reality. There are those who become possessed, there are others who go through hell in their homes and lives, and there is a demonic underworld that interacts with our world whether human beings admit it or not. Are all cases demonic in nature? No, but there are those which are, and the number in this day and age is on the rise. There are the mentally ill, the delusional, and those who initiate hoaxes, and cases that prove to have a natural explanation. Then there are those cases which are truly real and those who witness it, live with it, and research it see just how real the spirit world is around us.

"Another issue which can make cases very interesting and difficult is that just because there is a mental disorder does not mean that the supernatural is not at play. There are cases where I have worked with individuals who were bipolar, schizophrenic, and had other mental disorders who also had supernatural problems, too. This makes it easier for the demonic to get a foothold and work in the background because anything this person says will be seen as a result of their mental problem.

"The eyes also can tell you a great deal when dealing with the possessed. I mentioned earlier that those who go under possession often do not blink. When you look into the possessed person's eyes you can see that they are not there, and that there is something else at play. Looking into the possessed person's eyes is unforgettable. I am personally a firm believer that the eyes are the windows to the soul. After seeing these people, it is obvious that something is with them."

*What are some of the causes of haunting? How come some people go years without any experiences, then have phenomena occur? Why do others seemingly have problems their entire lives?

"One reason that comes to mind is when an individual has become cursed. When someone curses an individual, such as a practitioner, it is important to try to find out exactly how it was done. By finding out the type of ritual and the exact practice instated, it will make it easier to find out the desired outcome of the curse, and therefore instate a binding to cease the problem or reverse the curse. Curses sound rather silly and old world in nature, originating in the time of witches and myths. However, many able practitioners of many growing religions, such as Voodoo, Santeria, and the like, can inflict problems onto persons whether they want to believe it or not. These practitioners manipulate intelligent energy and cut deals with deities to have their wishes carried out.

"Generational hauntings are always interesting cases. In a generational haunting the cycle of phenomena will carry on through separate generations. For instance, a grandparent might be cursed or have some other type of catalyst for the haunting. The offspring of the individual will experience the phenomena, as will the grandchildren. These cases are usually very in depth and are extremely difficult to remedy.

"For instance, just a few years ago I worked on a case in which three different generations had been affected by the phenomena. A total of twenty-eight different family members were involved in this particular case. What transpired after digging deeper and deeper in the case was that the grandparents had been cursed decades ago. They seemed to know this, but did not put much credence into the notion. As I have stated, it is crucial to the resolution to know how and what type of practices were used in inflicting a curse. In this case, it is quite obvious that not only were the grandparents cursed, but their descendants as well.

"When a curse is inflicted on someone, the deities or the demonic will be summoned to carry on some type of deed as instructed by the person placing the curse. Since there is no time in the spirit world, this deity might be on its third or fourth generation of torment, but this in turn does not phase the negative energy.

This is what they were assigned to do and that is their present assignment. What the practitioner has to realize is that after, there is a price to pay for their services, and the curse or some other type of detriment will eventually catch back up to them. These deities do not perform their services for free.

"Another common and probably the most accepted of all the theories is that of an earthbound spirit which lingers on after the time of death. The spirit might linger by means of a tragedy that took their life suddenly, leaving the individual confused and not realizing that they have passed on to a different plane of existence. This is often true of suicide victims. This is not to say that anyone who commits suicide will remain earthbound, but it has happened.

"Other times, individuals will haunt areas or locations that they are close to such as their home or favorite establishment or even the workplace. When someone passes on and still is tied into this world, they tend to remain in that time period. This is why when many people witness these specters, they often look like they are from a different era. With death, they carry to the other side what was common and understood by them in life. When these areas are renovated, such as older homes, sometimes spirit activity will brew. This is no coincidence. Many times physical alterations to a home will bring out spirit activity because you are changing what is familiar to them, and the change is not appealing to them. The area appeals to them as it did in their physical life, therefore change can cause frustration and phenomena will pick up based on the spirits' reaction. We need to remember that homes, castles, and other emotionally attached places were built and occupied by families, sometimes even for centuries. The past often shows that the family erected a structure, the group using their own sweat and blood to build the home. Then they lived in the structure and passed it on to the next generation. It was not like today where we move in where we please. This people had homesteads where they were born, worked, raised families, and died. All aspects of their lives revolved around these homes. The tract of land proved to encompass every important aspect of their lives. Every bit of joy, every bit of pain, life, death, and all emotions took place primarily in this one particular area.

"I conducted a recent investigation where renovations seemed to be the mechanism that brought about the haunting phenomena in the home. To me, it was an excellent example of how everything will be dormant, then some mechanism will cause havoc to break loose. In this case, that mechanism seemed to be the renovations taking place as well as possibly the young children who the spirit identified with. Cases like this are very interesting and usually are not altogether negative. Instead, a human spirit is at work that identifies with the family, wants attention, or tries to coexist with those who have inhabited the home that once belonged to the spirit when they were alive.

"This case involved a single mother who had three young children. One was almost four and she had twins about nine months old. She had never encountered ghosts or the like in her life, and was not necessarily petrified, but instead concerned about her children and if the presence would scare or hurt them. While remodeling was taking place, a baby could be heard crying in the apartment even though the children were not present at the time. Screams and wails were heard. Also, when her landlord went downstairs for lunch and returned, he found very small footprints in white paint on the floor next to the kitchen area.

"The woman claimed to have experienced very little and wanted to ensure that the situation could be brought to a halt. The only items that were in the vacant apartment were a baby bottle, which was removed from the corner of the attic and later returned to the spot it was found, and also a crib mattress that was left in the other end of the attic undisturbed. She decided to give as little recognition to the spirit as possible, claiming the house as hers. Also, she contacted a member of her protestant faith to come and bless the premises. She has not been in contact since.

"It is interesting how spirit that is around or even dormant will sometimes respond to a change. This is one of the most common reasons why I have been brought in on cases that resemble human spirit.

"Another aspect of haunting and something I truly believe in is that our loved ones have the ability to cross over to help us, warn us, or interact on a need-to-know basis. This is something I have come across time and time again and have experienced firsthand with the apparition of my grandfather. I cannot believe how many cases have come in over the years that exhibit such a similarity to such instances. Many times, after people report such experiences, there will be some type of occurrence, such as a death in the family, a major accident, or some other type of change in the lives of the family. Based on many scenarios and cases I have been involved with, it appears that there is a strong possibility that in many circumstances, our loved ones return to help us cross over at the time of death.

"Another common phenomenon that is documented heavily is residual haunting. Certain areas, such as buildings, battlefields, and other places, seem to hold energy, which at some times without any real known reason, that plays back. These ghosts seem to not be intelligent beings interacting with the witness, but seem transfixed, reliving some moment in their lives. It is like a loop of video that is played back indefinitely.

"Anniversary hauntings are also a type of phenomena that has been quite publicized in books and television documentaries. In this, a spirit will appear or come back in some form on the date of their death or their birthday on an annual basis. Sometimes it will be a wedding anniversary or some other moment that proved to be emotional and significant for that individual. Time cycles often prove to be directly tied in to cases and how the appearances or outward manifestations occur.

"Many women who are pregnant experience phenomena. It often intensifies around the time right around the physical birth. Many believe that this is a deceased family member looking out for the unborn child. Also, after the birth many women report occurrences. It appears that spirit is attracted to such an important event and makes their presence known in some instances.

"One aspect of haunting you need to be aware of is that spirit tends to attract spirit. Where you have one spirit you almost always run the chance of having multiple spirits. Since they tend to attract one another, it is difficult because a negative spirit could be attracted. Spirit attracts spirit, whether it is positive or negative.

"Bringing closure to cases involving human spirit usually involves trying to convince the deceased that they are just that-deceased, no longer a physical part of this spectrum. Today many people want to cohabit their home with a spirit that has made its presence known. I happen to disagree with this very strongly. I feel that this spirit needs to move on and be with their family. They need help to cross over because they may be trapped or confused. By fulfilling known areas of wishes that were conveyed by the person while still in life, often the haunting will stop. This is a clear indicator that there was unfinished business that needed to be carried out before the person could move on."

*What is provocation and what is its purpose, intent, and outcome?

"Provocation is often very misunderstood. It can be used for both positive and negative means. At times, it is dangerous and is abused by many in the field of psychic research who rely on this technique. Provocation is the irritation, if you will, of the spiritual intelligence of that environment. By triggering an emotion of a human spirit or triggering a response by the demonic by means of religion, what typically results is some type of physical manifestation of the spirit. This should really only be used when needed to gain information or to prove the existence of some type of entity in that particular environment.

"Provocation can be very dangerous. An investigator who decides to provoke must take into consideration the family, making it fully understood what their intentions as researchers are and what they are doing in the family's home. Provoking will help assess which approach will be most effective. Provoking on a religious level will often infuriate the demonic, bringing about the arousal of phenomena by the malevolent intelligence.

"When something is indeed provoked, the ultimate question is how to get it to stop. Through the power of prayer, a person has to close and send back this energy that is manifesting. By calling on God, you can stop the phenomena and protect not only yourself, but also the family you are trying to help. If one provokes spirit, you without a doubt need a belief system behind you to counteract that which has been aggravated.

"Religious provocation will usually fail to work when dealing with human spirit. This is usually reserved for the demonic. In cases in which human spirit is the reason for the disturbance, often the family will be instructed to recreate a scenario or emotion that initially has brought about phenomena in the past to see if the spirit will make its presence known.

"On a negative level, often blessed objects and relics or holy water can be used to receive a reply. It is not necessarily the object that causes the response, but the prayers that have been said of the object. As I strongly believe and have had proven to me firsthand over the years, there is a great deal of power in prayer. You could have all the relics in the world and there would probably be no physical response. Bring a blessed object into a home where the demonic is residing and the chances are pretty high that something will occur. The introduction of that object to the immediate environment will almost always receive a response from the inhabiting entities.

"Personally, all of my religious articles and the holy water I use on cases are blessed by Bishop Robert McKenna.

"There have been situations where there are objects which are blessed by two very different individuals. One object blessed by a member of the clergy may not spark any response where a different object blessed by someone totally different will cause all sorts of phenomena to take place. The reason is that one of these people will have a strong belief while the other might be very weak in his faith; therefore, the blessings instated over the objects would be very different. Thought has substance and faith can vary up or down in its degree. Each person will have their beliefs, some weaker and some stronger than others, depending on the strength of their faith."

*What is your response to those who feel that the whole field is fake? Many will lash out saying that ghosts, haunting, the demonic,

exorcisms, and the like are mere fiction. How do you respond to such notions that are the total opposite of your experiences after several years of investigating?

"What bothers me about these equations is that of the cases that the disbelievers have said are hoaxes, most of the time they were never in the home. How can these individuals actually say that the case was made up when they had no dealings whatsoever with the case at all? They were not in the home, they never got involved and witnessed any occurrences, and they never even spoke with the family or the researchers. I respect people's opinions, and if you do not believe in all this, that is fine, but how can you debunk a case that was real, having no insight into what has transpired in the home? Debunking would mean to disprove the allegations that the home was haunted, but how can you debunk a case that you had not one bit of involvement in?

"This has been an issue for the Warrens over the years. One case, for example, was the funeral parlor in Southington, Connecticut that I talked about earlier, where I had many firsthand encounters. That case leaked out to the media, and all kinds of reports popped up in the press, including that the story was a complete hoax. I worked on that case. I witnessed the phenomena. I recorded many of the tapes, took many of the pictures, and spent most of my summer in that home. It was real and concrete. There was no fraud or planned hoax. There was no misinterpretation or mass hallucination. That case was real. These negative accusations have no basis. It really is quite humorous how there will be extensive evidence and documentation, eyewitness accounts, and so forth on any given case. All it takes is one person not even involved in the case who has no idea what is occurring in the home to say it is a hoax and it is then considered to actually be a hoax. I could never understand this. This debunker just says the word *hoax* and it is taken as truth even though they are totally incorrect and have no proof to back their allegations up.

"Others will come out and state that the only reason why I and others are in the field is for the fortune and fame. Well, if you have any idea on what the Work is really like, you will see this is completely bogus and another statement that has no credential whatsoever. I do not get paid for my research, plain and simple. I lecture a few times a year and receive payment for most of them. Basically, there are no monetary transactions made. On a great deal of the cases, it costs me money to investigate them. With many of the cases, I am reimbursed for my travel expenses, such as gas, tolls, and the like. I do not make a living from the field."

*What is your relationship with Bishop Robert McKenna? (McKenna is known for his involvement in numerous cases pertaining to exorcism.) Did you know Malachi Martin? (Martin was an author, a professor, and an exorcist who was known in the field of religious demonology.)

"I have personally known and worked with Bishop McKenna for well over twenty years. I consider him a personal friend. McKenna is a traditionalist Catholic bishop who heads Our Lady of the Rosary Chapel in Monroe, Connecticut. I have assisted in many exorcisms he has personally conducted over the years. He is one of the most devout, Christian individuals I have ever met in all my years. He means and lives by what he says. Bishop will go to any extent to help a family in need, and as a result, we have a trusting relationship. He knows that when I need his assistance, the case is altogether real and needs interaction. His knowledge of the demonic pertaining to the clergy end of it all is very deep. There have been many times over the years that I have spoken with him because of the crazy things that I have come across. He, in return, will try to help me understand what has transpired. Bishop has trained numerous clergy members in the area of demonology and exorcism and has worked with hundreds of people. He has worked with the Warrens, myself, and many other researchers to help break the cycle of the demonic and bring these people into the light of God. He has a unique gift that he shares with many people, but you will never hear him boast about any of it. He is a unique individual who will bend over backwards to help his fellow man break the chains of evil that are bestowed upon him. Bishop McKenna really is an exorcist because so many of today's dominant clergy fail to accept that these types of situations, in which people are dealing with that of a diabolical nature, exist, leaving the victim on thin ice with nowhere to turn for help. Many clergy simply will not help or fear to help these individuals. If the case is legit and Bishop McKenna is asked, he will work with the families and individuals to try to rid them of their afflictions.

"Malachi Martin was an extremely interesting man. God bless him, he is no longer with us. I had met with him several times in the last few years of his life. I had assisted him with a few cases he was working on in Connecticut. Malachi Martin was very educated, with concentrations in the areas of Semitic languages, the Dead Sea Scrolls, and other serious areas of study. As a Jesuit and professor, he had an intellect that was very unique. When you dealt with Malachi, you were dealing with an educated man who was extremely down-to-earth. He was an absolute trip. You never knew exactly what he was going to say, but you knew it was sincere and rooted in truth. He learned a great deal over the years firsthand. He actually was an exorcist and had experiences that many could not comprehend. He was a man of purity who would also help anyone who needed help. He, too, had compassion for those who had suffered at the expense of the demonic. He knew that the Devil was at work on this plane and dealt with members of this blasphemous squad in the past. I hope he rests in peace in the hands of the Creator."

The Black Widow Case

The Black Widow Case

Gazing around, as John discussed the critical aspects of a case in northern Connecticut, something piqued my interest. Mounted on a glossy finished, wooden plank was a full-length silvery sword. Its blade was a deep-set chrome, its handle looked like pewter used for the molding of antique silverware. On its handle a devilish character stares out, horns perking upward into two almost half-circles. I was curious of the story behind this peculiar dagger.

"John," I said while sitting in a chair in his office, "where did you get that sword?"

"That's from a case I worked on a few years ago," he replied. He began to speak of the circumstances surrounding his attainment of the sword, and the anguish some faced in the home from which it was removed.

"Honestly," he continued, "I'm not sure if it was a mere decoration or actually used for sinister purposes, but it was tied in directly to a man by the name of Jason and the affliction he endured while it was in his presence. He wanted it banished from the premises and had me remove it from his home."

From the Onset of Bereavement

The deafening sound of a garbage truck flew down a nearby street. Children were abundant throughout the neighborhood. There was no school today and little people celebrated a day where there would be no math or reading, a day to enjoy the scenery and notorious season that New England had to offer. Southern New England is known for its beauty and tranquility. On Sunday afternoons, it is commonplace for families to gather in the car and drive down many of the back roads and even the major highways to see the leaves changing colors or the sporadic hill and mountainous patterns reflective of a unique landscape that only New England offers.

Jason's eyes remained transfixed on New England's beautiful atmosphere as leaves slowly piled up, then blew away as fast as they had fallen to the earth. Leaning against a rake, Jason began to recall the fate of his ex-wife, which was revealed to him just hours beforehand. His previous marriage which had ended just a few short years ago was disastrous, but he still could not believe that Karen had taken her own life.

Jason drifted back into the house only to find the local newspaper strewn about on the kitchen table. On top of the heaping mess of paper, this morning's breakfast dishes, and a stack of mail was a picture of his late wife on the obituary page. "Crazy bitch," he thought, picking up the black and white image of Karen gazing out at him. "What was she thinking?" Jason thought without speaking.

Jason walked over to the living room chair and sat down, putting his feet up on the hassock. He closed his eyes, recalling the life they once shared. He never imagined his next glimpse of her would be in a newspaper due to such a tragic circumstance.

When Karen and Jason met, he loved her instantly. Her tall, slim figure and long black hair grabbed his attention immediately. When he finally worked up the nerve to speak to her, Jason was instantaneously entranced by her dark eyes, which gazed at him passionately. From that day on, they spent countless hours together courting, until Jason asked Karen to marry him. She accepted without hesitation, and a few short months later, the local justice of the peace married them.

One thing that was hard for Jason was the fact that he was Karen's fourth husband. Three times before, Karen was left a widow by the tragic deaths of her supposed lifelong partners. Her first husband died by the hands of a near fatal automobile accident, which eventually claimed his life. After four days in the hospital, he passed on. The second husband's cause of death was never conclusively determined, but Karen had found him lifeless next to her the next morning in their bed. Her third husband had suffered a mental breakdown and committed suicide. On a cold winter night, her lover went out drinking and came home only to mix his regular drink of whiskey with a large amount of painkillers. He, too, was found lifeless, this time on the dining room floor.

It bothered Jason deeply in his unconscious that he would be her fourth marital partner, but he was sure he would be her final. Never before had a woman gripped his heart as Karen had over the last year. Karen's love seemed to encompass him like no other, and Jason slowly lost any concern that remained in him over her outlandish past, truly believing their life together would be the definition of sheer perfection.

For the first couple of months, Jason and Karen organized their new life together. Jason moved in Karen's split-level home, sharing it with not only Karen, but also her three children from her previous marriages. Jason, although not a stereotypical father figure, took on the responsibilities associated with raising children. He sincerely cared about the three children, treating them like his own flesh and blood.

Things seemed to be picture perfect for the newly united family of five. The children did well in school and Jason was doing just fine at his job renovating homes. Contractors were banging down his door for his handyman skills, paying him top dollar for his services. Jason had always worked with his hands, installing dry wall, painting, some minor woodwork, and cabinet installation. Everything was fine, at least for now.

The Time for Unwanted Change Approaches

"Karen," Jason said with solemnity in his voice, "Do you want to take the kids out for dinner?"

Jason just landed a sizeable down payment for his upcoming work on an old Victorian just a few miles from his home. To celebrate, he wanted to take the Karen and the kids out to the local pub to grab a decent meal. With his recent long hours and the kids sporadically dispersed all over the place due to school and sports, he felt it was the prime opportunity to come together and spend quality time with his newfound family.

Sleepy-eyed and rather sarcastically Karen replied, "Take the damn kids and go, you know I already have plans."

Karen had started to cut back her hours at her job as a temp at the local dentist office. Work began to become secondary to her nights out with her friends. These friends were becoming increasingly apparent when Jason was at work or when he was going out with his buddies from high school. These acquaintances sometimes made Jason nervous because almost all the time when he came home, they were on their way out the door. His words to them were few and far between and Karen spoke very little of her weekly visitors. "Karen, what the hell is wrong with you lately? Your attitude has gone to complete shit. What about the kids? What about me? Don't you want to spend any time with us?" Karen gazed at him with burning eyes. She stood for a moment as if she were going to counteract Jason's interrogation. Without a word, she turned around and walked back to the bedroom, only the squeaks of the bedspring heard in the background.

Jason rounded up the kids and headed out. That night Jason could not really enjoy himself. Every time the kids mentioned their mother, he could not help but think of her attitude over the last month or so. She had become almost too quiet, whether at the dinner table or watching the ten o'clock news. Her soft-spoken nature had erupted into sudden outbursts of sarcasm and intense criticism. The children were often scolded for no reason, and upon Jason's defense of the children, a sure battle was to emerge. There seemed to be no way around some type of verbal altercation on almost a daily basis. It was at the point where he basically tried to avoid being around her, but this was, of course, beginning to destroy him internally.

Jason pulled up the driveway, as he had everyday over the last few months, but something did not sit right with him. He noticed three other cars in the driveway. Two of them he recognized immediately. The third was not a known vehicle, but he figured Karen's friend, Danielle, must have brought another one of her flings over to the house.

Once again, as Jason predicted, Karen's crew exited within about five minutes of his arrival. Jason's blood pressure began to rise considerably. He began to swelter with anger. Danielle, another girl whom Jason did not recognize, and two men nodded and greeted him, followed by a sudden departure. Jason fastened the door behind them, locking the deadbolt. "Damn it Karen, what the hell is going on?" Jason expressed with his fists clenched. "Who were those people? Are those bastards your little boy toys?"

"Shut up, Jason," Karen said firmly. "You know that I love you. How can you even insinuate such a thing? They are just my friends, why can't you just accept that fact and grow up?" Once again, Karen acted as if no explanation were needed, leaving Jason not only furious, but also undeniably confused by the guests who once again left as fast as they appeared. Jason sat up and watched the rerun of an old basketball playoff game, drinking a beer with his feet up on the table. He could not completely concentrate on his favorite sport, instead his mind wandered, questioning his own perspectives. Maybe he was overreacting. Maybe Karen needed some time to herself with her friends. They were not married that long and maybe she needed the social aspect of her friends to feel independent. One aspect was not sitting well with him though. Why had everything been so secretive? Why did they only come over when he was at work or when he was out for the evening? Jason took another sip of his beer and placed the empty on the oak end table. He grabbed the clicker and shut off the television. Jason arose and proceeded to the bedroom.

Jason stood in the doorway gazing at Karen. He loved her, but hated the turn of their marriage. They were like adversaries in a game of chess; the pawn was like the very love they thought they shared. Jason flicked the hall light off and headed to bed. He lay beside Karen, thinking and praying that their recent differences could be ironed out. Whatever was occurring was probably only temporary, at least that is what Jason thought and hoped for, praying that this was the beginning of the end of his recent distress.

Falling Deeper into Unrest

Jason lay unconscious in the bedroom. His physical body began to toss and turn as his unconscious experienced absolute fright. Jason's dream state was shrouded with horrible visions. Hooded specters danced like ravenous wolves around a blazing fire as defenseless bound animals were tossed into the blaze, yelping in excruciation from the burns inflicted from the crackling flames. Words that could not be deciphered echoed as from a distant source. Although audible, their exact speech could not quite be pinpointed. The evil aura of death and the relentless torture of creatures continued until Jason awoke from his slumber, which seemed to be nothing short of eternity. Jason sat up sweating, sheets drenched with cold perspiration from the vision straight from some foreign place he had just witnessed. He got up, went to the refrigerator, and grabbed an ice water and sat down in the living room, turning the TV on. At this point, the television was his only comfort. Jason continued to click through dozens of channels aimlessly, not able to quite forget what he had experienced in his dream. Jason felt that all the stress of his marriage had finally gotten the best of him. He knew he needed to talk to Karen and bury the hatchet before he really began to lose it.

The next day Jason talked with Karen over toast and coffee. The two made small talk and no real arguments started, despite the usual hostile atmosphere that so frequently surrounded the two.

Jason looked at Karen, "Honey, we really need to talk. Lately, we just don't click. You're doing your thing, and I've been doing mine and what about the kids? You never even seem to know where they are or what is going on with them."

Karen looked at Jason and apologized for her delinquency. "I know, I know," Karen said with only half sincere motions. "We'll make it all work out." After a few minutes, the two went their separate ways. Jason went to work and Karen went to her new temp job as a switchboard operator for the local telephone company.

Three weeks had passed and Jason's sleep was still scarce. Almost nightly, he was woken by strange feelings and often-unexplainable thoughts and perverse visions. Jason spent the majority of the night hours in front of the television half-dozing. He just felt uncomfortable in the bedroom. Attributing his feelings to the tense nature of his relationship with his wife, he figured that his insomnia was a normal side effect of a failing marriage; his dreams the result of stress, once again caused by his fear of marital failure. What had happened? Was he going completely crazy? How could he not have seen Karen's flaws before they were united as man and woman?

Early Saturday morning Jason sat on his porch as the kids played baseball in the yard. His cousin Phil was stopping by to pick up some paintbrushes and tarps to finish up his mother's failed painting effort. Phil pulled up in his pickup, getting out with his usual smile covered by heavy, scruff hair. The bearded man of twenty-five was one of Jason's closest relatives. The two had spent nearly every summer during childhood together, fishing and playing baseball in their grandmother's front yard. Recently, however, the two were drifting apart. Jason was becoming more withdrawn and kept to himself.

Phil approached Jason with open arms, hugging his favorite cousin. "Long time, no see," Phil said, his blue eyes fixed upon Jason. "When are we going for a beer or over to Clark's Diner? You're a stranger lately; don't be afraid to pick up the phone. I call you at least twice a week and never hear back from you."

Jason looked at him and almost burst into tears. "I don't know what's wrong with me. I can't take it anymore. My marriage might as well be done. Karen will be completely fine one moment and a complete loony the next. I think she's sleeping with someone else. Every week she has her cronies over and they walk out of here when I get home like I'm not even coming in the door."

Phil and Jason gazed at each other with neither saying another word. The silence gave heed to a few tears from Jason. Phil put his hand on his cousin's shoulder and led him inside. "Where is she?" Phil asked with apprehension in his voice.

"I don't know," Jason said in a low, yet wild tone. "She's gone most of the time, and when she's here, we fight. She barely acknowledges the kids, and she never seems to acknowledge me at all. We just don't get along anymore. She's completely nuts. I want out. I can't take her shit anymore."

The next day Jason got up early and started loading his truck. He told Karen he was going to stay with his cousin until they could work out their differences. Leaving that day, Jason had no idea that he would not return to the place he, for several months, called home. Within just a few more months he filed for divorce and the two never spoke again, their relationship terminated with axe-like precision.

Opening his eyes, Jason got up out of his chair, wondering what exactly had caused Karen to go over the edge. He could not help but feel some compassion for his ex-wife, even though things did not exactly work out for them. As his first wife, she was obviously an irreplaceable part in a chapter of Jason's. Although they bore no children together, Jason still loved her three children. He had heard through a mutual friend that all three were taken away from her last spring. Apparently, her temper and fits of rage that Jason had begun to experience before leaving had grown in frequency and intensity, and local authorities had been brought in several times before deciding to take the children away from her care. Jason even considered taking his stepchildren in, but starting a new life meant total separation from her, breaking any and all ties they had together, including interaction with her children.

Now, Jason had found a new love and had a daughter of his own. Their daughter, Cynthia, had been born two-and-a half years ago and they had been married six months after her birth. His new wife Denise was perfect in Jason's eyes. She worked as a realtor and was the perfect mother for Cynthia. The three made quite the stereotypical family, spending time together daily enjoying one another's company. Sure, there was the occasional display of tension, but nothing that could not be resolved by means of discussion.

The next few weeks were typical of the standard New England fall season. The onset of a long, cold winter was just around the bend. In a few short weeks, Halloween, the commercialized pagan holiday, would be eminent by eager trick-or-treaters disguised in their ghoulish arrays and ghostly vestibules. Typically, this night is the one evening each year in many superstitious belief systems where the dead are allowed to drift among the rest of humanity freely before returning to their eternal resting places. The next day would mark All Saints' Day, the day of repentance for all departed souls in the Catholic tradition. The end of these two days signaled the conclusion of fall, the remainder of colorful leaves crashing to the ground to be raked up and discarded until new ones appeared next year, marking the birth of new, earthly life.

Jason awoke drowsy. For the last few nights, he had risen from his slumber for no obvious reason. His sleep patterns had been disrupted by sporadic bouts of cold sweats. For seemingly no reason, Jason would wake up at various points in the night disturbed. Looking around the room, he never quite found a reason for the all too familiar sleep trouble. There was no physical commotion, nor were there any recognizable factors causing the lack of sleep. He could not recall any nightmares or any inner turmoil that was causing his sporadic sleep disturbances. He would simply just wake up.

Walking to the kitchen, Jason dragged his feet slowly across the darkly stained hardwood. Sitting at the kitchen table, Jason recalled the previous night in vivid detail. His mannerisms over the last couple of weeks were bizarre, and not only recognized by Jason himself, but by Denise as well. Twice already, Denise made comments on how withdrawn Jason had been, keeping to himself after arriving home from work. Jason would often retreat to his office downstairs, not even coming up to join his wife and daughter for dinner. He just did not feel like interacting with anyone most of the time. His mood had taken a total one-hundred-and-eighty-degree turn, alternating from calm and happy to quiet and argumentative. Jason would often snap at the most minor of problems. Under the guise of normal adult stress, Jason's newly formed negative attitude went almost unrecognized as the beginning of a far deeper problem.

The night before had marked the realization that something more was happening to Jason, something both confusing and unexplained in Jason's perspective. Not only was he frightened, but also he assumed that his sanity was slipping away from him. Jason was on the front porch smoking a cigarette when the he felt it was time to get down to business. He got up off the stairs and headed down to his office to write up his invoices for the week. It was a decent week, and he needed to collect for his services remodeling two homes that were just a few blocks away.

Sitting there, pen in hand, Jason felt uneasy. He had the feeling that something was standing behind him. He turned and saw nothing. The initial feeling of being watched surrounded him, a feeling that he had never really experienced before, but at this point it felt very real. A second time moments later, he turned yet again only to find nothing residing behind him. Feeling he was being completely ridiculous, he continued filling out the standard paperwork, licking the envelopes, and sealing them shut. It was at this point that he felt the touch. Jason distinctly felt what seemed like a human hand brushing down his back from his neck to mid-back. It had the weight of a hand and felt just like the touch of a human. Jason jumped forward out of his chair, facing the direction where the disembodied appendage had apparently came from, but yet again, there was no visible source of the sensation. Jason stood frozen in fear, unable to view the source of the disturbance. After several minutes, Jason headed upstairs, convincing himself he was nuts. However, he knew what he felt was real, as real as his wife's touch or any other person for that matter. Jason retreated to the comfort of the television for hours, until the experience seemed distant and inconceivable. He threw on his slippers and headed downstairs again with the intent of grabbing his invoices and bringing them back upstairs to throw them on the end table by the stairs. He needed to drop off those bills tomorrow to ensure payment for his work.

Jason flicked on the light and hustled over to his desk where he had filled out the paperwork earlier, but the invoices were missing! He knew he left them there, right next to his desk lamp. Jason jumbled some papers, looked on the floor, under the oversized desk calendar, and on top of his filing cabinets but found no trace of the documents. Disturbed, he stormed upstairs and plopped himself in the easy chair. Had he left them where he thought he did? He knew he did. After being touched, he headed upstairs immediately. There was no time for him to have moved the documents elsewhere. He had not even left the house and no one else had been downstairs, so there was no way that the invoices could have been taken out of his office.

Once again, Jason used the television to comfort his angst. He sat there trying to make the situation disappear from his mind, convincing himself that the papers would turn up. Little did he know that they would not until several days later.

Jason sipped his decaffeinated coffee. The bitterness made his lips pucker. He plunged one foot to the floor, lifting himself up to a standstill. Sugar was the only thing on his mind. All he had to enjoy this evening was his nightly cup of hot coffee, which became a pre-bedtime ritual. Tonight, however, he was still pissed. Everything in general was a blur to him. His relationship was diminishing, and he thought that his experiences were the onset of his sanity leaving him.

Jason stood, eyes transfixed on the doorway. What stood there was still and very dark, blacker than the black of a cold winter night. Whatever it was, it peered at him, hanging in the doorway with an aura of death. Accompanying the image was the odor of sulfur and what Jason could only recognize as the scent of decaying matter. The stench was enough to turn ones' stomach. The figure hung in midair, still but bodiless. Jason's eyes dried out from not blinking. What seemed like years came to an end with the torso-shaped black mass descending into the darkened kitchen, and with it the putrid smell, like flesh withering off of a corpse.

Jason's feet remained frozen to the floor. His natural instinct to flee never had a chance to kick in because of the fear instilled in him by the encounter. Even though the physical encounter was very real, he could not bring himself to believe his own eyes. The situation simply did not make any sense. There was no way in hell that such a figure was a part of the normal spectrum of life. It must have been caused by mental stress, or perhaps by the onset of some type of depression. The possibilities went on, the images of all types of reasons littering his brain, but somewhere he felt that perhaps there was something darker and more sinister than anything his imagination could concoct deep within the neurons of his brain. There was a deep-rooted problem which had surfaced, but was playing a game with Jason—a clear and concise plan to tear him limb from limb by working his senses and preying upon his most vulnerable human emotions.

Weeks went by, with each night marking a sinister overtone which hung in the houses' atmosphere. Jason's lack of sleep continued, wearing him down enough to cause outbursts of anger related to the most insignificant of events. Not only was the lack of sleep enough to create a hostile atmosphere, but also an emotion of fear dwindled around him. He waited for the next encounter with the being or beings which had appeared to him that night by the kitchen. Jason constantly looked over his shoulder, as if an unseen force was going to lunge on him. His had become a prisoner in his own home, locked in a world of mystery, wondering if it was all psychological or if it was a dark realty that he was taught to overlook—the stuff of mere superstition and medieval lore or a world that sometimes interacted with ours. Who knew what was really true?

It was Thanksgiving eve, the night before one of the most celebrated holidays in the United States. Denise had prepared much of the food that they would bring to her mother's tomorrow. The smell of pies and fresh bread lingered throughout the upper portion of the house. Cardboard cutouts of pilgrims and cartoon-like turkeys hung in almost every window. The center of the dining room table housed an oversized cornucopia filled with harvest items from the local farm. Denise had just retired to bed after many hours of cooking to watch some television while resting, and Cynthia had long been tucked away after an intensive day of playtime at the daycare center just a few streets over. Jason remained uplifted and alive with excitement for the upcoming day of celebration. It was the first time in quite awhile that he had felt even remotely joyous.

He sat still at the kitchen table thinking about his visit the next day with his in-laws and then later with his own family. Denise was downstairs, putting the laundry in the washing machine, not aware of what would occur.

"What was that?" Jason thought to himself. He knew he had heard something, but could not pinpoint which direction it came from. "Must have been a limb from the damn trees rubbing on the outside wall," he said in a low, murmured voice out loud to no one. The tapping emerged again, this time a little louder and longer in duration. What seemed like knuckles thrusting the walls kept building, growing more intense every minute or so. It did not make any sense, the sound was so basic yet unnatural. The invisible source of the noise drove Jason to a point of anger laced with fear of what he did not understand.

Jason stood up, moving steadily toward the increasing sounds, which had turned into knocks. "Knock it off," Jason said firmly with patience that had obviously been worn thin. "What do you want, you bastard, get out of here." He truly felt that the knocks surrounded him in the kitchen, mocking him as an inferior life form.

The knocks continued steadier than before, audible through most of the top floor. They seemed to surround Jason, growing louder following his demands to stop. Jason retreated to his office, turning on the radio to a talk show to hopefully ease his mind. He sat not only disturbed but also purely pissed. His mood was interrupted. Shrieks of terror engulfed Jason. He heard Cynthia screaming.

Within a matter of seconds, Jason was at her door. Almost running right through it, he tossed on the light and hugged his young child. Denise was only a second or so behind him.

"What's the matter, honey? What's wrong?" Jason compassionately expressed, his heart racing.

Cynthia stated that something was in her room. Jason could see nothing, but the air seemed thicker, heavy with a burden of disgust.

"What's wrong, Cindy?" Denise clamored. "Did you have a nightmare? It's alright, daddy and I are here." Denise's frown turned into a reassuring smile.

"There was a man, daddy, by my nightlight. He touched me," she said pointing in the direction where the intruder had disappeared.

"What do you mean touched you?" Jason said, trusting his daughter, but still confused. "He touched me on my arm," Cynthia was sincere in her efforts to convey her story. Denise sat back, consoling Cindy with words, but passing it off as that of an overactive dream which seemed like reality. Jason could not pass this off so quickly. Had the thing that had appeared to him be appearing to his daughter? Jason thought back on that night when the mass had appeared to him, he thought about his invoices that had vanished, then reappeared where he originally left them, and the feeling of being watched. Even tonight the tappings had occurred. What was happening? Maybe it was even more than his nerves. Jason realized that maybe his daughter had encountered the wrath of this entity which had made residence in their home, coexisting in the background of Jason's life, feeding off his fear, bearing witness to his entire life. For weeks now, Jason had felt like he was never alone in the house, as if something was around him or beside him.

After several minutes of persuasion, Jason and Denise calmed Cynthia down and retreated to their bedroom. Jason sat on the edge of the bed, his head leaning on his open palms. "Are you alright honey?" Denise's voice echoed through the desolate room. "She'll be fine, it was only a nightmare, all kids have them, and we've all had them."

"Denise," Jason said peering out of eyes that seemed to gaze right through her. "There is more to this, so much more, you don't understand, maybe never will."

"What do you mean?" "I mean I really don't think Cindy was having night terrors. I've been experiencing things and I don't know what is going on, but I need to make sense of it. I need to know what is going on. I just can't deal with it anymore. It's driving me crazy."

Denise said nothing. The two stared at each other, wordless. Denise really had no idea what Jason was suggesting. The two sat there, Jason exposing the hidden experiences that were plaguing him. Denise sat back, not quite understanding, but acknowledged his sincerity and his open-minded disposition. After about an hour of discussion, Denise just looked at him and hugged him.

"We'll get to the bottom of it," she said confidently. Denise herself had not experienced anything yet, but she knew her husband was completely serious. He had never lied to her before, and how could he have concocted such a story and more importantly, why would he?

A few days passed, and things seemed less tense for Jason after spilling his hidden thoughts and impressions to his beloved wife. Denise had gone to the store for her weekly ritual of grocery shopping, leaving Jason alone in bed. It was early and was Jason's day to sleep in. He awoke to a damp, cold feeling caressing his entire body. Jason opened his eyes only to find his window wide open. Jason emerged from the bed and used the crankshaft to tighten the window, then proceeded to fasten the double set of locks on the window. Jason lay back down, pissed that his wife would open the window on such a damp and dreary day. About an hour had passed, and Jason felt another icy breeze brush over his uncovered shoulder.

"What's wrong with her, why the hell does she keep opening the damn window," Jason thought, his face red with anger.

Jason sat up and put both feet on the floor. Standing up, he went once again to the window to crank it shut and latch the locks. After ensuring that the window was securely locked, Jason went to the kitchen to see why Denise had repeatedly opened the window.

Proceeding down the hallway, Jason noticed that the house was completely silent. The regular noises of his daughter playing, his wife on the telephone, or the distant sound of the television all failed to exist at this point in time. Jason peered out the living room window, and saw that her car had not yet retuned. Disturbed, he went down to his office and made a few follow-up calls to his clients.

Jason returned to his bedroom an hour later to shower and change, anticipating the arrival of his mother. As Jason approached the bedroom, he could hear birds and the basic sounds of nature as if they were just around the corner. Walking into the room, Jason stood in awe. What Jason saw both shocked and frightened him. The very window he had locked and shut twice was opened a third time.

Hesitantly, Jason approached the window, examining it for damage. The locks had been unbolted and the window was uncranked. Jason cranked the window shut and fastened the locks again. Moments later, he returned with an extension cord and a small piece of rope to tie the crank tightly to the leg of a nearby table. The extension cord served as a means for keeping the locks tied to the crank so the window could not possibly open. Jason left the room, hoping what happened was not real. How had the window opened up so many times, and after being shut and locked?

Jason showered, thinking about the experience, but still tried to pass it off as some weird coincidence or something that had a reasonable explanation. Jason walked out of the master bathroom, slipping into a pair of boxers. He glanced over at the window, which was still shut and locked. He opened his closet door, shuffling through his shirts. He came across his red flannel shirt, an article he wore almost religiously. Taking it off the hanger, he noticed the whole back of the shirt had been shredded. This shirt, worn by Jason several times a week, had been fine just a few days ago, and now the shirt looked like an angry pair of scissors had attacked it. From the collar to about an inch from the bottom of the garment, slashes were present. This was not the end of the situation either. He looked next to the ruined shirt at his other flannels, which appeared to have the same type of destruction inflicted upon them. Some unknown force had massacred a total of four shirts. As Jason stood at the closet, he made a connection. These were all shirts given to him by his ex-wife. Maybe Denise had slashed the shirts, but as Jason's mind rambled on, this theory made no apparent sense to him. He had always worn them, and Denise had never made any comments or initial reaction to their presence. She probably did not even know that Karen had bought these for Jason. He closed the door after finding a fully intact shirt. Walking down the hallway, he buttoned the light blue shirt, still feeling unsettled by today's events. What seemed like an end to multiple strange occurrences had today erupted into a few bizarre instances whose source could not be pinpointed.

Over dinner, Jason asked Denise if she knew anything about the state of his clothing. She looked at him as if he had ten heads. Denise appeared to have no idea what he was talking about. After dinner, Jason's mother departed, Cynthia was put to bed, and Denise and Jason started to settle in for the evening. The events of this morning had taken their initial toll on him, and he wanted to forget about what happened, thinking a good night's sleep would give him back the sanity he so desired. This, however, would not be the case. Jason's night, and his family's night, was just getting started.

It was about one-thirty in the morning and Jason arose to the same chill he had encountered fifteen hours previously. He turned toward the draft and the window was wide open again. A chill rushed up and down his spine. When he went to bed the window was secure. He had to explain to Denise why it had been tied the previous day. She could not grasp exactly what Jason had meant. Denise thought maybe Jason believed that he had closed the window, but really had not shut the contraption at all.

Jason turned on the light. Denise awoke immediately, weary-eyed and confused.

"Damn window is open again," Jason exclaimed. His face was serious and portrayed an intense lack of patience. Jason had it. He wanted to smash the window-pane with his fist. Better judgment kicked in, of course, and he stared at the glass and wood structure, wondering if it would ever remain shut. "If this nonsense doesn't stop, I'll glue it shut, Karen." He was in no mood for this to occur.

Denise said nothing, but instead rolled over, pretending that it never happened. She pretended to sleep, but lay awake with her eyes closed wondering what would be next.

Jason approached the window to find the rope laying on the floor. The extension cord appeared to have been cut, as if slashed with a serrated blade. The fibers were tattered and the wires within the extension cord were exposed. The locks had been released and the window crank had been opened all the way. He shut the window and went back to bed. It would be an hour or so before he could fall back to sleep. Jason could not fully grasp what had happened, nor did he want to understand it. He preferred to pretend it never happened.

At about three-thirty that morning, the two awoke to screams of absolute terror. Cynthia begged and pleaded for her parents, accompanied by the onslaught of wails of nightmarish terror projected as if there were a murder taking place in her room. Jason's hair stood up and his fraternal instinct kicked in to rescue his young child. Within a few short seconds, both Denise and Jason were through Cynthia's doorway, flicking on the lights.

"What is it honey?" Denise said with apprehension in her voice. Denise had an idea why they had been summoned by their daughter's screams, but she hoped that she was wrong. Was what affected Jason terrorizing their daughter as well? Denise received a response that was the direct opposite of what she wanted to hear.

Cynthia, face buried in her mother's breast, would not look up, saying that it was in the far corner of the room, her little fingers pointed, as she remained hidden. "It was over there, right over there. I saw it, it glowed and walked."

"Saw what?" Jason interrupted. He wanted to know what had appeared to his little girl. He wanted an immediate explanation. He wanted to see this thing, whatever it was. He wanted to know so he could fight it, but there was no intruder that could be beaten up or tossed around. Jason deep down knew that the intruder was not a burglar, but something he did not understand. Something he had heard stories on television about, but nodded his head, dismissing it as all mumbo jumbo and that of the mentally unstable or those craving attention.

Denise carried Cynthia to their bedroom, allowing her to sleep in bed with them for the remainder of the night.

Jason lay awake for the rest of the night waiting for something else to happen. Nothing happened, but Jason had no idea to predict what would be the next occurrence or when it would happen. He wanted to protect his family, but had no idea how to do it. What he was dealing with was lingering, disguised by being invisible and anonymous, not able to be pinpointed. How could he confront what he could not see?

The next day, Jason and Denise vowed they were going to search for some answers. Jason called his cousin and Denise subtly threw the notion out to some trusted coworkers that she thought they had a ghost in their home to see what people would say. Her coworkers seemed intrigued, but offered her no help. Instead, they referred to "bumps in the night" that they had heard growing up, or the tale they heard on television. The end of the workday arrived and there were still no answers.

As they sat at the dinner table, both Jason and Denise wondered what could be done about the impending situation. Cynthia had retreated to the family room and was coloring. The two sat there in almost complete silence, stressed from a lack of sleep.

"Honey, do you think Cynthia will play in her own room tonight?" Jason questioned, even though he knew what the response would be.

Denise, with saddened eyes, looked directly at him. She sensed the recent change in their daughter. She avoided her bedroom, making use of the toys elsewhere in the house. After the recent night terrors, things seemed to be falling into place. Their daughter was frightened to be in her own bedroom, even to grab a coloring book or a favorite plaything. Whether it was day or nighttime, Cynthia seemed to dread the room that was hers. Even in the brightness of daylight, Cynthia avoided any and all reasons for entering her domain. Time spent in the room consisted of sleep, whenever sleep was possible.

Denise opened her mouth slowly, "Jason, something happened to me today."

"What?" he replied both curious and disturbed.

"I believed you all along, I really did, but honestly I never really experienced much. Now I think something is really going on, there is something I don't quite get at all. I know I'm not cracking up, honestly."

Denise could not express herself without looking over her shoulders, as if to make sure she was not being watched. Her tone became much more serious and she almost could not blink. She was terrified, plain and simple. Even though this was her husband, she felt foolish telling him about today and was scared to even mention the events.

"When I was washing the dishes, I smelled something burning. I looked around the kitchen, but found nothing. The smell got stronger and then that's when I saw it. My scarf was on fire."

"What do you mean on fire?"

"I mean it was actually burning!"

Denise looked at him, and almost teared up right there in the kitchen. "My mother gave me that scarf, I love that scarf. That's not all either. There's more." Denise continued. She recounted her steps when she came home. Cynthia was not picked up as usual. Instead, her sister picked her up to take her out with her cousins. Denise had been alone in the house; at least she thought she was alone.

Upon entering the house, she placed her keys on the kitchen table as usual. A few minutes later, she sat at the table, only to notice the keys were no longer there. She searched everywhere, even though she distinctively remembered placing them right there next to the salt and pepper. Frustration led to absolute anger. She stopped her search and a few minutes later discovered her keys in the toilet. After removing the keys, she washed them off. Then she decided to wash the few dishes that littered the sink. This is when she smelled and then found her favorite scarf burning. There was no heater near the coat rack, and regardless, the scarf was suspended about four feet or so off the ground on a wooden peg, without any source of heat present. There was no heat or flame source nearby which might cause the spontaneous fire to erupt. There was just no way to explain it. Not even sunlight hit the object where it sat. That though was not the end.

"My angel is also gone," she said with hurt in her voice.

"Gone?" Jason asked.

"I found it in the middle of the kitchen floor ripped apart and charred. I came in about an hour ago and found it that way."

"Where is it?"

"In the trash," she said, tears now dripping down her milky white cheeks.

Jason went over and pulled what remained of the straw angel that was at one time elaborately draped with silk and a corset made of fine linen. It was absolutely mutilated. This was one of Denise's favorite decorations. It was given to her by her mother before she passed away a year earlier, as was the scarf that had been destroyed.

Denise knew that there was more to what was going on, but like Jason had never been exposed to any strange occurrences in her life. She was raised in a devout Greek Orthodox family, and her father once told her that such stories were ridiculous and a sacrilege to their faith. Ghosts and the like were nothing more than hallucinations sparked by an overactive imagination.

Jason listened intently, absorbing her testimony like a first-class detective. He knew that the recent events brought an ever-growing aura of hostility, fear, and downright confusion to not only their home, but also their lives.

That night, all was pretty quiet. The anticipation of events kept Jason up another night. Once again, his desire was to protect, but he felt helpless against an unseen enemy who possessed the wisdom of the ages.

The following night, Jason went out with a few buddies to the local pub. Denise did not feel like going and had a hard time finding a babysitter, so she stayed home to relax. It was about ten o'clock and Denise retreated to her room to retire for the evening. After a long struggle, she convinced young Cynthia to sleep in her own bed. It was the first time that week she was able to convince her to do so. Denise lay in bed, picking up a book she recently bought. She thumbed through the contents, but was too tired to settle down and break into the hardcover. She turned on the television, flipping through the channels. The room started to grow colder. She pulled up the blanket, engulfing her legs with warmth, which seemed to be disappearing gradually.

Denise started to shiver; the room had dropped several degrees at this point. Then the unthinkable occurred. She felt a tug on her nightgown. A tug like that of a man—strong, quick, and fierce. She felt something pinch her breast. Before she even knew what was occurring, she had jumped out of her bed from a sitting position, yelling and screaming as she ran down the hall. Denise did not know where she was going nor did she care. She wanted out of the house. There was nowhere to run, nowhere to hide. She and her family were prisoners, prisoners in the place they called home. There was nowhere to run nor was there anywhere to seek refuge.

Jason came home late that night and found his wife and daughter on the couch. Denise was wide awake and their daughter lay motionless in deep, deep slumber.

"What happened?" Jason asked her.

Her eyes were puffy from evident crying and she looked absolutely horrible. Her lips shaking, her words whispered with hopelessness. "It touched me."

Denise told Jason on what had happened that evening. Jason cringed with a sick feeling in his stomach. He knew help was needed; there was no doubt about it. What had occurred in their house over the last few weeks was nothing he could put his finger on. They needed a way out, a resolution to the ongoing dread that engulfed them. Jason walked to the bathroom to put cold water on his face, as if trying to wake himself up from some nightmare. The only problem was this nightmare was not a sleep-induced hallucination; it was a reality. Gazing into the toilet, he saw what he had not expected to see, his keys.

Finding Help

The next day Jason received a message on his answering machine from his cousin. Over the past few days, he had a chance to go on the Internet and found some web sites that he thought might help Jason find some direction.

Jason immediately called him back, hoping and praying that he had found some information to help ease the situation. His cousin gave him his findings and Jason browsed the computer, actively taking notes.

The southern Connecticut coast had received a light coat of snow over the past few hours. Sitting in his office, John was knee-deep in paperwork and audio-tapes. He was reviewing crucial aspects of a case in New York City which had been ongoing for over a month now. Surrounding John were hundreds of books, many of which bearing titles reflecting demonology, witchcraft, voodoo, religion, and spirituality. There was hardly any room to move in his three-room office. Hundreds of items were stacked neatly on shelves and placed randomly around. Each had its very own story. Some were mere collectibles, reflecting his interest in religious items and paraphernalia pertaining to the lore of the unknown. Other items, however, had been directly linked to many of the cases he had worked on over the years. With over twenty-five years of dedicated study in the field of psychic research, John had received items from the previous owners who wanted the objects removed, banished from their homes.

In one corner of the center room lays an old brown oak clock. The clock was brought into a home and phenomena began to occur. After an intensive investigation and the removal of the clock, the phenomena stopped altogether. Another object, a wooden head reflective of the African culture, stared out at the room with eyes that seemed to pierce one's flesh. The item, although only a foot high, emits a sinister and devilish sensation. The item had been used for the conjuration of spirits in incantation rituals, calling on deities to perform a desired effect. It too had been removed from a case in which the owner wanted nothing to do with the aura of evil conveyed by whatever was attached to the wooden head.

John took a long puff of his cigarette, smothering the rest of its contents in a nearby ashtray. Thumbing through his notes, he was interrupted by the ringing of the phone. John reached over to pick up the receiver.

"Hello," John said in a kind, gentle tone.

"Are you John, John Zaffis?" the obviously nervous voice said. "I'm Jason, we spoke the other day on the computer."

"Why yes Jason, sure I remember, what can I do for you?"

Jason did not know where to begin. Would this guy think he was a complete nut job? He must get crank calls all the time or calls from complete loonies, Jason thought. Maybe he would tell him to get some psychological help or maybe John would hang up on him. Jason's pulse was rapid at this point. This was the only option he had at this time, and what if John refused to help? Jason would have to deal with whatever this was in his home by himself, an undertaking he wanted no part of. He did not understand what was happening, nor did he know how to remedy the problem.

Jason took a deep breath and began to communicate as openly, honestly, and as detailed as he could. "Well John, I don't quite know where to start. I hope you don't think I'm crazy but..." Jason told his tale over the next half hour from beginning to end, including every detail he thought might be relevant. It felt good to air out his dilemma, just as it did on the night he opened up to his wife about what had been happening to him. When Jason finished his testimony, he waited for a click. He thought for sure two minutes into the conversation John was going to hang up the phone. The response he got was not what he expected.

"If what you're telling me is legit, you got a great deal happening," John said seriously. "If you don't mind, I try to work with people in person when possible. What about this weekend, Saturday evening ok? Myself and a few other researchers will come out and give it a look. I'd like to video your testimony and spend some time in your house, only if it is alright with you and your wife, of course."

Jason did not even give it a second thought. He gave his full consent and invited John to his home, giving him full permission to bring anyone who would be of any help. Jason hoped and prayed that what he had read on this man was true. If so, could John help? Jason could only hope, but he was desperate enough to try anything at this point.

The next few days were full of eager anticipation for the investigative team to arrive at their house. However, all was not quiet on the home front. Phenomena were increasing in intensity. Just when things were dark, they got darker. Jason was plagued by nightmares and could not sleep for long periods of time. He was being brought to an ultimate low, marked by extreme irritability, feelings of helplessness related to the unseen force, and a heavy burden of absolute despair. He could not keep focused at work because of his incessant thoughts surrounding the situation at home. His bouts of quick, unpredictable anger had also created tension between himself and Denise. Minutes after the altercations, he would look back, finding no real concrete reason for the squabbles.

Denise was poked in her lower back while washing the dishes and saw a large black shadow creep slowly down the hallway later that same evening. Also, after finally putting Cynthia to sleep in her own bed, another frightening assault occurred. Cynthia complained her covers had been lifted off of her and thrown some six feet away. Also, for two nights in a row, tappings would begin in almost any room the family stayed in for an extended period of time.

Saturday morning had come, and Jason and Denise could not wait for John and the other researchers to show up. They were hopeful that the team would not be thrill seekers or complete crackpots. They appeared to be legitimate, but Jason had no knowledge about the field of psychic research. He was running out of time and patience. No one else was of any help and John was the last resort.

There was a knock at the door. Jason answered and introduced himself immediately. John introduced himself and four of the investigators that had come along with him. There was Diane, an attractive woman in her mid-thirties. Although a nurse by trade, she had been on dozens of cases which involved anything from satanic ritualistic abuse to homes infested by the demonic. The same was true of David and Ruth, who were a married couple and had been going on investigations with John often for over four years. Finally, there was Brent, a local college student who had been interested in the occult and its workings since childhood. John set up the camera in the kitchen to tape the testimony of both Jason and Denise. They recounted every experience from beginning to end, detailing each event as if it had happened yesterday. The last few months were nothing short of terrifying and had begun to wear their patience, sanity, and marriage down to the last possible shard. Each day, the situation seemed to get worse and worse. Jason's recurrent nightmares and Cynthia's constant complaints of harassment by foreign beings were absolutely draining mentally.

The group stayed after the interview to see if anything would manifest. In situations pertaining to such strong activity, it is not unheard of for researches to witness or experience phenomena. Denise took David and Ruth to her bedroom to show them where much of the phenomena had taken place. Jason remained in the kitchen with the other researchers while John toured the lower level of the house.

David immediately noticed something in the bedroom. It was unnaturally cold. The rest of the house was warm and comfortable, but this room was very different. It felt at least ten or fifteen degrees cooler. There were no windows open and no doors in the vicinity leading to the outside where a possible draft may be the culprit. Cold spots frequently appear in cases and often represent the onset of phenomena to come. An entity needs a fuel source in order to physically manifest itself, and often the heat or any viable energy source will act as a conductor for the spirit to manifest as some type of phenomena. David kept it in the back of his mind to discuss with the group later.

Meanwhile, John remained downstairs while the others walked around upstairs, getting a feel for the home and interacting with the family. John had an idea that there was more to this case than he initially thought when he agreed to investigate it. During the interview, John's head was repeatedly touched by what seemed to be unseen fingers. Disturbed by this, John kept silent, so as not to influence the other researchers or the family so that an accurate depiction of experiences that night could be conveyed.

John plunged in Jason's desk chair and sat attentively. He remained transfixed patiently. He knew he heard something and wanted to know exactly what it was. John was immediately drawn to the area after a rapping noise was heard. Sitting there, John could not believe his ears. Frozen still in the chair, he listened as synchronized taps emerged in the room from within the walls. It was similar to Morse code and continued incessantly. John had heard taps on several other occasions. In many cases, a human spirit was the source and in other cases it was that of the demonic.

In many cases at the beginning of the onset of phenomena, it is difficult to determine the exact difference between human spirit phenomena and occurrences pertaining to that of an evil, demonic entity. It is not until the case progresses that the difference between the two becomes apparent. Demonic phenomena will intensify significantly and will target individuals to break down their free will into nothingness. It is then that the entity will attempt to win over the soul and induce possession.

David did not like the feelings he got in the house. He had become very weak and tired over the course of the previous hour; his energy seemed to be pulled from him.Brent was in the bedroom with Denise when his attention was drawn to her.

"It's touching me!" Denise screamed in absolute shock. Everyone gathered in the room rapidly, which at this point had been recognized as ice cold with a low-lying stench that resembled natural gas. "It grabbed my arm, I swear it did, I swear."

David and Ruth tried their best to calm Denise down, reciting the "Our Father" and other prayers of their Catholic faith. John and Brent doused the area with holy water. After a few minutes, the situation calmed down and everyone returned to the kitchen. Jason put on a pot of coffee before retreating to the porch with John for a smoke.

Jason looked at John, but no words were needed. Both were thinking on the same level and knew that this was the beginning of a long night of putting together the pieces of this horrible puzzle.

Looking at Jason, John exhaled. "You got some real problems kiddo, some real bad problems."

Contacting the Clergy

John sat at his desk. Picking up the receiver to his telephone, he recalled much of the testimony Jason and Denise had given the night before. The phone began to ring on the other end of the line.

"Hello, Father Karl, it's John Zaffis."

A gruff voice reflecting an older gentleman replied, "Hi John, good to hear from you. How are the wife and kids?"

"Great Father, no complaints at all."

Usually when John and Father Karl spoke, it was not to discuss anything of a positive nature. Their relationship had been formed out of dealing with many of the severe haunting cases that John had worked on himself or with the Warrens.

"Well, what can I do for you, John?"

John began to unravel the details of the case to him bit by bit, recreating the scheme of terror that had been inflicted on the family in recent times.

"I'm sending some researchers up to the house tonight to set up some audio and video equipment. I'll be meeting them up there around nine o'clock or so. We'll probably spend the entire night there again to see if anything kicks up."

Father Karl agreed that, if necessary, he would bless the house, or maybe even perform a High Mass in the home, if need be. Father Karl worked on about two dozen cases over the years and recognized the grip that negative stalkers from another realm often inflict on normal, everyday people. He knew that all too often, clergy in his own faith and all mainstream religious practices tend to dismiss such cases as mere superstition or mass hallucination. Today, the notion of evil is recognized mainly as the choice of men to take part in negative avenues. Basically, the idea of an intelligent evil or malevolent forces outside of basic comprehension is seen as mythological and evil, nothing more than a state of mind stemming from psychological desires. This may be primarily true, but Father Karl recognized those occasions where there was an external agent behind the fiasco, an enemy shrouded in secrecy and covered up by the doubt in men's hearts. Although many of the faithful and even the clergy believe strongly in God or some type of Supreme Being, the recognition of the Devil was frequently overlooked as an old superstitious monster with no real root in anything besides mere false notion.

That night at about nine, John met up with Jason and Denise. Diane and Brent had been there for about half an hour, talking with the two and setting up recording equipment. The group sat, engaging in conversation and discussing the case in general.

Jason looked at Brent, eyes fixed closely upon his face. "What do you want?" No one knew exactly what was going on. "I know right now you're questioning yourself, wondering what exactly I am feeling. You also were wondering what practices I have taken part in. Well, the answer is none."

Brent did not answer, but stared right at Jason, both amazed and frightened. "How did you know what I was thinking at that exact moment?"

"I don't know, it just happens. Every once in awhile, I know what people are thinking. Over the past couple of weeks, I just seem to take in thoughts; they just pop into my head." John immediately jumped in to figure out exactly what was going on. "You mean to tell us that you can pick up on our thoughts?"

"Yes."

"How often?"

"Not all the time, but pretty often. It started a few weeks ago. I thought I knew what Denise was thinking, but was too scared to confirm if my instincts were correct. I never asked her what she was thinking at that particular time. So am I crazy or is this part of what is going on?"

John sat in the overstuffed sofa chair that was not really comfortable. It was far worse than he thought. Whatever it was that targeted Jason had penetrated deep, far deeper than he initially thought. If Jason's thoughts were becoming oppressed, then there was not too much more to think about. Tomorrow, John would call Father Karl immediately and set up an emergency visit to the house. John was to recommend the almost unthinkable to Father Karl: an exorcism.

The Rituale Romanum charges and commands evil spirits to leave in the name of Jesus Christ. Although the ritual dates back many centuries, it remains virtually unchanged in an era of constant change. Kept in the background of most faiths, exorcism is used as a tool to rid those who suffer from true possession from a foreign, alien intelligence whose ultimate goal is to have complete control over the individual. Many cases arise, but so few reach the point where exorcism seems to be the only solution. Many religions instate the rite of exorcism, and even though doctrinal differences separate the religious groups, the rite seems almost universal in regards to its goal: to free the oppressed or possessed from the negative spiritual presence, which is usually tightly wrapped around them.

John sat at his desk once again to call Father Karl and suggest what he thought was the most viable option. The previous night marked the onset of tappings, odors, and rushes of cold air in the house. Some people complained of being touched. Instead of the phenomena occurring in the night, it had intensified, occurring even in the onset of daylight. Jason and his family were on edge, knowing full well that the oppressive being or beings were closing in. No one spent any time alone in the home, and a close eye was kept on Cynthia, who had been complaining more than ever about the man in her room.

"Father, I have reason to believe the case has intensified even more," John said, hesitating. This was perhaps the most severe case he ever referred to Father Karl. The case demonstrated the classic progression of the demonic from entry right down to the onset of possession—in this case, transient possession in which the demonic force comes in and out at its whim. Although the concentration of the phenomena was around the family, it was now obvious some type of invasion had occurred into Jason's body. His thoughts had become obsessive and he knew by means of that which plagued him what many people thought, displaying a preternatural means of clairvoyance. There was no doubt that an exorcism of the home was needed, and also the initiation of the ritual over Jason as well.

"We've dug even deeper into the story behind the story," John exclaimed to Father Karl. "The phenomena started shortly after his ex-wife committed suicide. She was obviously involved with the black arts and was a practitioner. After piecing it together, Father, it seems that a curse has been placed upon Jason, or else some type of ritual was invoked to have something reside within him. Jason's ex-wife was devastated when he left. The fact that her three previous husbands passed on mysteriously makes me believe that he might have been the intended fourth victim in the scheme."

"I also removed a sword that was given to him by his ex-wife. He kept it above the bed where he and Denise slept. It's hard to tell, but it might have been used in some type of ritual. He begged me to take it out of his house. It is one of only a few possessions associated with her, but certainly the most bizarre."

"Anything else I should know about, John?

"Jason has been sleeping on the floor of the little girl's room. She seems to be the direct target of some of the physical phenomena. The poor kid is absolutely terrified and cries for him almost nightly."

After a long, extensive conversation, Father Karl concluded that an exorcism was necessary. He would talk to his superior in the morning and set it up as soon as possible. Father Karl hung up the phone and looked out his window at the weeping willow tree that blew in the wind. There was not much that bothered him. He lived a life devoted to God and had the opportunity to perform work alongside the people in his community. He engaged in his normal, everyday duties as a priest, such as conducting mass and absolving the sins of his parishioners in the sacrament of penance. However, this was a situation he dreaded. Knowing full well that the demonic was present in a home was a reality, a terrifying and realistic truth. The next morning, Father Karl set up the exorcism, after approval was given by the archdiocese, for Friday afternoon. It was Monday and he knew that Jason and his family needed to rid their lives of the predatory force which wandered about them, but this was the best he could do. Father Karl needed at least three days preparation for the clash, taking the basic steps of intense fasting and prayer, hoping that with the intercession of God, tthe demonic energy would be banished from the home.

The Demonic Intensifies its Clutches

The next few days would be nothing short of hell for the three people, especially Jason. Jason was the recipient of horrible nightmares, causing little to no sleep each night, no matter how hard he tried to ignore the images. A sensation of being watched was constant and almost the norm in the house that week, the clutches of the force closing in, increasingly stronger.

Denise also knew that the demonic had begun to manifest more freely. Foul odors were noticed more frequently and randomly. While folding laundry after dinner, the living room filled with a stench resembling the smell of rotting meat. Within a few seconds, the smell vanished mysteriously, but not before chilling the room by about ten degrees.

To try to maintain their composure, Denise and Jason decided that they should take Cynthia to their mother's house and then go out to eat together for a relaxing meal, insofar as they could relax. Upon returning home, all the lights in the house were on, along with all of the ceiling fans. Earlier, before leaving, Denise left only the night-light in the bathroom and the hallway lamp on.

Wednesday marked the onset of rappings at nighttime, which, although they were not extremely loud, persisted until the morning hours. It seemed that once dusk arrived, the intensity of the phenomena steadily increased until daylight reappeared.

The Exorcism

Father Karl approached the house. He slowly walked up the stairs to the front porch and rang the doorbell. He knew that what he would confront today was nothing short of evil in its purest form. Perhaps the ritual would go smoothly without any outward interferences taking place, or maybe he would experience chaos beyond comprehension. The thoughts of the possibilities ran through his mind, but had no effect on him. It was Father Karl's faith and belief in God that carried him into the house. For Father Karl, the last few days marked a period of cleansing and intimacy with God through prayer and fasting. Father Karl knew that the force plaguing Jason and the rest of the family waned in comparison to the power of the Almighty Father. He wondered if today would be the day that the force was cast out of their lives, or would it take several more attempts. Father Karl knew that if intercession took place, the demonic would be banished. After ringing the doorbell, he made the sign of the cross, praying that he would have the strength to carry out the exorcism.

Jason swung the door open, looking at Father Karl. "Hello Father, please come in and sit down."

"Are you alright, Jason? John tells me that this week has been a little intense for you."

"I'm just nervous, Father. I want it all to be over."

Father Karl looked at Jason with a look that could stop a train. "It will be alright, son. I promise that it will be alright."

John pulled up to the house with David and Brent. The three entered the house and sat down with Father Karl and the family. Within a few moments after some preparation by Father Karl, the rite began.

Denise sat on the other side of the room with Cynthia, her right knee shaking up and down. Denise had not slept well all week. The pressure was at its worst the past few days. She prayed silently, hoping that today would mark the end of their struggle.

Father Karl prayed with the vigor of an army commander, "In the name of Jesus Christ we adjure and bind thee, all spirits not in worship to the Holy Trinity." His sincerity and power were expressed in the tone of his voice and the power behind the words he launched outward throughout the house exorcism. He sensed that they were not alone, but at the same time, there was no outward manifestation at this point. After about forty-five minutes, the exorcism of the home was complete; the question remained on whether the diabolical force was giving in or not.

Immediately after Father Karl finished the house exorcism, he looked at John, saying, "I think it is time, John, get a kitchen chair for Jason to sit in."

John followed his wishes and put the chair in the living room and signaled Jason to come over. As asked, Jason came over and sat in the chair. The rite was begun and within a few short minutes, all seemed calm.

"We plead the blood of Christ against you evil spirits, and by its power, seal all spirit entry points or portals," Father Karl said sternly. He sensed that Jason was coming under heavy oppression, and maybe even the onset of actual possession. The room was growing colder, but not because of a draft. It was an unnatural cold that seemed to present itself, dissipate, and then repeat the process.

John closed his eyes and began to pray in a deep state. He had noticed that Jason had not blinked in at least five full minutes and also sensed the moving coldness.

"O Father in Heaven, in Jesus' Name," Father Karl continued.

"Fuck you, you swine, you filthy fucks!" Jason blurted out. David and John immediately interceded and restrained Jason, who began to come out of his chair shaking like a madman. His eyes were wide and still refused to blink. Jason rocked violently back and forth, trying to get loose, trying to grab Father Karl. "You'll die! Die like me! Die like me!"

Time was progressing and the exorcism was continued, just as concentrated as when it began. Father Karl would not break. He continued on with a heart driven by sheer faith. Cynthia began to scream. Father Karl, undistracted, continued on and ended up performing a light exorcism over the girl. As the unseen force was buckling, it seemed to have gravitated toward her.

The exorcism carried on and within another fifteen minutes, Jason settled down considerably. Father touched the wooden cross to Jason's head without a fight or a second look. After several more thorough prayers, the rite was complete.

Father Karl began to pack his things into a leather bag. He took off his purple stole, kissing it before folding the fine linen. He looked around the room and nodded at John and the other researchers. It was a matter of minutes before he shook Jason's hand and received a hug from Denise. He blessed Denise and went on his way. The exorcism, as was usual, had taken its toll on Father Karl. He was drained physically, mentally, and spiritually. He had ultimately come face to face with the hierarchy of the damned.

Looking Back

John becomes very serious when reflecting back on this case, his lighthearted demeanor changing to a monotone and somber presentation. The case obviously burned deep into his memory as a reality, which occurred to real people, surrounding real events in a real home.

"When the case came to the point where an exorcism was necessary, Jason was broken down to the point where everything around him had been crushed. His sanity was becoming part of the past. After an extended period of time, exposed to phenomena associated with fright and confusion, this normal, everyday man was at the end of his rope. Jason just wanted it to stop and could not understand why he and his family had been the target of evil intent.

"When speaking with Jason, you could see a very intelligent young guy, a hard worker, and a family man. He never thought in a million years that such occurrences were genuinely true, nor could he believe that they would happen to him. Jason went through a situation that I would agree does not happen to many people, but nonetheless still occurs. This is not the first case or the last in which I will deal firsthand with someone going down a destructive road. Luckily, Jason began to realize what was occurring and wanted to do everything and anything to get rid of the negative intelligence that surrounded his life.

"To say Jason was destitute is an understatement. Here we have a successful handyman and loving father who was broken down to the point of physical and mental exhaustion. Sleep depravation and mental oppression by the demonic had worn him down considerably. He could not eat or sleep normally; his marriage began to deteriorate, as did his job. On top of all of this, he was genuinely frightened. There is no way to prepare for such a change in one's life. It is an unexpected twist that few will directly experience, but still is a reality for an unlucky few.

"After the exorcism, I stayed in contact with Jason, trying to help him to understand what happened and how to counteract the situation. He truly desired to keep this force from reentering his life. Days and even weeks after such an event, the demonic will linger and try to gain reentry into the oppressed or possessed person's life. It is crucial to have some type of positive weapon as well as an understanding of the situation to prevent the force from gaining the reentry it so deeply desires.

"Jason was able to get back into the swing of things by going to church, taking part in his sect's activities, and trying to find a relationship with God. It was a slow process of recovery for him, but I can say that Jason found his way through it all. Today, he is still self-employed and is doing quite well working in his field, and his marriage is stable and strong. Jason stood up after it all, was able to realize what happened, and took control of his life. He knew the potential threat that remained dormant and wanted all doors to it to be closed permanently.

"Not too many people come out of a situation like this without some type of life-altering realization. Many will become religious, while others will have a new respect for that which they thought was mere myth. No one leaves a home like Jason's without some new outlook on the schemes of life and what lies beneath the surface.

"People will often question their experiences, wondering if it was his ex-wife who was around him, or was it something else? Regarding spirit, you have the potential for other spirits to be around, too. Spirit attracts spirit. Jason's late wife was very involved in the occult, and was a heavy practitioner of the dark side. With Jason leaving her, she might have been quite angry. Perhaps Jason was to be the fourth husband to die while married to her. She could have sent an entity toward him. The underlying issue still remains the same, however: Jason had problems reflective of the spirit world that needed immediate attention. Without help, who knows what would have happened to either Jason or the rest of his family."

The Santerian Curse

The Santerian Curse

It seems that every year that goes by, multiple cases come to John's attention, hundreds of cases from a multitude of sources. Some prove to trace back solely to psychological causes, while others may reflect activity pertaining to human spirit while still others transcend the basic boundaries of popular spirit manifestations. Others integrate great power, a manipulation of energies that naturally occur on earth. These energies can be channeled and abused by truly evil forces feeding off of man's perverse desires. Calling upon deities for a particular outcome seems like a fanciful extension of one's imagination, but this, however, is not really the case. Not all who seek to dominate and control and to harness this energy fail in their attempt to conjure these unworldly beings that are calloused with none other than the deepest hate and deception. Many individuals run into serious problems when the day comes for repayment. Those energies are intelligent beings who collect before you are ready and with interest. Their fee, however, is far greater than the average dollar. It is the soul, the sanity, the peace of mind, and the essence of life. By bringing the bidder under its control, this force will try to take everything from you, stripping you of your pride and trying to lower you into a state of absolute fear. By becoming a slave to these forces, you can fall into their trap, becoming their puppet, being directed in such a way that your life becomes not a gift, but instead a struggle. Many are brought to their lowest emotional state, giving in, leading lives of fear that may result in suicide to escape the struggle which inhabits all aspects of their lives.

The following case is one that I was able to work on with John. He told me about it for several weeks before the visit actually took place. I knew through his preliminary work that there was something more to all this than just what popular media refers to as a "ghost." This was as real as it gets. It would be one of those cases where the researcher is tested to great extents. There was so much intensity as far as what was happening in the house and the state of emotions of the family involved. I knew that my trip to Maryland with John would not be a relaxing vacation. I had been on other cases with him, but this one felt different, the known logistics darker, and the possibility of danger was far greater.

On the trip there, John shared every detail that was reported to him with me and another researcher who was present. John's gut feeling was telling him that there were real problems and that the case was deep. John spoke specifically about Sarah and Eric, the very couple we would be visiting, who had been systematically attacked.

After several hours trekking to Maryland, we finally arrived at the house. The house was far from ominous. It was located in a typical suburban neighborhood just like any other. Initially, I walked in skeptical and ready for anything. If it was psychological, then the paranormal explanation could be largely discounted. If it were a human spirit-related case, I was ready to accept that as well. I went in with an open mind, ready to try to make sense of what might be the reason behind the madness. I, however, had not been ready to hear the stories that emerged from the mouths of this seemingly normal duo.

Apparently, there were supposed physical manifestations, noises, psychic attacks, and a generalized fear running rampant on an almost daily basis. This type of case seems far-fetched, but occurs, as those who experience it will attest. The researchers, clergy, and the families involved all play an intricate role in proving that the presence was not a hallucination or a hoax.

It was not until I got involved with this work that I realized what actually occurs in situations involving violent hauntings. No book, television show, interview, or the like can prepare a person for this type of experience. It is the word "experience" that is the key. Nothing about this realm makes logical sense until you witness these occurrences firsthand. It does not matter if you are on the researcher end of the spectrum or the family struggling to rid the force. Seeing, smelling, touching, and witnessing the phenomena compels you to believe.

"This case is reflective of many of the other intense cases I have seen over the years," John says very seriously. "It has so many different avenues tied in that it all can be related to the case, fueling what is occurring in the home and more importantly, to the people. Sarah has something with her that wants absolute control. She seems to belong to this thing and every time something comes between her and it, it will lash out. Her case is rare and I don't want people to get the impression that this type of situation happens to most people. This would simply be an inaccurate statement. Although we have elements tied in which incorporate forces that many do not want to believe in, the fact remains that they are very real.

"This woman through her own will and volition had conjured something dark and sinister and was not prepared for the consequences which ultimately would be bestowed upon her. Her case is delicate because not only would religious assistance probably benefit her through approved rituals for eliminating the entity and weaken its tight grip, but a deep personal change is also needed to break the cycle that she had initialized through her own free will.

"Several years earlier, Sarah had activity start to occur when she lived with a previous boyfriend she was planning to marry. Sarah really became interested in the occult and joined a local coven to learn some of the alternatives to organized religion and thought. This, in itself, is not harmful, but the road she chose proved to be the path less traveled, and with good reason."

The Search For Meaning

The heat was too much to bear. Wrapped in a dark, oversized shawl, the old woman walked slowly down the dark path. Weeds stuck out of the earth, protruding upward, entangling one another into complete suffocation. The piercing gaze from behind struck her down as if they were casting stones. She was shunned, ordered to go on her way, and the sinister looks from the country folk indicated two options: leave or be killed. Up the path she continued, knees cracking as the hill became steeper and steeper. Turning one last time, she saw those blazing eyes transfixed on her, still evident of hate and remorse for her existence.

Sarah flung out of her bed, sweating profusely. Heart pounding, her composure was not essentially gained for quite some time. This nightmare seemed so real to her. It had occurred to her a few times previously over the last several months, each one more detailed and vivid than the last. After several minutes, she put it all behind her and headed to the shower. Her dream was vivid, as real as actually experiencing it, emotion stapled into her mind as if it happened in her own backyard. In the shower, Sarah continued to reflect on the nightmare, trying to make sense of the mess in her emotionally unstable state. A few minutes passed and the vision faded. She exited the bath, washing herself clean of the confusion and torment that her unconscious was spitting forth into her dream state. After getting ready, she headed to her car to make her trip—a trip she would have been better off not taking.

Sarah glanced left to right, looking for Main Street. She knew it had to be somewhere around here. She had driven only a few towns over from her house, but she was unfamiliar with the area. At the next set of lights, she found her destination and turned right onto the ordinary main drag that stretched through the middle of the town. While cruising slowly down the street, she saw the sign, "Realm of the New Age." She had heard about it from one of her friends and saw the ad in a local newspaper. Sarah had been long intrigued by the supernatural realm and how these witches had used the energies of the earth to gain an upper hand on life. Perhaps it was all sheer mythology living on into the modern day, carried on by a bunch of gullible followers. Regardless of what the reality happened to be, she was determined to find out what it was.

At this time, Sarah was engaged to Matthew, a tall and slender man with a taste for the finer things in life. He owned several pieces of property including many profitable storefronts in town that generated an impressive income few receive. In total, a dozen pieces of rental property, a successful financial consulting firm, and some wise investments had provided Matthew the means to support himself. Her life was prosperous as it was, but she craved much more—a search for the truth, a quest for meaning and knowledge, or understanding. She craved individuality and power—a sense of true inner self.

Sarah turned the engine of her car off and reached to the floor for her purse. Walking into the shop, a little bell began ringing, indicating her presence.

"Hello, madam," a low but comforting voice expressed happily. "Is there anything that I may assist you with?"

"Yes," Sarah replied to the soft-spoken woman, "Can I ask you a few questions?" Without any hesitation, the woman replied, "Of course."

"Well, I've never been anywhere like this before. I don't really know what I'm looking for but...." Sarah conveyed her seemingly lifelong interest in the occult and how she wanted to delve deeper to see what it was truly like. She continued to make it clear that she had no prior experience or exposure, but a sincere desire to learn.

After a cup of coffee and about twenty minutes of conversation, the shop owner felt that Sarah should consult with some local practitioners who she had worked with in the past. She could see Sarah's genuine interest and curiosity reflected through the expressions on her face and tone of her voice. Sarah gave a telephone number etched on the back of a business card, and Sarah was on her way after buying a few books and candles the woman had suggested. At home, Sarah sat at the kitchen table, wondering if anything would come of this experience at the shop. Was it all complete bullshit? Was there truth to the idea of something more?

Reaching Out

After calling the mysterious number, Sarah had her first invitation to classes that were held every Tuesday evening in an apartment downtown. She would, of course, go alone so as not to anger her future husband with matters that he felt were outright ridiculous. Telling her fiancé of such matters would serve to stir up an argument. Sarah wanted to tell her brother, but the truth was that they hardly ever spoke.

Christopher and Sarah were never really close. The two had grown up in constant competition with one another. When one of them experienced some success, it was a given the other would have to try to come out on top. Although Christopher was sincere in Wiccan beliefs, Sarah did not feel at all comfortable confiding in her own flesh and blood. Instead, she would venture by herself to this apartment and see what these people had to say.She was introduced to the half a dozen people gathered here for their weekly meeting. She noticed that these people were not eccentric or mentally unstable, but instead were down-to-earth people. There was no cost for the session, but a deep-rooted belief in what they were doing, which bonded the tightly knit group together.

While interviewing Sarah, it was obvious that she was moved by the experiences which occurred that night with the psychic group, many of whom were actually practitioners in witchcraft.

"They were very serious," she said. "There was no doubt about it that these people were sure that what they were involved with was real and rooted in their belief system heavily. I remember sitting in a circle with the other people present. Everyone was in a deep meditative state, and one of the members was actually taking us on a mental journey. I can remember feeling ice cold, even though it was a warm evening. During one of the meetings, several members of the group claimed that in the circle by me, they saw the images of animal-type figures. I had not seen them, but the others had. After several meetings, I turned away from the group. The members were very open people and truly cared about me, but the situation was getting too real for me, and at the same time, truly frightening. It was as if the gates had been opened to my inner self, and it honestly scared me at the time."

"These animals," John tells, "are usually referred to as familiars. Familiars are often spirits that are called upon and assist witches and others who are involved with magic."

"My brother found out about my excursions and was nothing short of insanely angry," Sarah said. We had always been rivals, always outdoing one another, and my involvement in such a group without his approval was seemingly forbidden. He would not talk to me for months, and to this very day we seldom speak unless brought together by a family gathering of some sort.

"Going into my home after the last meeting with the coven was different. My awareness and mind seemed to be thrown wide open to virtually anything. My senses were wide awake; I can't really describe it any other way. It was as if some veil had been lifted from my face. I quickly comprehended much of what I had learned and experienced with them and through my reading. A gateway, in a sense, had been partially opened."

"At this point, Sarah was starting to experience the first stages of phenomena in her home," states John. She claims that she was seeing shadows, mostly out of the corner of her eye. When she looked in the direction of the dark silhouettes, they would disappear. She also heard sounds which were audible, but could not be deciphered, which is often referred to as magical whispering. Many voices and sounds are heard, just like a muffled conversation coming from another part of the home. Sarah was obviously very nervous and pulled herself out of the class, but it did not end there.

"She continued to read in order to educate herself, trying to figure out what was going on and what was being performed at her past group meetings. She was intrigued by one of the high holiday celebrations she witnessed in regards to the winter solstice. The whole altar had been lavishly decorated and she wanted to know the exact intent of the rituals performed. As her research progressed, so did her experiences in the home. The voices persisted, as did the appearances of shadowy figures. Windows were opening by unseen hands, and the telephone would frequently ring once during the middle of the night. Of course, there was no voice on the other end of the line when she picked it up."

With her sessions ended and research almost terminated due to fear, Sarah contacted her brother on the issue of spirit manifestation. Her brother proved not to be very helpful. Instead of trying to explain or help his sister, or at least comfort her, an argument ensued. Sarah was reprimanded and told that what was occurring was punishment and payback for dabbling in a world she was not familiar with.

Within a few short weeks, her relationship with Matthew was diminishing into nothing more than a constant battle. Sarah became very irritable, even more so than usual, and the two fought like young schoolchildren over anything that arose throughout the course of their interaction on a daily basis.

At this point, Sarah tried to take matters into her own hands. From her reading, Sarah had come across basic rituals that were meant to provoke suffering unto a recipient deemed worthy of such an action. Simply put, Sarah placed a curse on Matthew. Her anger and disappointment with him was so strong that she felt compelled to do him harm, not in a physical sense, but instead to ruin wealth, sanity, and soundness of mind.

After about three months of seemingly constant arguing, the sudden collapse of Matthew's business, and a severe physical altercation, the two split and went in complete opposite directions. Sarah vowed to herself that she would never speak with Matthew again. She wondered why her life had dramatically changed, but could not quite figure out what had happened in the few months that her life was turned upside down. Her ritual could not have actually come into play, or so she thought.

For the most part, the activity seemed to calm down until the touching began again. Sarah claimed that scratches emanated on her body, usually depicting a mark similar to a scratch that would be inflicted by a small house cat. The welt would be there for a day or so, and then disappear without any trace of scarring. The situation was steadily increasing and the Catholic Church had performed the rite of exorcism over her after an investigation into the source of the problem was performed. She contacted a family friend, a priest, because the situation was too overwhelming for her to handle. It wore on her life heavily, bringing her to the point of depression. For about ten years, all was quiet except for an occasional outbreak of phenomena that was fairly insignificant in nature. Sarah carried on and lived her life with no real trace of the supernatural world. A few years went on with no significant paranormal occurrences.

Sarah began working at a local hospital as a nurse's aide. She had one daughter who was now seven years old. Her daughter was not born out of wedlock, but by a temporary relationship with a boyfriend which lasted only a few short months. Sarah and her daughter, Crystal, lived in a suburban neighborhood in a three-bedroom house, complete with an inground pool. Sarah had inherited a large sum of money from her father, who had passed two years earlier, and felt that he would have wanted her to use it for a nice home for herself and his only grand-daughter. She worked long hours and money was, by all accounts, not really an issue. This past year had been exactly what Sarah needed. She had a steady job for the first time in years, a beautiful young daughter who was intelligent in school, money to take care of the bills, and a new man in her life who she had absolutely fallen in love with. Although only together for a year, they both knew that marriage was in their near future.

Eric was a tall, hardworking man. He was built like an athlete and had the heart of a loving family man. He loved Sarah dearly and could not wait to live with her. They had been talking about it for months and he was waiting for the sale of his condo to go through. A few weeks later, his property sold and as scheduled, he moved in.

According to Sarah, there were no signs of an oppressive force for a few weeks, then it was as if a freight train hit them head on. Sarah convinced herself that no harm could come to her as long as she ignored the entities which lurked in the dark. "I began to notice something was around a few weeks after Eric had moved in. I started seeing the shadowy figures which I had seen years before in my house. I ignored them and did not dare to tell Eric. I assumed it was natural and perhaps the result of nerves relating to the stress of moving him in. If they were indeed what I thought they were, I decided that if I did not acknowledge them, then maybe they would respond similarly by ignoring me."

This would not prove to be the scheme of things that ensued in the household. A few weeks into Eric's move, many things changed in the household. The initial beauty of the home and the promise of a happy courtship took a backseat to the frightening ordeal that would take place over several months. Sarah and Eric were just starting their lives together as a live-in couple, but a presence disrupted this, attempting to make their unity a more challenging undertaking than either could have anticipated.

With both impatience and despair, Eric looked at us to tell of his ordeal. "At first, I thought that it was some berserk nightmare, but the only problem was that I was not asleep. The first night, things happened to me that I cannot explain nor do I really want to think about. It was hell, that is the only way I can describe it—hell. Any bit of reason I have cannot begin to delve into what is at play here. It all seems so illogical to me.

"I was laying in bed with Sarah, it was probably around eleven o'clock or so on a Friday evening in February. I remember it because I just had a conversation on the phone with my mother and we were talking about my sister's birthday party which would take place the following day. I had just turned off the lights and Sarah knew I was coming to bed but was half asleep herself. At the time, she had not told me about the shadows, the strange noises, or the unexplainable cold spots in her house. She did not tell me of the nightmares or the objects that had moved seemingly on their own. Basically, I was clueless and had no idea that anything had or would have occurred so far.

"I lay there, trying to get more comfortable, and turned, facing the window instead of facing Sarah. In plain view in between the two windows it stood, but it was not the only visitor that night. I closed my eyes and turned away, questioning myself, and shortly turned back, but it was still there. I can only describe it as a monk-like silhouetted figure, standing about five feet in height. It was dark and shaped just like a human wearing a dark robe. The figure remained there in full view for quite some time, peering at me. It had no recognizable facial features, but I got the impression that it was glaring at me. After it left, I got up and had a cup of coffee, not knowing quite what had happened. It was not a monk and did not really wear a robe, but that is the only way I can describe it to this day. The situation was so bizarre. Although I know that I saw it for a relatively lengthy period of time, I try to forget about it and pretend that it never happened.

"That was the first time I had ever experienced anything of this nature. I knew it happened, but my mind denied the situation completely. It was driving me nuts because it was so real, but still so out of the normal scheme of life."

"This black, seemingly robed figure has been quite commonly perceived in many situations where people are affected by the demonic and visibly see an entity," John said.

Laypeople and even many saints and theologians, when coming under diabolical attack, have reported blackened monk-like shapes. They have described such a figure as peering and watching over them. Other times, such figures have become violent, physically attacking their victims, but almost always under the veil of invisibility.

Eric's first encounter was not his last, but instead was the initial onset of the impending terror. Eric decided to initially keep this encounter a secret. At the same time, Sarah kept her isolated secrets and her past a secret as well, afraid of the very consequences of revealing what was occurring.

The Grip Intensifies

Sarah walked barefoot down the stairs to the basement to throw in a load of laundry. A deep-rooted sense of apprehension engulfed Sarah to her core. She hated the basement and only went down there when someone else was home. The reason for this was that a few weeks ago when she was in the basement, the dark low-level beings circled around her like a sadistic carousel. She could see them circling just a few feet from her body, but as she turned, the ominous shapes were no longer visible. She wished that her peripheral vision would not detect these characters, but she had no way of shutting off their images. After returning her attention to the laundry, they would start to appear again. The game of cat and mouse was cruel and yet mysterious because any attempt to identify the grayish black beings came up empty-handed. She at that time left the basement and retreated to the kitchen where she grabbed her car keys and went to a local coffee shop to kill time until Eric arrived home. Once again, she kept the incident wrapped in secrecy.

Prior to this, downstairs was never an ominous section of the house. In fact, she particularly liked this portion of the house. It was cool and was perfect for storage with the open floor plan. There was never a reason to fear the cemented room. Despite her newfound trepidation, she headed down into the depths of her house yet again about a week or so later.

At first, she placed the clothes in the washing machine and added detergent to the heaping load. She hurried, trying to get her chore done as quickly as possible, so exiting the basement would be sooner than expected. A pungent, dank odor filled the room instantly. Sarah gagged and was almost brought to her knees by the stench. She dry heaved frantically and headed to the stairway. The dim light above the washer blew out as she ran into the upstairs hallway. Unfortunately, this would not be the last of her encounters with the demonic, which initially had been dormant all these years, but began to come back with a vengeance.

"This case was absolutely severe and on a scale of one to ten was certainly up there in regards to its intensity," states John. The problems she had years before with the demonic were waiting in the wings for the right opportunity to strike. This is exactly what I mean when I stress that there is no time in the spirit world. Something you do or encounter may take years to have repercussions, but the opportunity is there for some real problems. The force which had plagued her years earlier took its time and waited for her to be truly happy and find someone that she really loved and who loved her. I got the impression that through trial and error, this force felt Sarah belonged to it and would not accept any interference in tightening its grip around her. To the entity, Sarah was destined to submit. Eric really was an obstacle and would be dealt with.

"I feel this way," John stresses, "because everything went haywire once Eric moved into the house. When they were intimate, the phenomena escalated. The more time they spent together, the worse the activity became. Things really were almost nonexistent until Eric moved into the home."

Sarah hoped to bring some relief to the spiritual infection that hid in the seemingly barren corners. At this point, not only were physical manifestations occurring, but heavy oppression began to set in. She was a complete wreck, wondering everyday when the demonic entities would strike again. Her house had been transformed from a place of rest and solitude to a place inhabited by darkness and fear. This game, however, is what the demonic does best—remaining anonymous while instilling fear and disrupting the normal scheme of life, mentally weakening the target to the point of relentless despair.

I remember being in this home on the initial interview with John, listening to some of the extreme situations these people had gone through. During the interview, a smell like natural gas and sulfur emanated in the room and disappeared within seconds without a trace. It was puzzling nonetheless. Also, John had been tapped upon his head a few times, causing him to be somewhat concerned. Most of the time during a visit or an interview, nothing paranormally related will happen. It will often take many extended periods within a home to experience the events that occur. On our second visit to the home, I was wandering around on my own while John spoke with Sarah in the kitchen. I walked from room to room, taking in the place. I distinctly remember walking into the bedroom and doing a double take. The room I had been in seconds previously had taken on a life of its own. The bed, which was perfectly made just moments earlier, was not quite so perfect. Some paperwork had been strewn on the floor and pictures on a mantle above the bed had changed places. There were no windows open, no other people in the home except the three of us, and no access to this room without going by me. This amazed me. It was a matter of mere seconds for the occurrence to take place and not a sound was heard. It was the first time I had really witnessed the physical displacement of objects. My blood nearly froze and my heart nearly stopped. I knew that any doubts I had regarding the legitimacy of this case were quickly diminishing. This was the real deal, an authentic case involving a powerful being capable of manipulating the physical environment and who seemed to toy with those in the house, not out of fun but out of detestation—a servant of revulsion and of disgust that thrived on torment and pestering. The torment had begun and would continue for Sarah and Eric.

An Unexpected Intruder

Eric pulled up and took the key out of the ignition. He grabbed some of the papers in the backseat and headed to the back door. He rifled through his pockets to find the keys he had just inserted into one of them. Unlocking the door, he placed his keys on the kitchen counter and put the papers on the table. He took his jacket off and kicked off his shoes. Heading to the bedroom, he made sure not to wake Sarah. He turned on the hall light and approached the doorway. Eric instinctively went to check on her as he always had before settling down and watching television before he went to bed. Eric was not prepared for what was to occur.

Hovering around Sarah were deep, black shapes. Eric froze, feet stuck to the floor, eyes wide open, gazing at the perverted display. After a few moments, he backed up a few steps and turned away from the direction of the bedroom. He paused, sweat rolling down his brow. What was happening? How could the same shapes he witnessed before be back again? The shapes were just like the one he had witnessed that first night, but this time there were many more. He headed back into the room, although scared to death. The shapes had disappeared.

"The first time it happens, and the second, the third, and so on," Eric says, somewhat trembling, "you think that your nerves are frayed. It doesn't seem real, but you know that it happened. To this day, I try to doubt what I have encountered so far, but I cannot deny the fact that what has happened is real. It is just as real as waking up and going to work every morning or interacting with someone.

It is a part of the lives of some and I wish I was not one of those people. I never asked for any problems nor did I invite anything to manifest on purpose.

"When I saw the dark shapes around her and on her, I got the impression that they were insinuating sexual acts or portraying something sexual in nature. Maybe it was meant to scare me or show that they had the upper hand, I don't know. I do know that they were there, I'm positive of that. I feel ridiculous even saying that, but they were there and appeared to me physically."

John articulates a key aspect of the onset of oppression. "The method of operation pertaining to that of the demonic is often a cerebral attack directly targeting people when they are alone. When alone, they are more susceptible and of course more fearful than if something occurred with even one person around. It is not rare, but almost always the norm, for one person to be targeted while others experience absolutely nothing within the home. This makes the sufferer of the attack alone and ten times more vulnerable in the battle for dominance. When alone and afraid, energy is thrown off of the individual, and they (the entity or entities) feed off of this, causing the manifestation to grow in intensity.

"Many of the cases I have worked on are quite similar regarding how they begin. The children will often be the first to experience what is taking hold. When and if they bring it to the parents' attention, they are usually shunned. This, however, would be a normal reaction, basing the child's testimony on probable overreaction. Children, the more open victim, will accept it for what it is and recognize the onset of terror and will feel alone and separated, fueling the wishes of this astute being. Often, months go by and naturally the intelligence builds strength before the parents or adults of the household notice it. Usually when this happens, it is a real bad situation, to say the least.

"There are also a couple different ways that this particular manifestation could have taken place in Eric's presence. There is the possibility that it was a physical manifestation. Most of the time, however, it will be the appearance of the being in the mind's eye. The entity will portray itself as it wants to appear, and essentially be projected to a particular person. Also, it could have been a combination of the two theories. Either way, something was still present and scaring him."

Eric Becomes the Focus

Sarah stirred the boiling water. Her daughter, Crystal, was gone, away at her aunt's house for the weekend. She had gone to spend time with her cousin who was visiting from Florida for the month. She gazed into the pot, losing herself in the thick steam pouring upward from the kettle. Reflecting on her life, Sarah realized just how fruitless it was when these so-called "things" were around. She had tried over the last few days to ignore what was occurring, but how could she? This world was not completely foreign to her, nor was it forged in fictitious allegory. She stirred the water as the white froth flooded over the side of the pot, not noticing that the overflow was even occurring. She was lost in thought and sorrow. The mind games had developed into an onslaught of terror. She never knew when they would manifest and always thought that the entities were present, ready to pounce on her. It was a battle waged in the realm of the physical and mental. She felt at this point that these "things" had the upper hand in both.

Sarah continued on, setting the table for both her and Eric, peering ahead into the living room. She noticed that her usually neatly organized environment had been altered. Set on the end table were pictures of Sarah and her family, friends, and Eric. She went over to the table, thinking the cat must have knocked the pictures over. When she picked the pictures up, she noticed nothing out of the ordinary until the one of Eric was turned over. It was still covered with the glass front, but the picture itself was completely destroyed. His face had been scratched out on the picture, as well as his chest. Everyone else in the picture was perfectly intact. Tears befell her as she sat down on the floor. Sarah broke into prayer, hoping that her fears were an overreaction. The picture however, had seemingly been removed, destroyed, and placed back into the frame.

"Actions of the demonic intensified after Eric moved in," John notes. "She had experience several years ago which had tapered off into an almost dormant state. Previous years earlier, she had something attach to her that waited for the opportune time to strike again. The unseen entity saw Eric as a threat. It was the first time she really loved another person and Eric returned her love. This being saw Eric as a barrier between them both, and the entity and wanted Eric eliminated. She was a belonging to the entity, and Eric was a threat to the total control, domination, and degradation that it was inflicting upon Sarah.

"People think you are crazy when you speak about people being oppressed or possessed by the demonic," John explained. Just because it falls out of the norm of thought, people automatically feel that it does not exist. What is at the root of major religious traditions? At the root is a battle that reigns on between good and evil, a personal quest to find the truth and to be connected to the Divine without falling into the stumbling blocks. The only problem is that there is a roadblock along the way, that roadblock being evil incarnate. Once again, I stress that such circumstances occur regularly all over the country and the world, but not every frightening situation of peril of human nature is the result of the demonic. Human beings can obviously create their own travesties, but there are cunning forces that have the ability to influence, and in rare instances can wreak havoc on an individual.

"Sarah's struggle at this point was at a turning point. The grasp became tighter with each waking moment. It seemed that almost every day, something would occur in the home. Bangings, objects disappearing and reappearing seemingly at random, putrid stenches, intangible voices that would flood a room then dissipate, and noxious nightmares were common. The moving of objects and the destruction of precious objects, like the photo of Eric, deliver a frightening message—a message letting the person know that they are around watching your moves, letting you know that they are always there. The most frightening aspect for Eric at this point was the figures.

"These figures were rare, but were still present over the preceding months. At one point, a figure was seen during daylight. Demonic activity can happen anytime in a haunted house, but usually occurs in the darkness of night when all natural light is absent."

Eric recalls his daylight encounter. "I was in the kitchen talking with Sarah, when in the doorway to my office, I saw a black form just standing there. It was about five-and-a-half feet tall and had the shape of a human, but at the same time it was not really an accurate resemblance of a human being. Its eyes were deep sunken and it made my skin crawl. It was only there for a moment, maybe a few seconds, but it left me with the realization that I was not crazy. It was as real as you and I, as clear as day. I know what I saw.

"At this point, I had to sit and talk with Sarah about all these encounters. My nerves were shot and I needed to air out my concerns. We spoke until it got dark about all that I had witnessed, all that she had seen, and she informed me about her past experiences before she even met me. We both agreed that it was real because we both experienced similar things without knowing that the other one was going through such a dilemma. Piece by piece, we figured out that if I was to stay here that we needed to do something. We tried a few local groups, but received no real advice or substantial remedies. Eventually, we were referred to John and called him immediately."

Before any investigation was pursued, Eric and Sarah tried to identify and combat what was going on in the home and their lives. Eric is a Catholic and loosely participates in his religion. Sarah is very weary of the traditions of organized religion, and although not opposed whatsoever to the concept of a Higher Being, finds it hard to confide in some type of church-based atmosphere.

Eric brought Sarah to church one afternoon to pray. "She looked so uncomfortable when we got there. It took us several minutes to even get out of the car.

She really was frightened, completely apprehensive of the church. Going up the steps beside her, I thought that she would never make it into the cathedral. When we did get in, we were inside for about ten or fifteen minutes. She just could not deal with it anymore. I got the impression that something was bothering Sarah, even though I could not see or even sense anything around her at this point. She did not seem completely opposed to the idea of religion, but instead was uncomfortable with the initial practice, as if it would cause her to go through more suffering rather than alleviating the struggle she was having."

Sarah's struggle and fear is not uncommon. Many have had messages given to them in which the demonic intruder instilled a verbal threat or a threatening impression. After working with John on several cases, I sought out clergy contacts. I met one morning with a very respectable priest who I was referred to by another member of the clergy. This priest had confronted firsthand the demonic and knew those who had experienced the wrath straight from hell's legions. This priest looked at me and began to tell of a situation where a woman was heavily oppressed by a force which threatened her with death if she received the Holy Eucharist. While attending Sunday mass, she would never get communion due to the threats which besieged her. This woman really thought that these voices would strike her down and kill her if she received the body of Christ. After a meeting with a priest, she was told to ignore the danger and receive the body and blood of Christ. She was threatened even more by the time she went to mass the following Sunday. She did, however, ignore the wicked commands and went to communion. She has never been bothered since.

"Mental oppression," John elaborates, "is all part of the struggle that these victims must endure. This can be more frightening than the physical mayhem because it is a direct assault on the sanity of the individual.

"This is the same of nightmares in the dream state. Certainly there are normal, everyday dreams which take place while sleeping, but this is not what I am referring to. Instead, many of these victims and even researchers will be given warnings, premonitions, scare tactics, and the like to frighten or to deter them. When someone is fed information that they should not know, or shown a future event related to the case, it becomes quite clear to me what is going on. In the dream state, we are wide open and completely receptive if something from the spiritual realm chooses to communicate with us. Deep sleep is similar to trance states or deep meditations where communication can take place. A frightening nightmare can be traumatizing for many individuals who are experiencing a demonic outlash."

Looking For Answers

Initial investigations are usually done after interaction with the family has gone on to some degree. During the investigation, researchers will often try to piece together the situation with the information available and based on the testimony of the families and personal experiences at the haunted site, a primary view as to what type of phenomena taking place will be the desired result of the trip. Is it demonic? Human spirit? A psychological issue? This often becomes a long, drawn-out scenario to piece together and determine the origin of the situation at hand, and if proven to be genuine, it will likely take even longer to bring about a resolution.

The following is part of the original audio between John and Sarah during a firsthand interview. Some points that Sarah did not think played a key factor in her problems certainly have added to her dilemma. Sarah thought that her brother could be part of the reason that her problems had escalated due to the anger and jealousy felt by him. No one wants to believe that a beloved family member would do anything to harm him or her, but it certainly does happen. This becomes obvious upon examining popular media. Child abuse, incest, spousal abuse, and virtually any other unspeakable crime have been committed against loved ones. The motives are unique in each situation, but hatred and resentment often fuel the attack. This field is not any different. Just because the effects are not easily recognized as actually physical hitting does not mean that the possibility for injury does not exist. Cursing is not unfathomable. Instead, cursing is real and concrete because thought indeed has substance. Thoughts have influence, power, and intent which make them a real energy, which although immeasurable, does create and cause a desired outcome in many instances.

John: Can you describe any of the practices your brother was involved with?

Sarah: He was into areas of spiritual enlightenment and other aspects of the world which magic is readily encompassed. He relied heavily upon astrology and candle magic to steer him in the right directions. He really believed that witchcraft was the key to life in order to solve life's mysteries and gain the power to deal with everyday situations. Growing up as a Catholic, he strayed maybe in his early teens, claiming it was all complete lies and that we are all our own god. I know that Christopher did not stay to the old proclaimed ways of white magic. He definitely dabbled in other areas and warned me of the repercussions of dealing with such energies. He liked experimenting whether what he was doing was deemed good or bad.

J: Were you around when he performed any type of rituals, prayers, readings, or anything on that level?

S: Yes. When I actually was in between homes he let me stay with him. It was the first time in awhile that we were seemingly getting along. I can remember that he thought I had some real spiritual issues and that I needed cleansing because of the high degree of negativity that, according to him, surrounded my being. I didn't totally agree, but listened to his feelings on matters pertaining to me and my present state. I remember him setting up a circle of multicolored candles and can recall him inviting me in to help cure and bind the spirits that were afflicting one of his close friends. I refused and thought maybe he was a bit off balance and wanted him to stop immediately. He went about his business as I sat there and later finished the ordeal. He claimed that while in his circle that I refused to enter, he saw small, short, dark animal-like figures in the room. He claimed that if I entered the circle, I would have seen them, too. It was disturbing to me and was not the last ritual that I heard or saw him perform. He acted very strangely in my opinion. I don't want to analyze something that I may not totally understand, but the thoughts, sayings, and attitude were so bizarre and almost sinister. Within a week or so, I moved out and once again we were not getting along so well.

J: How does your brother feel about Eric and yourself? Is he angry or does he disapprove of your relationship with Eric? Does he ever mention anything about your relationship with him?

S: He doesn't really even speak to me at this time, but the last few times I saw him, he was very negative about Eric. He doesn't even really know Eric and has no reason to dislike him. In my opinion, I think he was truly resentful and even envious of him, because Eric had my full attention. I think naturally that Christopher is extremely jealous. We have always been competitive, but it's on his end. I do not want to compete with him, but every time I get ahead, he wants to be just that much further in front of me. There never seems to be any type of common ground. He is not happy unless he is more successful and has the upper hand, no matter what it is.

J: Well, you certainly have a great deal that could, and in my professional opinion, does tie in. You have your past experiences with witchcraft, which led you down some frightening roads. Once you discovered some of the elements which are out there, you had the opportunity to experience them. Also, your brother may be partially responsible for what is happening through his practicing or perhaps sending a curse or an attachment to gain an upper hand over you. Something obviously does not want you and Eric together. Something is targeting him because it views him as a threat to your ownership by another party.

S: Say that it is true that my brother is partly responsible for this in order to destroy my relationship with Eric or because some entity from my past claimed dominance over me. What is the next step?

J: Honestly, there is not a clear-cut answer and there is not some quick fix to the problem at hand. We need to start with the basics and win one battle at a time. First, I would suggest some type of search for a higher, spiritual power. I'm not trying to push the idea of religion onto you, but I think your situation has proven to you just what can be out there. If you acknowledge the negative side, there must logically be a powerful pure side that needs to be addressed. You can fight as long and hard as you like, but these things that plague you have the upper hand. They respond to religion and this appears to be the only way to rid them from your life. Sure, I could arrange for a blessing, an exorcism, or some other method to try to alleviate what you have here. The real change needs to take part on your behalf. You need to fight it with a positive outlook and faith.
I know it's hard, Sarah; it always is. Going back to church is often the farthest thing from many people's minds, but look at what you're against. You know it's real, and now Eric does too.

After the interview that lasted for several hours, more was on the table than John thought. There was so much more to the case than just a woman living in a haunted house. This was a very dangerous situation.

Sarah brought up an unfathomable concern, which did not surprise John at all. He heard similar situations before described to him in detail and knew it to be true of many other cases.

"It was one evening after we got home from dinner," Sarah began to reveal. "Well, we were becoming intimate when I noticed the black things all around Eric. He did not really respond verbally and even hurt me while we were having intercourse. Honestly, he's never been like this. It seemed like he was in a trance, not responding to my voice. These black things remained around him and in the room the whole time we were together. It was dark, but I know they were there. The figures were so vivid to me. In my darkened room, they made their presence known, kind of like a pitch-black haze that stood out and moved freely about, remaining much darker than the rest of the room."

A great deal of guilt was also stressed on behalf of Sarah. She continued in the interview with John, feeling that somehow she was partially responsible for the backlash directed at Eric.

J: Why do you feel you are somewhat responsible for the experiences Eric is having?

S: One night, I was stressed and Eric came home from his mother's house. I was completely out of line for giving him a hard time, but I did. I began to question him, interrogating him on why he had been at his mother's house so much recently. Honestly, there was no real reason to get mad, but as I said before, I was very stressed and angry in general. I was probably just looking for anything to start a fight. Well, after an hour or so of arguing, he stormed out and left to go to his mother's house. I, at that time, was so enraged, filled to the brim with anger that I told all that was in the house to get him. I ordered the beings to leave me alone and go right for him. It seems ridiculous, but since then, his experiences really intensified.

J: I know what you are saying, I really do. Basically, you sent these entities at him. No formal ritual was performed, right?

S: No. John, I don't know what I was thinking at the time. I was so overwhelmed and completely angry that I just lashed out. I just tried to channel it all toward him, blaming him for the discord in the home and in our lives. Afterwards, of course, I knew that this was not his fault. I wish I could just take it all back and start over.

John explains Sarah's actions. "Sarah's mistake could obviously tie in to the end result. There are so many factors that branch off into the reasons why all these problems are occurring. What really matters in her sending off the forces at Eric was her initial intent. She claimed that she 'totally tried to have him overrun with disaster and wanted to bring about his destruction.' She was mortified that she had directed it all at him, and was absolutely regretful and disappointed in herself. Reading into it far deeper, you can see what was probably going on. What was with her saw Eric as a threat and wanted him eliminated from the big picture. What better way then causing dissention between the two people? Couples naturally have conflicts which often lead to bitterness and anxiety. The strain, however, was directly caused by and related to aspects of the supernatural realm. They were not arguing over money or some other small occurrence, but instead fighting over the entity which was targeting them. She was lacking sleep and sanity after dealing with the constant barrage of phenomena, and she was at the breaking point from it all. Her stress was caused by the spirits of the home."

The Dreams of Iniquity

Why was Sarah having the reoccurring nightmare in which she was targeted by angry humans who sought her destruction? The dream state is a very complex and mysterious realm. There may be no way to physically prove that it might have a direct correlation to the case, but dreams must still be taken into consideration. It may be a strange nightmare caused by the unconscious for an unknown reason. It could be an assault to instill fear by an outside source. Dreams can essentially be viewed in one of two ways. Sometimes dreams come through as prophetic or incorporate instances which in no way could be produced by a person's imagination. In Sarah's case, there is a possibility that it could tie in with her past. Reincarnation, past-life regression, and such terms are often met with frowns and disbelief, but in Sarah's case, there is a possibility that they tie in to her existence.

Through experimentation, Sarah thought that perhaps in an alternate life, she was a witch. Why might this be? She tried to explore the possibility of past lives with a therapist who was also a believer in the occult, which suggested the possibility that she practiced the religion of the earth hundreds of years ago. This theory cannot be conclusively proven. The fact remains that the dreams persisted and were confusing in nature. After she pieced it together, perhaps she was a living human being more than once, and this curse upon her followed her not only through generations, but also lifetimes. Was the dream indicating aspects of her past life? Perhaps she was killed or at least shunned by a practice she took part in during the distant past.

"This is one aspect which can be particularly difficult about a case," John emphasizes. "Sure, you can get the pictures, the audio or video, or physically experience something. What makes it hard are the intangible things, like dreams, information fed directly to the mind, and other aspects which are virtually intangible. You can't touch them, necessarily prove them, or measure them. Therefore, they are simply dismissed. Where a legit case is concerned, they need to be looked at just in case they tie in somewhere else."

The Physical Attack on Eric

Eric paraded to the mailbox to retrieve the mail and paper as he did every morning. However, this endeavor would be short lived. After retrieving the parcels, he never quite made it to the door. Instead, he collapsed in agony, screaming for his life. He lay helpless on the driveway until Sarah heard his cries. She immediately called an ambulance and Eric was taken to a nearby hospital. On the way to the hospital, he screamed and complained about his back and the pain that cascaded through the lower region of it.

Eric has had back problems in the past, but the circumstances are what make this injury all the more unique. His agony on this day could have a deeper derivation. The medical field could not pinpoint the cause of his torture. According to his diagnosis, it appeared that the discs in his lower back had been severely crushed as if he had been repeatedly smashed with a hard object. There was no physical object that had damaged this sensitive area. Fluid had been released and could potentially lead to partial paralysis, and the possibility that Eric would not be able to walk again.

Of course, it does not make any sense to solely blame the supernatural realm for such an injury, but the possibility exists that the main cause is supernatural in nature. The following recollection sums up the reason why this assault had taken place.

John seriously explains the possible reasoning. "When Eric and Sarah had conversed and shared their experiences, Eric expressed that he wanted it all to end. Eric was acting as a protector, but soon realized that there was nothing he could do to protect Sarah. This situation had escalated and was out of his control, completely.

"I cannot explain to people enough that resistance to these forces does not always work. When you have such forces on the higher levels, as they were in this case, you need to combat it with more than just resistance. It responds to the fundamental beliefs rooted in positive spiritual beliefs and the deeds of evil need to be undone. Eric, however, had done just the opposite. He, in a sense, had joined forces and gave in to the evil plan.

"Eric heard of a local Santerian priestess. He approached her for help, hoping that there was something that she could do to rid both his life, and, more importantly, Sarah's life of the demonic entity plaguing both of them. He was willing to try anything. By his fury, impatience, and genuine fright, he fell victim in a deeper sense. Essentially, he cut a deal. A deal that would essentially not be fulfilled unless he gave something as an offering.

"Many moons ago, when African people were removed from their own soil, the culture migrated as well as the people. These people kept their religious traditions very much alive, and integrated concepts from the areas they were moved to. As tribes intermingled, different concepts and ideas were adopted, giving heed to many sects of Santeria. Just as Christianity has thousands of its own branches of belief, so does Santeria. Some are positive; some are negative as in many other societal beliefs.

"Popular anthropology claims Cuba as the true home of Santerian beliefs. As African descendants were exposed to the Catholic beliefs of their Spanish dominators, a new precedent was found in regards to their beliefs. In order to continue the praise of their deities, also known as orishas, they would conceal their worship by praising statues and relics of the Catholic tradition, mainly the saints.

"Therefore, we can view Santeria as a mixture of African heritage and the Catholic religion. It encompasses belief in natural forces, and is complete with rituals and practices. Many of the diverse sects within the Santeria belief system see the positive side, in which the orishas prevail as the soul survivors and dominant powers, where others view the evil side as the dominant force. This negative side is often referred to as *ajogun*.

"The initial deal he cut was very complex. She gave him one of three choices. As a price to pay, he would have to give up his eyesight, his hearing, or his legs. He agreed hastily to give up the use of his legs, not knowing if this would be a full-fledged payment or the stuff of movies. After about two-and-a-half weeks, this attack took place in the driveway. Since he already had minor back problems, this made it easier for the attack to take place, leading to his hospitalization. It gravitated to his weakest spot, his back, and hit hard. It reminds me of other situations where someone will have some type of a weakness, and during an exorcism, the demonic will attack that weakness because it is a unique and effective foothold to cause suffering. For instance, someone with a heart condition may have severe heart palpitations during an exorcism. I cannot fully understand how this is done, but it is and I have seen it in many situations where I was a witness. Eric had offered his ability to walk and was having that exact threat posed to him."

This retaliation was real. Upon our second visit to the home, Eric was still in the hospital. When John was talking with Sarah, all I could really think about was the reality behind Eric's attack. At this point, I realized that this was definitely the heaviest case I had been exposed to, and I now knew why John had prepped me and insisted that my guard be kept high." These are the rare types of situations that occur with some of the cases John receives. Many think of the world of the supernatural as pure fantasy or low-scale activity, like doors slamming or the occasional cold spot. Cases of this magnitude show how deep and how extremely dangerous some cases truly are. Obviously, the family or the targeted individual bears the brunt of the grief and aggravation, but the researcher and certainly the clergy involved are often targeted for their involvement in such matters.

This was, however, the last time John would hear from Sarah and Eric. They were very eager to rid their lives of the terror that had been unleashed, but did not want to fight it with all of their might and positivity. Instead, immediate gratification had its grip on them, and they consulted with a Santerian priestess, a curator of the black arts, and several other investigative organizations; they even tried some homegrown remedies. They were unfocused and very discombobulated about which direction to take. They did not put their hearts into solving the issue, but instead wanted an "extermination" to be done.

John continues to reflect on the case. "Sarah told me just days before my arrival at the house that she tried to rid the home of the problems she had endured. She had lined up white candles and salt in a circle, challenging the spirits to come out, and ordered them to leave. Her intent was to end the whole nightmare, but instead, she provoked what was there lurking in the camouflage of invisibility. Eric was in the room with her observing as she tried to bring forth and expel the beings from the home. He saw dark figures in the background by the wall as she summoned and commanded these same beings to leave the home. Later that night, Eric claims that he "saw them having sex with her again." He was referring again to the darkened profiles that he saw before on other occasions.

"I can only hope for the best," John says sympathetically. "I know they have a long, hard, and possibly deadly road ahead of them. I can only pray that they get focused and find the direction they need to go. Honestly, I don't foresee a resolution to this case. Since my last visit to the home, I knew right there and then they had given up and decided to call it quits. I knew it was the last time I would speak with either of them. They hoped the situation would just go away on its own, but they know and I know that that will never happen. Instead, things will just get worse, and even more dangerous than they are now.

"The door opening for possession is a very fine line to cross, but they have all the attributes for this to eventually happen. The situation occurred in chronological order of the demonic scheme thus far, and when I left the case this was what was possibly destined to happen next. I've seen it several other times and anticipate that this will happen with either Sarah or Eric, even though I still hope that this will not be the case.

"What will happen? I do not know. There is just so much tied in with this one particular case. Evil relishes in the destruction of mankind, and Sarah and Eric were heading farther and farther down that path. Even if they kept in contact and fought to revoke the force, I feel that if an exorcism was performed, it would have been performed over both of them. There was definitely the possibility of an entity coming through either of them at the point when I spoke with them for the last time."

Terror In Litchfield, Connecticut:
The Case of Pat Reading

Terror In Litchfield, Connecticut: The Case of Pat Reading

In 1988, a case was opened in Litchfield, Connecticut, a story that had a horrific impact on the lives of one particular family. The Reading's, an average hardworking family, saw the opening of a door to another spiritual domain. This domain is not the substance of fairy tales or ancient mythology, but instead a direct war that ensued for over 14 years with the demonic hierarchy itself. Although the worst hurdles have been overcome, attacks do still occur sporadically.

Pat Reading, a slim, kind-hearted, soft-spoken woman resembles one of your favorite aunts. By simply walking through her door, you are guaranteed a warm cup of coffee and something to eat. Invariably, she will sit you down and ask how you are doing with complete interest. However, this normal woman would become the direct target of a deep battle wrapped with religious fervor. Pat, a Catholic woman, could never imagine what was in store for her for many years to come. Her plight has been lessened somewhat, but occasionally a negative energy peeks its head back in to try to gain reentry into her body. Every day remains a struggle that will seemingly continue all the days of her life. Years of complete agony and fifteen exorcisms later, Pat has some type of comfort in knowing that a higher power has freed her from the grip of near-death encounters with the demonic hierarchy from the depths of oblivion itself.

"I never thought in a million years that such things could occur or really ever existed," states Pat empathetically. "You hear the stories, but there does not seem to be a rational explanation at the time."

After years of dealing with the oppressing spirits, Pat has ultimately received an unwanted crash course in religious demonology.

"When it all started, I, of course, tried to find a reasonable explanation for the events taking place," states Pat. "Before this, I had never had an encounter with any type of spirit phenomena. I guess I believed, but I did not have any evidence to back up the existence of such possibilities. When you go through it firsthand, you are forced to believe. I don't care what anyone else has to say. I don't care if I am put down by skeptics or those who feel such things are silly or pure nonsense. I know now that there is good and evil and that there is sometimes a clash between the two."

Pat does not speak of everyday clashes, but a clash rooted back to the very scriptures that modern and ancient religious groups alike site as their doctrine: the Bible itself. Many use the Bible as the source of their beliefs, but choose certain passages as they see fit to coincide with their belief system. When viewed as a whole, the Bible is just that—a battle between good and evil. The Bible could be viewed as a manual for how to evade the cunning of the Devil and to embrace the unconditional love of God.

The phenomena started shortly after a violent sexual attack directed at Pat, which took place on her own property. The perpetrator to this day remains unidentified. The first traces of infestation were strange feelings, noises, knocking, objects moving, and the like. At first, Pat claimed that she did not quite understand what was happening. From a typical lifestyle to an almost immediate transition to hellish events, Pat's life took a twist from a catalyst of unknown origin.

Pat's first truly bizarre occurrence began one morning in the dining area of her house, which abuts the kitchen area. "A cup of tea toppled over, yet none of the tea came out," states Pat. "The tea remained in the cup, although it should have been a complete impossibility for this to happen. This happened at the very beginning when the phenomena began to occur in my house. I was absolutely amazed and could not explain the incident and still cannot to this day. It was at this point that I realized that the phenomena I was experiencing was not only in my mind. It was something that was around, and at this point, had made its presence known yet again. This incident with the cup of tea defied all rational thought. How could it topple over with its contents remaining inside? It was as if the tea was frozen solid."

In another instance, Pat and her daughter, Michelle, were home by themselves, and the bangings started on the doors at opposite ends of the house. Inside, the animals were going absolutely berserk. To seek refuge from the pandemonium, Pat and her daughter, who was sixteen at the time, went out into the yard and sat in the family station wagon. It was broad daylight and the two were, of course, frightened and greatly confused. The house had seemed so different over the last few weeks.

"We sat in the car as a means of escape," says Michelle. "We did not know what to do and had no idea what was going on. I was just a teenager at the time, and to see my mother so scared added to my own fear was really too much to bear. We thought the only way was to hide outside in the yard and wait for my father to come home. At the time, we couldn't possibly stay in there. Our thoughts were that we might see or experience something we didn't really want to encounter. It was all just too bizarre to even fully comprehend. It didn't seem plausible or even something that was possible, although we both had witnessed phenomena at this point."

The two sat in the station wagon for some time. They stopped talking about their theories of what was going on to escape the uneasiness that beset them that day. Within a matter of a half hour or so, they were paid a visit by whatever was lurking within their home.

"I sat there with my mother," states Michelle, "but the comfort of sitting in the car came to an end. The car slowly started to shake, but it had not yet been started and there was not a key in the ignition. We didn't even have the keys because we had fled the house so quickly. It picked up in intensity until the car was rocking back and forth like people were jumping on it. You could also hear scratching on the windows all around the station wagon. We moved closer together and embraced one another. We didn't know what to do. There was no one anywhere in sight and it was broad daylight. There was no visual explanation for the rocking or the scratching on the windows of the car. We knew what we had experienced was real, but still were quite clueless of what this was and why it was in our lives."

"Another concern I had," Pat reveals, "was that seemingly every time we would go out as a family, or one of us would return to an empty house, all the furniture would be rearranged. It was as if it were systematically set up and moved for some unknown reason. Things were not just knocked over or misplaced. Instead they had changed locations."

John adds to Pat's testimony. "I remember when this happened, too. Just leaving on a day-to-day basis almost ensured that upon arrival back at the home, everything would rearrange. This did not just happen two or three times, but instead was a very constant characteristic of the case."

With the onset of the knockings and other actions of the spirit or spirits, Pat and her family sought out help. There was a pertinent question that was gleaming in the minds of all the members of the Reading family. Was there actually help available? Were there credible individuals that would even believe them?

The process of seeking help was not easy. Pat discusses her discovery and the attempt to contact these ghost busters who often go unheard of in the background of religious fervor. "I was at work and one of my coworkers suggested that I give Ed and Lorraine Warren a call," Pat says, looking up. "She said that they dealt with hauntings and might be of some assistance. Trusting her opinion as I had when telling her what was happening at home, I thought giving the Warrens a call might be a good idea."

Both Ed and Lorraine Warren agreed to meet with the family and try to figure out what was going on within the once peaceful home.

Coming Under Diabolical Attack

Possession is a debated term that turns heads the moment it is even brought up. Initially, many believe it to be nothing more than an allegory rooted in ancient times and based on an overactive imagination. Psychology tends to support the theory that it relates to mental disorders, such as schizophrenia or multiple personality disorder. Although these theories are accurate in some cases where spirit phenomena is not the reason behind the madness, other cases resemble an external agent at work behind the scenes where intelligence is a factor. A battle ensues to gain control over the will and quintessence of the possessed. It is not because those in the field of demonology want to believe that spiritual matters are at hand, but because they truly exist. The psychic researcher will seldom deal with matters of pure possession because of its rarity, but the opportunity still lies for this seemingly unnatural action to take place. Most of the time, the spirit manifestations will not get to the point where possession will take place. If something is truly happening to an individual or family, the phenomena is usually caused by a human spirit or lower-level demonic intelligences, and chances are that the situation will be identified, resolved, or at least lessened to a bearable degree. With possession, the battle is being won by the prime adversary: evil incarnate. When possession has occurred, it is as if a celestial law has been broken. The unthinkable really has happened when true possession occurs. The demonic appears to be one step ahead of the individual, and ultimately needs to be counteracted to head off any further issues, such as stress, fear, physical assaults, mental torment, and even suicide or murder.

By overpowering the individual, the demonic force will either cohabit or dislodge the human spirit, and temporarily cease the will of the possessed. When this blasphemous act occurs, the ultimate insult has taken place, and the individual is defiled to animal-like proportions, outward manifestations of intense, unnatural phenomena, and terrifying moments for anyone immediately involved are quite commonplace. Total degradation may be the temporary result, but help can occur by the will of a pious member of a multitude of religious sects. By means of purity, a clergyman will risk himself, his very core, to save a fellow brother of humanity. It is not he who casts out the stubborn spirit, but an outside interaction by a Higher Being. People cannot cast out demons and devils, it is through God that expulsion is complete. An exorcist always casts out evil in the name of "Jesus" or "God." The terms used may be different, but the meaning is the same. Calling upon the Great Being is used because eternal goodness is the only way to cast out such blasphemy. After this, the factor of free will becomes even more crucial. The individual is seemingly always targeted for reentry and needs to be very careful not to allow the banished tormenter to gain the power it once held. Still, the power they have may transcend that of humans, but they fear that which revolves around God. The entities know they will be banished and know their time to meddle in the affairs of humans is limited.

Possession remains to this day highly controversial. Eyewitness accounts, substantial evidence in the form of video and audio recordings and even photographs, and passages rooted in the beliefs of all major religious doctrines do not seem to be accepted by mainstream society, which tends to frown on the idea that such acts of spiritual or essence possession are even possible. It really boils down to a matter of faith to believe that faith substantiating that both good and evil powers exist and roam the world in search of followers and those to dominate, torment, and destroy, therefore disgracing the cosmic creation or existence of that particular individual.

"When the attacks take place," says Pat, "I do not have a recollection of what happened during the attack period. I was asked several times if I could even remember part of the possession, but for some reason, I never had any idea of what had happened to me. I couldn't recall the verbal assaults I put forth, the bizarre violent outbreaks, or the animalistic attributes which I played out while overcome by the force. When these instances were revealed to me, I really couldn't believe it or even begin to accept it."

Michelle, looking at her mother, speaks up in a nervous tone. "When she would come under possession, she would start to act strange, almost like something was beginning to bother her. She would seem very disorientated. When the first bout took place, we were home alone together. I was in the living room folding laundry, and my mother was in and out of the kitchen doing her normal everyday cleaning routine. She seemed like something was wrong, but I had no idea just how wrong this occurrence would be.

"She started to walk slower and slower and her legs gave out. She cursed and flailed in the room right next to where I was. She looked at me, but she didn't seem to fully be there and was definitely incoherent to my words. She was in her own world. I was scared and my fear had to do with her physical health. I knew that what was around was overpowering her and I panicked. My mother had been sick for quite some time and I didn't know how her physical well-being would be affected by this subjugation.

"I stayed on the floor holding her and could immediately tell that there was no way that she was going to be able to get up on her own. I carried her to the car where her convulsions continued, as did the mumbling and sporadic cursing. I drove her down the street to the shrine and immediately carried her in, still fearful for her welfare. I dragged her up to the altar and prayed. I put holy water on her and just kept praying, asking that she be spared from the torture that had been inflicted on her that day. After five or ten minutes, she seemed to be mildly coherent. I brought her back to the car and drove her home.

"This was the first time that I had ever seen such a spectacle. I knew it was real. After all, I had been experiencing many of the same things that my mother had witnessed. My concern for her well-being was very high at this point. I questioned her health during the attacks. I didn't know if her life would be taken or whether or not her health would plummet to an even worse degree."

This would be the first but not the last of Pat's episodes. Over the next several years, the demonic spirit would continue to meddle in the family's affairs and possess Pat several more times. The struggle had just begun, and at this point in time, was only gaining strength. Two Catholic exorcisms were performed on the house and on Pat. They, however, were not successful. Although the attempts to release her from the hands of evil were fruitless, the Reading family continued on, not giving in to the devilish fiend or fiends which worked in the shadows of the dark. If anything, religious values were intensified. It is often said that God will not allow something evil to happen without the birth of something pious, positive, or righteous. Pat, as well as her family, grew in faith and in hope, not willing to accept the satanic strike as their downfall. They may be standing seemingly alone, but they knew that an invisible positive force was still watching over them. The struggle continued, but the Readings fought harder.

"I can remember thinking that there was no way that I could win this battle," Pat recalls vividly. "This mentality was only temporary though. To have this frame of mind would have been completely absurd. Without the help of God, there would be no way for me to pull through. Facing the demonic or any other frightening situation would be completely impossible on my own. Since these entities have the upper hand over humans, there would be no way to combat these forces without help from above."

"Pat, at the beginning, was destitute, but she never lost hope," John notes. "She knew that facing darkness such as this would be difficult, and as a result embraced God as her fuel for battle. The demonic relishes in the demise of people, and what better way to endorse this than by making them feel alone. Through faith, Pat was willing to exchange blows with the help of a Supreme Mediator."

"Also," Michelle intercedes, "I can remember my mother and I praying to the saints for help, mainly Padre Pio."

Padre Pio was a Catholic clergyman who died in 1968, and is most known for his life in which stigmata plagued him. Stigmata are believed to be the appearance of the wounds of Jesus Christ on ordinary human beings who were chosen for reasons which are unclear. Padre Pio was considered to be a modernized, pious man of the church, who has been considered for canonization as a saint.

"During one of the exorcisms that was performed here in the house," Michelle states, "an odor emanated after the completion of the rite. The smell was of roses, not the smell of an actual store-bought bouquet, but instead a thick, resonating smell of roses. This was experienced by all those present and remains a constant positive memory in my mind. It was often said that the smell of roses was one of the recognizable characteristics of Padre Pio's intercession in spiritual events. The feeling after this smell arose to all of those present was of hope and positivity."

"Essentially," Michelle continues, "faith was the only peace of mind my mother had through her ordeal. Sure, she had us and our support, the researchers that she could call, but a deeper meaning based on faith in a High Superpower was what gave her the strength to carry on." John sits and recalls the phone call he received one night while sitting at home. "It was a night just like any other night, and I had come home from work and heard the phone ring. I had no idea what to expect and certainly got more than I had bargained for on that evening. Michelle was on the other end of the line and was beside herself with confusion and fear. Her mother had gone under possession again and it scared the living daylights out of her."

The attack on Pat lasted for approximately fifteen minutes. Michelle was in the living room watching television when the possession took place. Pat began cursing and convulsing, spitting all over herself as profanity continued to be powerfully vocalized. She also was on all fours, growling and biting at Michelle just like a rabid dog. The furniture had been turned over and everything around was strewn about, either out of place or broken. Michelle did the right thing by praying until the attack ceased. Michelle found her mother wrapped around the toilet and had to pry her out from behind it. Pat had no recollection of what had happened again and was very weak, barely able to speak.

"The demonic," John elaborates, "will do anything to lower humans to the ultimate lowest forms of degradation. Making the human host writhe on all fours like a dog, blasphemous cursing, spitting and vomiting, and inhuman-like squeals and yelps are the fundamental nature of possession in regards to lowering the host to animal-like extent."

Michelle looks at John and I with a somber expression during the interview. "When these attacks on my mother continued throughout the years, it was not her who was in control."

John agrees and continues. "Mental illness is just that—mental illness. Possession, on the other hand, is altogether different. The two can be very similar except for one huge difference: the possessed does not just exhibit the outbreaks that can make these two seem the same. Possession will have a long history of external manifestations that are usually witnessed by family and friends, researchers, and the clergy. Possession has the odors, cold spots, visual manifestations, speaking of unknown languages, revelation of private and unobtainable events and circumstances, and even sometimes attacks on individuals present among the possessed by unseen hands. The two occurrences, mental illness and possession, parallel one another, but it is quite obvious after putting a case together to see what is at hand.

"Skeptics are quick to jump to the conclusion that all apparent cases of possession are mental illness. This is downright ridiculous because the evidence has not been examined by these people. Sure, I have been on cases which I have proven to be related to psychology and I consequently referred the affected party to a psychiatrist. On the other end of the spectrum, I have been witness to true cases of possession and had to get other researchers and the clergy involved.

"Pat's case reveals the demonic nature of the situation that she came face to face with. I know her case was the real deal because I was a firsthand witness to many of the events. I saw her under possession, I witnessed the external phenomena; there was no joke here. This case is one of the more memorable ones I have encountered because of its severity. I don't think that anyone who entered through the doors of this house went away without experiencing something during the peak of this case.

"One evening several researchers were up at the house, documenting anything that might happen. With her case, there was so much going on that I'd say probably every researcher that went into that home experienced something or gathered some type of evidence. It was later in the evening and Pat began to act strangely. She went under possession, but did not sadistically attack or have the outbursts that she had in the past. She was again not herself. This night, however, was marked with a new twist. She looked at the different researchers one at a time and revealed very personal experiences and situations that they had been through. Many of the researchers left in obvious distraught after being mentally assaulted. She had knowledge that was otherwise unobtainable, so personal that many of the researchers could not comprehend how this act was even possible."

The Many Diversions

"In order to gain access," John reveals, "the demonic will often throw up diversions to permeate even deeper into the individual they try to dictate. When dealing with such a cunning force, one's guard needs to be up all the time. Retaliation on investigators and an intense turn for the worst in regards to the individual experiencing the brunt of the attack is all too real. Each case, unique in its own right, must be handled carefully. It is rather difficult and sometimes impossible, but staying one step ahead is essential in dealing with the hierarchy of evil. Trying not to fuel the situation is a necessity, not an option. Opening doors further and giving superfluous recognition will only allow the grasp to tighten. Roadblocks will be thrown in the way to try to ensure that the possessed will not get help."

"I remember being down in the basement one afternoon," Pat states. "I will never forget the beauty of the woman I encountered. She was gorgeous and was dressed in white. I was, of course, startled, but cannot forget exactly what she looked like."

"At this point in the mix," John vocalizes, "the demonic needed to intensify the hold it had so far. In my professional opinion, based on the circumstance, the white lady in the basement Pat had encountered was a diversion and only a diversion. I do not think it was positive at all even though it portrayed beauty and grace, nor do I believe that it was a human spirit. Instead, by Pat's intriguing desire to determine what this entity was, she inadvertently let her guard down just enough for the sexual attacks to break into existence. It was around the time of the appearance of this form that Pat was soon forcibly raped by the malignant entity. This is the case in many of the investigations I have been involved with over the years. In this case, the incubus saw the open door and struck hard, trying to degrade her even further, trying to make her even more vulnerable and alone.

"Sexual attacks in themselves are one of the most vile forms of malice and hate. Imagine experiencing such an action like this, but unable to defend yourself or fight off your attacker. This is often the hardest thing to understand in such a case for the victims. It is all too real, but at the same time, so hard to accept because of the almost unnatural pretense of such an act."

An incubus is believed to be the demonic spirit which sexually attacks women where the succubus attacks a male victim. Although demons appear to be genderless, they can take on any form they choose and strike both men and women, depending on the given circumstance.

As the situation become more portentous and threatening, an exorcism was to be performed in the home. The exorcism would be done over Pat and in the home to try to banish yet again the oppressors of eternal life. The exorcist, Bishop Robert McKenna, would be the clergyman to undertake the battle with the keepers of immorality.

Pat was bound to an overstuffed living room chair just in case the demon came forth with vengeance and aggravation from the prescribed ceremony. Other researchers were present during the event and noticed that the crucifix attached to the wall was bleeding from its eyes. The relic was of much importance to Pat. It was a gift from her mother that she truly cherished. The eyes of Christ continued to bleed as the exorcism progressed. Afterwards, it was thought that this was probably a diversion to take the emphasis off of Pat and her delivery from evil. Samples were taken by one of the researchers who had a deep law enforcement background and were immediately tested for content. After testing, it was determined that the substance which bled from the relic was not of human or animal origin. The blood-like substance was of an undetermined nature.

"I saw this relic bleed," said Michelle. "Blood oozed from the crucifix steadily. Bearing witness to this was extraordinary. It was unfathomable at first because you could wipe the blood away from the crucifix and more would seep from the relic. This also happened on multiple occasions and many who were here witnessed this event and documented it."

Even today, a few faint stains remain on the wall below the image of Jesus Christ, standing as a permanent reminder of the phenomenon.

Some time later, Bishop McKenna performed another exorcism over Pat, in which she indeed went into a state of distortedness, the demon present again, once provoked through the Latin language spoken with aged prayers of the Lord. The exorcism lasted for about an hour. After it was over, Pat complained of pains and was examined. On her stomach, three crosses were etched deep into her skin, an event documented by still film and video. Her body had been restrained during the exorcism, but the fresh wounds indicated some type of abuse had certainly occurred while the possessed state had transpired. She appeared to have been physically assaulted by invisible hands that beleaguered her in the vulnerable state.

Repelling the Dominion of Empty Promises

After several experiences and thorough documentation of Pat's endeavors with the oppressing and possessing blasphemous tormentors, the rite of exorcism was to be administered yet another time. Past attempts had reduced the physical, mental, and spiritual attacks, but within a few weeks, the pain would sneak back into Pat's life, as if through some invisible window. An attempt to rid Pat of this torment would be made once again, but this time the effort would be moved to Our Lady of the Rosary Chapel in southern Connecticut. The exorcist, Bishop Robert McKenna, would again perform the rite in the name of Jesus Christ to hopefully experience divine intercession from above. Through intense preparation, the bishop equipped himself with faith to combat forces as old as time itself. Present at the exorcism were Michelle Reading, a few of the sisters or nuns from the convent on the premises, and many researchers. They would all bear witness to the ritual in this house of the holy.

"My main concern," Michelle recalls, "was my mother's health yet again. I prayed and begged for the removal of the spirit from her and that which was always around her, but I still feared that she would physically be in jeopardy due to the writhing and intense nature of the possession if she went under. She had already lost a great deal of weight and at the time was one hundred and eight pounds. She was very frail and weak."

McKenna, armed with holy water and relics, would deal with the blackened angel of pride, his piety put to the ultimate test. His attack would be an ultimate battle of faith with the hopeful intercession of the Divine to discharge the enemy of sin and disaster. The exorcist is essentially a warrior of God, standing up on behalf of the virtues of charity and compassion. Freeing the captive consciousness is obtainable only through faith and a positive intercession.

Pat was led up the front stairs of the church and was led to the first pew in the chapel. Within a few moments, the confrontation was marked by a sign of the cross. The antediluvian ceremony started and it would not be long before the tyrannical force of doom would surface.

Pat sat in the pew, the normal function of blinking ceasing to occur. At first, she seemed quite docile, dazed as if in an altered state of consciousness. Remaining bound with five large men behind her, her demeanor changed once the force was confronted with phrases and lexis of biblical inspiration. Pat became irate, looking those present directly in the eyes: a gaze so inhuman, so distant, and the polar opposite of her normal behavior. Grotesque facial contortions marked the onset of the dark seraph's arrival.

Pat kept looking into the top left front portion of the church. Those at the exorcism describe what they can only depict as a wispy, black presence that lurked in the corner.

Michelle recounts the event, "There was actually a black being there that remained through most of the duration of the exorcism. It was not just a glimpse, but also a physical representation of something that decided to hang around during the rite. I remember that even Bishop McKenna noticed the shadowy figure.

"My mother was looking at everyone present in the eye, then quickly glimpsing back to the black form that remained in the left corner. She became even more distraught when the demon was provoked to reveal its identity. What possessed her fought even harder at this point, trying to ignore Bishop McKenna's commands in the name of Jesus Christ to reveal itself. It was an absolutely hellish standoff."

The spitting and attempts to bite intensified along with the verbal assaults. Later, the language proved not only to be Latin, but also backwards English. The figure in the corner remained there, as if peering and overlooking the entire event as the attempt to expel the dark entity continued.

Michelle continues her description of her mother's state of possession that warm summer day in the church. "She became even more aggressive and broke out of the ties and wanted to ravage Bishop McKenna. She was one hundred and eight or ten pounds at this time, but was completely filled with forcefulness. It took about five people to keep her from acting on the aggressive state that had befallen her. Each second, her strength seemed to grow stronger and stronger until the pew actually cracked due to her violent behavior even though she was heavily restrained. As Bishop McKenna continued ignoring the demon's blasphemous words, the demon grew more and more infuriated. At this point, I was really afraid of what would happen to her. She was so brittle at this point and this exorcism was needed to hopefully end her suffering. This was the day that would make or break her. She could no longer endure the physical, sexual assaults, the stress, or constant sleep deprivation. I really wasn't quite sure how much more she could take. I truly felt that this was the day which would decide the fate of my mother."

Bishop McKenna had to back off and retreat a few steps back because she was becoming so enraged and inhumanly strong that it was almost impossible to keep her from assaulting him. The demon seemed to want to lash out and kill the bishop.

At this point, her facial features changed even more substantially where she looked remarkably different. Her pupils were dilated and kept moving in different directions. Additional researchers present had to help restrain her because her strength was too much for only a few men to handle. There were at least five people helping to restrain her throughout the ceremony, and from this point in the exorcism on, as many as seven were needed to restrain her. All the people present still could not keep her completely at bay.

Michelle continues, "At this point of possession, it was quite obvious that her soul, her essence, however you want to identify it, was pushed aside. I never believed that this could happen, but after living it, seeing all this happen, and speaking with my mother who had no recollection of the events, it really came about as a real, concrete experience."

A psychic cold befell the area even though it was summertime and very hot weather. Her eyes began moving in opposite directions from each other, giving a wild look to her already contorted expression."

"This is quite common," says John. "When something manifests and it uses the energy around or from people, the temperature will usually drop significantly to the point where it is obvious and noticeable. With all that was going on, a great deal of energy was being used when the possession took place."

"Pat at this time was very sick and is a small woman to begin with. Her strength was too much for several decent-sized human beings to hold her down. When she was possessed, she was totally overrun with hate and pure disgust to anything that even remotely represented God."

After about one hour, the rite was over and Pat was weakened to the point where an ambulance was actually called, for fear for her health was even greater at this point. She was, for all intents and purposes, in and out of consciousness. She was brought to Bridgeport Hospital and was followed by Michelle and a few of the nuns that were present during the ceremony. Her blood pressure was very low and her body bruised from all the necessary restraining that had taken place at the chapel. After a few hours of observation, she was released from the unit and was brought home by her daughter to rest.

"Pat had many bruises and etchings on her body," states John. "The bruises certainly could have been caused by the restraints as well as those who had to control her while she was under possession, but the deep scratches were obviously from an outside party as they had been in the past during other attempts to rid the possessing demons."

"To this very day," Pat stresses, "something will make its presence known on a daily basis. Sometimes, it will be the lights going on and off. Other times, the faucets will systematically turn on. Each day I am reminded in one way or another that something still lingers. Other times, it is a feeling that something is around, in the room, or in the house with you."

"I think what we have here now," Michelle continues, "is a combination of sorts. There are times where it seems the demonic is around, maybe trying to scare, threaten, or intimidate. If given an opportunity, I'm sure it would try to rear its head back into the picture for another opportunity. Other times, we have occurrences that resemble something that you might find on a poltergeist case. During my mother's struggle several years ago during the height of everything, it was quite common to find some of the furniture rearranged. Sometimes phenomena like this will occur. I also feel that there is human spirit here. Is it a previous owner? I don't know, but it appears to reside here. The house exemplifies that which could be deemed haunted, but thank God that the awful oppression that once besieged this home, mainly my mother, has been removed.

"There was a time where I thought these entities would actually kill her through all the physical stress they caused on her body. I believe that God has freed her, and I am thankful to the researchers and the assistance of Bishop McKenna for helping to bring relief to the struggle, which at one point seemed to be everlasting."

"If I can stress anything, it is that these types of situations can and do occur," states Pat. "It's hard to comprehend unless you've been through it. I really want people who are facing the same types of problems to realize that there is help out there. I know what happened is real and it must be remembered that God is stronger than any demonic presence."

The Raven

The Raven

Jeff lay completely still in his bed. Pulling the covers up over his head, he pretended he did not hear anything. Working up the courage, he ever so slightly pulled the covers down enough so his mouth was partially exposed.

"William? Did you hear that?"

Quite normally, William responded to his brother's question, "Hear what, that tapping?"

"Yeah," Jeff exclaimed.

"It happens all the time. What do you think it is?"

Jeff did not respond for about thirty seconds, but it felt like much longer, "I don't know. It starts every time we go to sleep, doesn't it?"

"Usually I notice it after the lights go off," William responded. "Maybe it's mom and dad playing tricks on us; that wall is in their room, too."

"I don't know, why would they tap all night?" Jeff continued to lie there wondering what all the commotion was. At the inception of nighttime, he would finish up his homework and watch the news with his brother and father. By that time, his little sister, Erica, was in bed for the night. She was only five and was not allowed to stay up past nine o'clock like her brothers: William, age twelve and Jeff, age ten. Jeff noticed the rapping noises one night after powering off the light and wishing his brother good night. The following night, the two spoke of baseball and the new girl in school. Once William dozed off, he noticed the steadiness of the incessant raps. Ever since, this clamor had been consistent and noticeable even to his brother.

"Get up, time to get ready," Rosemary called up to the boys. Rosemary was a young woman of thirty-four whose hair was long and jet black. Her slim, yet tall and attractive figure was maintained through her job hustling at the local restaurant, serving tables. She was a hard worker and also took part-time classes at the local university to get her degree in elementary education. She married her husband, Bruce, just twelve years earlier after the two met at a local restaurant. She was a waitress and he was the part-time bartender working his way through school.

Bruce was a short, stocky man, thirty-five years old and the owner of his own real estate agency. Shortly after marrying, the two bought their home where they continue to reside to this day. The Victorian house was a bit of a "fixer upper," but both of them saw the potential for a beautiful home and could not resist the charm of the old home.

Jeff walked slowly down the stairs, eyes still half shut. He did not want to get up after getting little sleep from his night filled with unavoidable thoughts. Even though he dislodged the night noises from his mind, he still had a trace of apprehension, not knowing what the pestering noise was caused by. Was it faulty wiring? A mouse trapped in the wall? He did not know. He just knew it was a little disturbing to not know the cause of the noises.

"Don't forget your report, Jeff," Rosemary stressed. Jeff compiled a report on both his Irish and his Native American heritage. Rosemary was from a deep Native American background, while Bruce was mostly Irish. His grandparents were born a few miles outside of Dublin at the turn of the century and eventually moved to the United States.

Jeff collected his materials and went out to the school bus with his brother.

"I was thinking about what you were saying last night," William said. "Any ideas of what it was? I was thinking more and more about it after we talked. I stayed awake most of the night listening to it."

Jeff interjected immediately. "So did I!"

William looked at Jeff curiously. "Whadda ya say that we wait up tonight and see if it happens again? I'll stay up if you do. Does it sound like a deal?"

"That's fine. At least we'll know if we're crazy or not."

A few moments later, the yellow school bus pulled up and the two entered its door, making their way to the back of the bus as they always had. The two embarked on a mission to determine the cause of the noise, but this was only the beginning. The tappings were the only phenomenon picked up on so far. At this time, the boys as well as their parents and younger sister, had not experienced or witnessed anything really concrete. Their saga would only intensify from that moment on.

After school, William and Jeff ran upstairs to get their homework done. The baseball game was on television at seven o'clock, and they did not want to miss their beloved pastime because of algebra or history. They took a break for dinner, then parked themselves in front of the television. They swapped their favorite baseball cards, a pregame ritual before every Yankees game.

Jeff looked at William, making sure that no one was looking.

"When do you think we should go to bed?"

William looked at his brother after verifying that no one else was around. "How about nine, we'll have to go to bed about then anyways."

"Sounds good," Jeff stressed with excitement in his voice.

The two boys continued trading cards and watched the baseball game. Before long, it was nine and the boys went upstairs even though the game was only in the eighth inning. Climbing into bed, Jeff reached for the light switch.

Jeff turned the knob, saying, "Ready?"

"Go ahead Jeff."

The two lay motionless and silent, waiting. After a few minutes William decided to speak up.

"You hear it?"

"No," Jeff replied.

"I don't get it," William said. "It happens all the time; why not tonight?"

"I don't know what to tell you," said Jeff.

Both lay there for about an hour before drifting off into sleep, waking the next morning to disappointment.

Jeff's New Friend

Caw! Caw! Caw!

Bruce rolled over to face Rosemary, "What the heck is that?"

"Sounds like a bird to me," she said.

"It better knock it off, or I swear I'll kill it," he continued.

Caw! Caw!

Bruce got up out of bed and went into the bathroom to brush his teeth, and Rosemary went to wake up the kids.

"Get up," she announced as she had every morning of their lives. "Get up now or else you'll be late for school."

Jeff turned over and looked at his clock. It was seven. He had a long day ahead of him. First, he had school and after school, he had an intramural basketball game. He got up and opened his dresser drawers, picking out the clothes he would wear that day.

William rolled out of bed and looked at Jeff, "Did you hear it?"

"Hear what?"

"You know, those noises."

"No, you?"

"Yeah, I did," William replied to his brother. "This time it was different though."

Jeff looked at him and said, "How so?"

"There was, well you know, the taps, but there was also scratching."

"You mean like something scratched you? Were you hurt?"

"No, not that type of scratching. It was in the walls."

Jeff did not say much at this point. He was playing games with his brother, trying to filter the information that William presented to him. Jeff also heard the noises, but did not want his brother to know. Jeff heard the noises while pretending to be asleep and had an experience which transcended the noises that both of the boys heard.

The previous night when the noises were most prominent, Jeff felt a sensation like something crawled onto his bed. Their cat, Freckles, died two years earlier, leaving no logical explanation for the thing that crawled up the side of his bed, around his waist, and disappeared.

William continued to talk about the audible sounds, which could be heard the previous night. Jeff continued to play dumb for fear of either alarming his brother or being seen as crazy. He did not know which.

Rosemary made the children breakfast and was basically pushing them out the door a few seconds before the bus was at the foot of the driveway. She waved to them as they got on the bus, Erica at her side.

Caw! Caw! The crow continued to scream. She looked up into the nearby oak to discover an immense, black crow perched about twenty feet off of the ground, staring down. She shut the door, and moments later, forgot about the intense squawk that carried across the yard.

After Erica was picked up by her grandmother, Rosemary returned to the kitchen to hit the books. She had the day off from work and had an exam the same night at seven o'clock. She sat at the table, reading through her textbooks, thoroughly studying the material she needed to know. She remained deep in thought, in a peaceful deep zone of reflection, trying to absorb and comprehend what she just read. She turned around swiftly to find nothing there. She thought she heard something. What did she hear? Who knows? There was certainly a noise, but she could not identify where it was coming from. Moments later, she again heard a low bang, a noise like a fist lightly thumping a wall. She looked around and did not really think anything of the occurrence. A few minutes later, the same noise struck again, this time much louder than the previous incident. This time around, she decided to investigate the occurrence, not frightened, but instead curious. She stood up, heading over toward the kitchen sink. She peered into the dining room, but saw nothing. She turned and looked down the hallway. Still nothing. Rosemary shook her head.

"I must be going crazy," she thought. She turned and walked back to the table.

Thump! Thump! Thump!

Her eyes nearly bugged out of her head. She looked around, but saw nothing. Whatever it was came from directly overhead in her bedroom. She remained frozen, the footsteps she just heard still in her mind. Instead of going to investigate, she sat down at the table to resume studying for her exam. Needless to say, she did not concentrate too well for the remainder of the day.

Jeff pulled up to the house later that afternoon with his best friend, Joe. Joe's mother picked up the duo at basketball practice and was dropping Jeff off at home. They turned onto Jeff's street and were only a few houses from his.

Jeff looked at Joe, "Hey, do you want to come over for dinner? My mom won't care."

"Hey mom, can I?"

"No," she replied. "You need to study for that math test you boys will be having tomorrow."

Disappointed, Jeff said his goodbyes and shut the door to the station wagon, waving goodbye and thanking Mrs. Lee for the ride. He headed up the walkway to his house. His attention was drawn to the old oak tree in the yard. There sat a raven looking at him intently. Jeff stared back, seeming to make direct eye contact with the creature. He headed to the door and turned the knob. Peering back at the black bird, he continued the staring contest with the intense, black creature.

Jeff threw his books on the table. "Hey mom, you home?"

"I'm in here," she called from the kitchen. She still sat at the table half studying, half thinking about the peculiar footstep-like sounds that had come from above. The two talked of their day, and within a few minutes, both William and his father had arrived.

"Jeff! Jeff! Come here," William summonsed.

"What?"

"Tonight, do you want to wait up again?"

"No, not really," Jeff said, answering William's question. "I think it's just a squirrel or something. Who cares? It'll go away soon."

However, Jeff did not agree with William's perspective, yet he made sure to try to plant the seed for his brother in order to forget about the noise and discourage him from pursuing its cause. Jeff did not want to go to bed that night. What if the walking ensued on his bed? What if the noises continued? Maybe it was his imagination, but the chance that it was not his imagination frightened Jeff. Jeff sees each hour awake downstairs as one less hour spent in his room in which the darkness of night was so uncertain and unpredictable.

Bedtime came from out of nowhere. Before William and Jeff knew it, it was time to turn in for the evening, retiring to their upstairs quarters. Jeff anticipated that nothing would happen; at least he tried to convince himself of this.

"William, do you think that I'm nuts if......?" Jeff stopped dead in his tracks. The lights had only been off for a few minutes, but the taps became harder, louder raps. Both sat quietly before William worked up the courage to speak out.

"A squirrel, huh?"

"What do you think it is, Jeff?"

"I don't know," he responded. "I just don't know."

The boys sat up and listened as the commotion continued and began to fade. It was not until midnight that Jeff rolled over and fell to sleep from complete exhaustion. William, however, was not going to get off that easily. Instead, he would be the target of tonight's tumult in the room.

William felt his covers being slowly, yet progressively tugged until they moved about six or eight inches toward his feet. He wanted to call out to his brother but could not. He did not know why, but he could not vocalize his distress to his brother who was only feet away from him; his words seemingly stuck in his throat. He felt something around the bed on his left side. It was not visible, but he sensed its presence. William closed his eyes.

"Now I lay me down to sleep."

William still sensed that the entity was there.

"I pray the Lord my soul to keep."

He kept his eyes clenched shut, not daring to open and possibly catch a glimpse, even if there was nothing of a physical nature present.

"If I die before I awake, I pray the Lord my soul to take."

William remained frightened, not willing to fall asleep if there was something indeed in the room with him and his brother. However, once two o'clock arrived, the feeling of the unseen entity no longer existed, and William drifted off into sleep.

The next morning, William did not speak of his feelings or his impressions of the previous night. He, instead, was fairly quiet and quite shaken up by what took place in his own home. After breakfast, William headed out to the bus without his brother.

Jeff peered out the window, seeing his brother walking down the driveway. Jeff grabbed his premade lunch and proceeded toward the door to join his sibling. He opened the door, unhinging the latch. Making his way down the sidewalk, Jeff caught a glimpse of the bird. Its stature was large and upright. The bird sat staring down again, following Jeff's movements. He did not really think much of it and continued down the walkway toward the mailbox where the bus would soon pull up.

He kept looking back, the raven still keeping watch over Jeff. When the bus arrived, he got aboard, and the image of the large critter was lost within moments. Jeff and his brother, along with their friend Joe, exited the bus after it pulled up to the gym of the school. William made small talk with Joe while Jeff listened. Something, however, broke Jeff's concentration: the noise. What was it? Jeff looked around. About twenty yards from the school, it sat: a large raven suspended on a branch. Was it the same one? It seemed to be. The same large mass was noticeable as well as that stare which still gazed at him intently. Jeff felt a chill go down his back. He quickly ran into the gym where he met up with some of his friends from school.

Later that day, Jeff's father picked him up after a basketball game. The two made small talk on the way home. Jeff's mind was elsewhere though. He was very confused about what was occurring at night in the house, especially in his room. There was more to it all, but he had not quite figured out what it was. Jeff struggled to understand the significance of the ominous crow.

After dinner, the usual watching of television, studying, and chores took place. Little Erica sat in her room playing with her toys, waiting patiently for her father to join her as he promised.

Erica smiled, "Hi," she said happily. "Who are you?"

Not surprisingly, there was no answer to her question.

"Do you want to play with my doll?"

She continued with a few questions directed toward her visitor.

Bruce and Rosemary sat in the opposite room. Rosemary looked at her husband with mysterious eyes. "Who is she talking to?"

"I don't know, are the boys in there?"

"No, they're upstairs," she replied in a puzzled tone.

Bruce got up out of the easy chair and crept ever so slowly to his daughter's room.

"Honey, who are you talking to?"

"No one, daddy," she said. "It's just the shadow guy."

He looked his daughter directly in the eyes, "The shadow guy?"

"Yep, the shadow guy."

"Who is this shadow person?"

"He comes around sometimes. Sometimes he's here and other times he isn't. Sometimes he passes through the closet door."

Bruce just shook his head and told his daughter that if the shadow man came back, to say "hello" for him. Bruce acted as if he accepted her so-called imaginary friend. He remembered having fake playmates as a kid and accepted it as nothing more than the mentality of a young child.

Rosemary went over to the kitchen table where Jeff was studying for his history test. "Why don't you get ready for bed and get a good night sleep."

"I'm alright," Jeff answered immediately. "I think I'll work a little bit longer."

Jeff, of course, was trying to prolong his stay downstairs, trying to be inconspicuous about the apparent diversion of the bedroom.

"Hey mom?"

Rosemary looked at Jeff, "Yeah?"

"Can I sleep on the couch tonight? I think I want to watch some television before I go to bed."

Rosemary looked at her son hastily. "I guess…that's OK?"

Relief befell Jeff. He thought about the possibility of staying in his room and did not even want to deal with that prospect at all tonight. He figured that staying on the couch in the living room would solve his problems. At least if he was in the living room, the thing in his room could not hover around him or tap on the walls, right?

William was frightened out of his mind, heading to his bedroom without the comfort of his brother, but he did so anyway. Tonight, however, would be his night off. Instead, others would feel the presence of the intellect that lurked within the confines of the old Victorian. The half-moon lit up the night sky as the pitter-patter of rain droplets bounced off the roof. The distant sound of screeching tires could be heard, then the silence of the night fell over the suburban neighborhood. It was one-thirty in the morning; Bruce lay awake. He could not sleep. As soon as he dozed off, he would wake up in a matter of minutes. His struggle persisted all night. After trying to sleep for a few hours, Bruce decided to get up. It was quite warm, and he decided to go out for a smoke. He sat on the porch, thinking about the day to come. He had an important meeting that was to start promptly at eleven the next morning. His mind continued to wander as a cat cried in the distance. Flicking the butt off the side of the porch, he slid back inside, trying not to wake Jeff who lay silently on the couch. He continued down the hallway toward the study, where he figured he would check his e-mail. Bruce logged on, sitting in complete darkness, except for the blue and white shimmering light that cascaded from the screen, engulfing the room in a bluish haze. Each moment that went by caused him to grow drowsier until he finally decided to head back to bed.

Bruce checked up on Jeff in the living room. His son lay there, motionless, deep in sleep. Bruce was immediately startled by something on his left. At the glass sliders, a large black raven stood, looking into the living room. Bruce remembered the annoying cackling that erupted just a few mornings before. He went to the glass sliders and smacked his fist on it, scaring the creature away.

"Damn bird," he thought to himself.

He headed back to his room and decided to lie down for a few hours.

The next morning, Jeff lay on his bed, once again thinking about whatever it was that lurked in the home. When he was starting to drift off into sleep the previous night, he could hear objects moving around in the next room. He heard what sounded like the kitchen chairs being pushed in and out several times from beneath the table, and another sound like cabinets continuously opening and shutting, creaking and squeaking. Most disturbing was the cold sensation that surrounded him after the noises, just like being smothered by cold air. It was an uncomfortable feeling that embraced him and downright scared him. It was rather unnatural.

Jeff put both of his feet onto the braided rug and stood up. He extended his arms, stretching away the knots caused by sleeping on the small loveseat. That is when he saw it. At the sliders stood the raven peering in at him, watching him carefully. Jeff went over and stood by the glass sliders, making eye contact with the huge burning eyes which stared right back at him. This raven had quite a facade. It was far bigger than any normal crow he had ever seen. He recognized it, of course, as being he same winged specimen that followed him the previous day. After several minutes, minutes that seemed like hours, he opened the door and shooed it away.

Rev. Jun and John Zaffis after an exorcism in Massachusetts.

Fr. Malachi Martin and John Zaffis in New York City

Bishop Robert McKenna and John Zaffis after an exorcism in Connecticut

Ed Warren and John Zaffis in Connecticut

Ed and Lorraine Warren and John Zaffis at Borley Church in England

John Zaffis among his collection of itms removed from haunted houses

Psychic energy from a very old haunted town in New England

More psychic energy at night in an old haunted town in New England

Psychic energy in an old prison in Connecticut

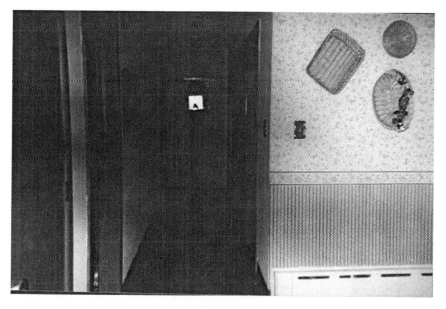

Negative energy coming down the hall as it was seen by eyewitnesses
on a case in Rhode Island

Things were thrown off the table as I turned away from it to talk to the family. This is the typical type of poltergeist activity you can witness in a home. Vermont

Boothe Park Homestead. Purportedly haunted by many of the Boothe descendents. Stratford, Connecticut

This photo is from the Boothe home. The coffee pot is levitating off of the old wood stove. (zoomed in lower-right to show levitation) Stratford, Connecticut

The Boys (clowns) were removed from a home after the person picked
them up at a thrift shop and psychic activity began to occur in the
home. Connecticut

This statue was removed from a home in Maine after it was mysteriously
moving from room to room

This idol was removed from a home after a young man had been using it in his rituals. New Jersey

Psychic mist in the basement of a New Hampshire home that was
reported to be haunted.

Spirit activity in an old haunted New England restaurant.

Psychic mist photographed in a New York museum that I was asked to investigate.

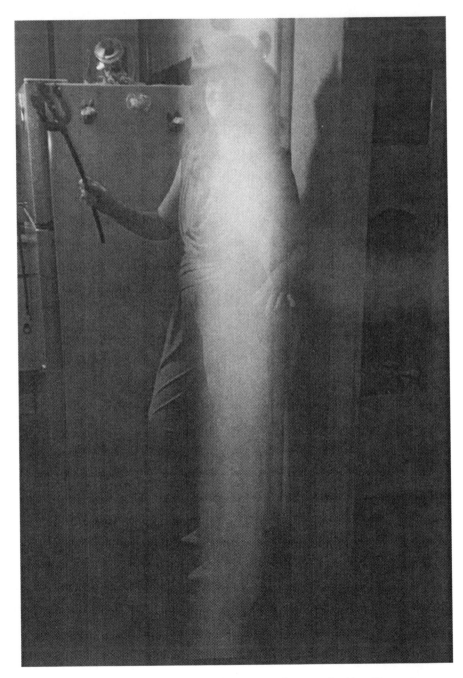

I believe this is some type of psychic energy photographed in a Connecticut home.

Photograph of a gray mist taken at Ground zero, New York City while attempting to photograph the cross.

Father Larry Elward and John Zaffis after an exorcism in Maine.

Location where John Zaffis saw the appearance of an inhuman spirit in
Connecticut.

This is a photograph of the raven that appeared frequently at a haunted
location.

The Revelation that Something Resides

It was Saturday morning, and the kids slept in. Rosemary moved about the house, cleaning while Bruce mowed the lawn one last time before the cold weather tapered off the grass' thick, green texture. Bruce pushed the lawn mower into the shed and began the journey back into the house. He noticed something outside Jeff and William's window; it was the raven. The big black contour was perched just outside the window like a loyal pet.

"Why the hell won't it leave?" Bruce continued to think about the bird. It really was not a big deal, except for the occasional squeaks and squawks, but it always seemed to be around. He had never really seen anything like it. The creature was a rather extraordinary display. When it flew, the raven's wingspan was quite expansive and its height and weight were probably almost double that of the average crow.

Bruce went into the house.

"Rosemary, where are you?"

"I'm in here," she responded.

"That crow is back. Did you ever really see how huge it is? Come on, it's outside, I'll show you."

The two went outside. There it was, still perched. It seemed to vaguely recognize their presence and continued to stare intently into the house.

"Get the camera," Rosemary said to her husband. "Let's get a picture of it. No one will believe the size of this thing."

Bruce went into the house and grabbed the camera from his desk. When he was coming out of the office, he bumped into Jeff.

"Hey kiddo. Come see this crow, it's huge."

Jeff nervously replied to his father's request, "No, I'm all set." He obviously remembered this bird and did not wish to see it again.

Bruce went outside, but Rosemary stood disappointed.

"It took off," she conveyed to him. "It just got up and left." The two were frustrated that the regular guest had vanished before they got a snapshot. They headed around the house, and there it was on the railing of the deck.

"Quick, take a picture," she commanded. Bruce snapped several still photos until the camera ran out of film.

"That's all," he said. "We're out of film."

They walked slowly up the stairs, trying not to startle the raven. They walked past it without even a glance from the large beaked bird. It was almost intimidating to be in the company of this bird.

They shut the sliders behind them and looked up to see Jeff on the couch watching television. Rosemary noticed something very interesting. The raven was staring at her son intently, studying his movements and taking in his character. She thought it was strange that the raven had moved and realized it was at first perched on her son's window and now moved to the deck to watch him in another room. She did not really think too deeply about it, but considered it to be a strange coincidence.

Bruce opened the sliders again and called to the raven. It looked at him slightly before turning back to Jeff's direction where its eyes remained fixed on the boy. After a few short moments, it came up to the threshold, without any apparent fear. The raven actually entered the home, showing no concern for itself, and seemed to gravitate toward Jeff. A few minutes later, the raven exited the house and flew away; the mystery of this ominous bird became even more difficult to decipher.

The Onset of the Sleepless Nights

Rosemary came down the stairs from the second floor, "What are you guys doing?"

"Nothing mom," William and Jeff answered simultaneously.

"Why aren't you in bed?"

Jeff looked up at his mother. "We figured we'd have a sleepover party and watch movies."

"Ok, but don't stay up too late," she retorted.

Rosemary left the room, and William sighed with relief, "Thank God she didn't make us go to bed. There is no way I'm sleeping in there." William and Jeff spoke earlier and actually told each other of the tales that something had besieged them over the last few nights. Jeff complained that he was constantly being touched. Jeff was not really uncomfortable with this occurrence, but felt more confused than anything about the crow, which had followed him to and from school for several days. Also, the crow remained near the house and looked into the windows at him and watched Jeff while he was in the yard. His uncertainty of the crow's motives created anxiety within Jeff, but he still did not see the crow as a threat of any sort.

William's experiences were altogether different. It sounded as if marbles were being rolled across the bedroom floor, and the taps continued within the walls more frequently after his brother slept downstairs for three nights in a row. He also felt something push down on his pillow suddenly, causing him to jump up from fear. He felt as if he were being watched, and, while taking a shower, he felt a sudden cold breeze emanate within the confines of the room, even though the bathroom upstairs does not have a window where a draft could have submerged him.

After sharing their stories outside away from the house earlier that day, the boys decided that they would keep the stories to themselves and would try to avoid being alone at night. If they decided to stay in the bedrooms, they would do so together. If they retreated to the living room, they would move into the room together. They decided to adhere to the old saying about there being safety in numbers.

Upstairs, Rosemary wrapped herself in a bulky cotton towel and walked down the hallway to the bathroom. She ran the water until it was hot and draped her towel over the drying rack. She lathered her hair vigorously and reached for a bar of soap. Suddenly, she stopped dead in her tracks. What was that? Something smelled horrible, almost like feces. She covered her face with a facecloth, trying to avoid the stench that just arose in the steamy air. After a few seconds, she took the linen away and the smell was no longer apparent. She rinsed off and stepped out of the shower quickly. Heading down to the bedroom, Rosemary's heart raced frantically. It seemed ridiculous to her, but she felt scared and uncomfortable in that bathroom. There was no one else there, but it seemed like a thousand sets of eyes were transfixed upon her naked body. She quickly dressed and went to lie down.

The boys continued to talk about sports and made a few jokes, making small talk as they always did. After about an hour, both boys started to tire out and both began to nod off into sleep. William was the first to be affected from trying to rest.

"Jeff! Wake up!"

Jeff arose immediately, "What?"

"It just pulled on my sleeping bag. I swear it did."

"Are you alright?"

"Yeah, I just want it to stop."

Both sat up and put the television on and watched the news. It would mark the beginning of a night where sleep would be scarce, if they got any sleep at all.

Rosemary lay in bed upstairs. Bruce was still out with his old college buddies while Rosemary struggled to sleep at all. She tried and tried again, but to no avail. Each waking moment marked the onset of discomfort; the very thought of her bathroom encounter made her relatively uneasy. The incident held no specific meaning for Rosemary, but she saw it as altogether strange. It was a feeling she never really had before and she wanted to get to the bottom of it. It reminded her of the day that the footsteps were heard above her while she was studying in the kitchen. She continued to lay awake, pondering the possibilities even though she could not determine an explanation.

"William, what's that?"

"What's what?" William looked at his brother, expecting to hear that he had been touched or that he saw something.

Jeff was obviously very serious, "Listen, listen very carefully."

"What is that? I hear it on the stairs," William said. A definitive thump, like heavy footsteps or banging, could be heard coming up the stairs. It approached closer and closer until it was at the top of the stairs. One last boom was heard and then the noises ceased. It was as if something was coming up the basement stairs that led into the living room. The noise continued to remain absent.

William looked at Jeff hastily. "Go check it out."

"What are you, crazy?"

"No. I just don't want to go over there by myself," William emphasized with deep concern reflected in his facial features. "How about we go together?"

"Fine," Jeff replied. The boys rose to their feet. They expected to see a fiend from hell itself, a ghostly image, or maybe a vicious wild animal. Together, with each one of their hands on the door, they turned the knob and thrust the door open. There was nothing there. They were so certain that they heard something approaching them up the stairs that this was impossible. Whatever it was had not descended down the stairs, nor had it come through the door. Where was it?

At the same time upstairs, Rosemary began to fall asleep, but not for long. As she entered her twilight state, she heard a distinctive laugh. It was a far-off sound, but was not in her head; it was definitely in the room. She sat up and looked around, but saw nothing: not a trace of any presence, which could have caused the unruly outbreak. She continued to sit up for a few minutes, thinking that perhaps her fear from before had affected her unconscious. This theory of hers would prove to be incorrect. She could hear creaking in the far right corner of the room—creaking like something was pacing back and forth. The sound was persistent, and she had the impression that something unseen was there. She looked in the corner and did not know what to think. The darkness was moving. The blackness was darker than the rest of the room and it continued to move, engulfing the night. Uneasy, Rosemary got up and went to the kitchen to get a glass of water.

To Rosemary's surprise, she saw the boys still up, "What are you guys doing awake so late?"

"Mom, can we tell you something? Promise you'll believe us?"

Rosemary looked at them, "Sure, what is it? Is something wrong?"

Both of the boys went into detail about the recent events that hit the household. She sat quietly, dumbstruck by their stories. They were both old enough to convey their thoughts and impressions clearly and concisely. Rosemary kept her recent experiences in the back of her mind, making the boys' testimony even more credible. She decided, without verbalizing her decision, to tell her husband about all of this, and perhaps he had an experience to tell as well, or so she hoped.

The three sat in the living room, Bruce returning extremely late after a night out with the guys. "What are you guys doing up, all three of you?"

"We're just watching television, we couldn't sleep," Rosemary said to her husband. Both of the boys remained silent. She decided to wait until the next morning to tell Bruce. Rosemary still thought that she might be imagining many of the events, but what about the boys? How could it be caused by her imagination if both Jeff and William had experiences, too?

During the discussion the following morning, Bruce maintained that he did not really feel anything concrete, but that he did have one encounter a few weeks ago that grabbed his attention. He was downstairs working on the plumbing when he heard someone call him from upstairs. Bruce claimed that it sounded like one of the kids, but they were all at their grandmother's house, and Rosemary was at the grocery store. On that day, the house was deserted. He forgot about the experience, and until now, had just passed it off as a figment of his imagination.

Even though Bruce did not want to believe the evidence that was presented to him by his wife, he still kept the possibility open that maybe something supernatural in origin was occurring. Bruce recalled that while growing up, one of his best friends, Charles, claimed that the home still housed the previous owners' spirits, even though they died years earlier. Since then, the possibility of ghosts and the like existed in Bruce's mind, but he simply did not have the experiences to say that they absolutely exist. However, he felt compassion for his family and kept it in the back of his mind that there might be more to it than simply overactive imaginations. It scared him to think that something he could not understand was at play.

Bruce and Rosemary agreed to monitor the situation and be open if anything was to occur. Over the next two days, nothing of a paranormal nature occurred. The only strange reoccurrence was that of the raven, which had continually been following Jeff to school. The raven would wait outside and then trace Jeff's steps back home and wait for him there.

The following Tuesday evening, Bruce was in his study, and the kids were sleeping in bed. Rosemary was reading in the bedroom with only a lamp on to illuminate the abnormally quiet room. Rosemary heard the shuffle of footsteps that headed down the wooden hallway and stopped after a few seconds. They continued once more, then stopped again. She got up and went to the doorway. She found her husband in the doorway of the study looking down the hall.

"Did you hear that, Rosemary?"

She stared back at him, "Yeah, did you?"

"What was it? It sounded like somebody walking."

Both returned to their tasks; Rosemary resumed reading and Bruce his paying of bills. They acknowledged the incident and felt that they should ignore it and maybe it would go away. Later that night, the family went to bed as usual. They slept without any disturbances at first, but their luck would change. It was just after three o'clock in the morning. The house was silent and all was calm. Bruce was the first to awake from the sound, followed immediately by Rosemary, and then Jeff. Bruce could hear the television, being that the volume was excessively loud. He rose to find the house in complete darkness except for the light from the television set. He quickly turned it off. Heading back toward his bedroom, he flicked on the hallway light. Heading down the lengthy hall, he saw something in his peripheral vision. It was William, curled up in a ball with his quilt in Bruce's study. Confused, he woke William up.

"William, why are you sleeping in here?"

"The thing was touching my shoulders and sat on my bed," William replied. "I couldn't sleep in there."

Bruce told his son everything would be fine and walked with him back into his bedroom. Bruce went back to his own bedroom and looked Rosemary in the eyes. "We need to do something. The kids seem so uncomfortable. I could see it in their mannerisms the last few days. The boys won't go downstairs without one another, and they hate going to sleep."

They both agreed that after Rosemary's class tomorrow she would seek out some type of advice, but from whom? They were not sure. They wondered if they should speak to a priest. They were not familiar with religion and certainly were not regularly attending church. It was not the type of situation for law enforcement. They would have to think this one through long and hard.

Rosemary anxiously headed home and thought that maybe the phone book would have some type of spiritual organization that may be of assistance. She found a local metaphysical shop and called for advice. They instructed her to put salt in the corners of all the rooms and light incense to ward of the menacing spirits. Rosemary did not think doing this would remedy the situation and she was not sure if she would find any help.

Rosemary continued with her search, actively taking notes. She worked up the nerve to call a local clergyman, but was instructed to get her family back in church and try some prayers within the home after having the children professionally examined. She again was not completely satisfied with what she found, so she tried the computer in her husband's study.

She browsed for hours through a multitude of sites and sent a few e-mails. Later that night, she received two responses and called the so-called ghost busters. The first group was run by a young man named James who thought that she might want to pursue the help of the clergy, thinking that since the children were being targeted, immediate assistance was probably necessary. The second group scheduled a time to meet at a local pizza shop and would follow Rosemary and Bruce back to the home to see what they could come up with. After the initial investigation, Rosemary never heard back from the group. James called back, but Rosemary's second try at contacting a priest was less fruitful than the first attempt. He did not feel that the church could be of assistance; however, he called Rosemary back.

James referred her to John. "I know of a researcher not too far from your neck of the woods. His name is John Zaffis. He has worked on virtually thousands of cases. Give him a try."

Rosemary was given contact information and contacted John without delay. He agreed after staying in touch with her for about two weeks to head over to the house to help piece it together and see what would be needed to try to remedy the problem at hand.

The Investigative Process Begins

"Who's this guy John that's coming over tonight?" Bruce asked his wife.

"He lives in Connecticut and performs investigations for people that have a haunting taking place. I think he has a regular job but does this stuff on the side."

"Oh, when is he coming?"

Rosemary replied that John would be there within a few short hours. She had spoken with John earlier and confirmed that he would arrive that same night at about eight. She was nervous and hoped that he could shed some light on what was going on in their once peaceful home.

John pulled up in his blue station wagon. He sat for a moment and took one last sip of his coffee before exiting the vehicle. He had a feeling in his gut that the case would not be entirely positive. The whole trip to the home was a disaster.

First, he had lost the directions and had to go home to get duplicate copies. Also, he was lost in town for about a half hour. Usually when many things go wrong like this, more ties in with the case than meets the eye. He approached the Victorian home, stepped onto the porch, and rang the bell.

Rosemary and Bruce both answered the door and welcomed John with warm handshakes. Both were eager to see if he had the answers to solve their problem.

Rosemary looked at John curiously, "So are you going to get rid of what's here?"

John smiled at her, "I'll see what I can do. Honestly, I can't just zap what's here and banish it from your home. There is much more to it. It can be a rather lengthy process eliminating a ghost. Let's sit down and try to make sense of what is going on here."

They sat at the dining room table while John set up his camcorder.

"I'm going to ask you a series of in-depth questions," he said, looking at the both of them. "I may ask some things that are personal, but it is all for your benefit. You'd be surprised how some things tie in to what's going on. Rosemary, let's start with you."

John interviewed them both for about an hour or so. He reached up, powered off the camera, and lifted his cup of coffee to his mouth. After taking a sip, he placed it down and looked at Bruce. "Do you want to show me around?"

"Sure," Bruce responded to the request. "No problem, let's start upstairs."

After touring the house, John sat back down at the table and began to speak with them. "I think first thing you should do is get Erica baptized. You said that you were Catholics, but not actively practicing. That's absolutely fine. We all go through it, but let's start at the beginning here. What you got here doesn't seem overly pleasant. I think counteracting it with faith really would be the best idea at this point. I'm not trying to push the idea, but maybe going back to church wouldn't be such a bad idea. You did mention how you were thinking of it anyway."

They spoke for another hour or so, and then John left. On the way home, he recalled what they said and thought about the case in general terms. He saw the potential for some real problems. What stood out right off the bat was that everyone in the home had some type of experience. This, generally, is rare as far as hauntings go. Most of the time, only one of the family members, or maybe a selected few, will experience paranormal events. What the family thought of as maybe a typical ghost was, for John, more reflective of the infestation process in which the demonic begins its barrage and assault. John thought that things would probably begin to intensify as the factors involved became more easily identifiable. Also, the fact that they were seeking help to alleviate the problem could intensify the situation.

The following day, Rosemary contacted John and let him know that no one in the house had experienced anything after he had left. He agreed to call them this weekend to check up on the situation.

Soon after, Jeff came home from school to an empty house. He had no idea that his parents had been contacting organizations. Both Rosemary and Bruce felt that it was better not to scare the children anymore than they already were or fill their heads with misleading thoughts.

Jeff kicked of his shoes at the front door and went up to his room to change. He put on his green corduroys and began to pull them up. He turned toward the door and looked out into the hallway. He could have sworn that a black, smoky image passed by with the blink of an eye. He put on his shirt and headed down to the kitchen. Jeff stood in awe. Every single drawer and cabinet was open. He did not know what to believe. Could this be a joke? Why would his mother have them all open? Then he thought of the "thing." Maybe the thing did this. He went around and shut all the cabinets and drawers, goose bumps appearing all over his body as his hair stood up. He prepared a snack and put on the TV. He sat very uncomfortably. It was as if eyes were fixed on him from some undetermined place in the room. He sat, still trying to concentrate on the television program, but of course, his mind was elsewhere.

That night was probably one of the more chaotic nights in the home. Bruce sat watching the football game, and the lights in the living room flickered off and on. Rosemary felt an icy cold brush by her on the stairway. When the lights went off for bedtime, poundings emanated throughout the home. They were audible by all in the family. No one quite knew how to react to the noises. The next morning, Rosemary called John, and he agreed to return to the house.

That Saturday, John went to the home. He set up a tape recorder and asked of any experiences that occurred since he was last at the house. This time, the children were there too, and William and Jeff were interviewed while Erica played in her bedroom. Usually, the children would be left out of such a situation, but they too knew all too well what was going on and that they were the targets of many of the manifestations.

After the children went back upstairs, John approached Rosemary, who was putting on another pot of coffee, "Were you able to speak to Father Gregory?"

"Yes, I was able to see him."

"What did he say?"

"He agreed to baptize Erica and said that we'll talk about what is going on here at the rectory on Monday."

"Excellent," John said enthusiastically. John hoped that the family's local pastor would be of some assistance in their time of need. Even though they were not avid churchgoers, both Bruce and Rosemary saw it as an important time to embrace their religion and get back on track.

The Intercession of the Clergy

Monday could not come fast enough for Rosemary. She was at the rectory promptly for the eleven o'clock meeting. The large white residence remained shadowed in the presence of the immense cathedral, which resided just a stone's throw away from her car. It was a beautiful church that decadently displayed many of the saints, picturesque images of angelic figures, and depictions of Jesus Christ's life in the form of stained glasswork. Outside, a sign eloquently read: "Embrace the Faith of Our Lord and Savior." She rang the bell and was greeted by the housekeeper who led her to Father Gregory's office.

Father Gregory was a priest in his mid-sixties who had been the pastor at this particular parish for twenty-two years. Although modern times mark a lack of followers, his masses often packed into the church. He was very approachable and had a very comforting smile, which comforted those who belonged to the congregation.

"Father," she said hastily, "what do you think is going on with my family?"

"I don't know, Rosemary," he answered honestly. "I am not well versed in areas of the supernatural. I have known priests and monks who specialize in this theological area, but I simply lack the experience in dealing with such matters. I have only encountered one such instance in which a family had noises and objects that were moving around their home. That was many years ago when I was fresh out of the seminary. Until now, I have not really had to deal with such spiritual matters as you are experiencing."

Rosemary looked rather frightened and disappointed. This was not the answer that she wanted to hear from a member of the clergy. Wasn't the clergy supposed to be familiar with such issues?

Father Gregory looked at Rosemary, "Relax, Rosemary. It's all right, dear. I want to take a ride over there later today. I'd like to bless your home, Rosemary, as long as it is permissible by you, of course. Hopefully, this will take care of your problem. I need to make my rounds up at the hospital, but I will be over around four o'clock."

"That would be great, father," Rosemary said, filled with hope. She went home and sat in the bedroom on the bed, studying for her exam next week. She prayed that Father Gregory would be able to end the madness through the intercession of goodness based on the ritual prayers he would recite throughout the home.

As planned, Father Gregory arrived at the home, bag in hand. Out of his bag, he took out holy water, a soft leather prayer book, a small glass cylinder which contained blessed oil, and some blessed candles for her to keep in the home. He put on his stole and began to recite the prayers. She remained in the living room and prayed as he went room to room, blessing the premises. After about twenty-five minutes, he was finished. He came back and sat with her. The two spoke for awhile about what occurred. Father Gregory ensured her that this would probably remedy the situation and wished her peace.

"I'll see you Sunday at the baptism," Father Gregory professed as he closed the large wooden door. He headed to the car and was off after putting his bag in the trunk.

"Thank you, Lord," she thought, hoping that anything that had been around was terminated and cast back to where it came from. However, this break was only temporary. For about two days, there were no signs of any occurrences until the night before the baptism of the daughter.

Not Quite Banished from the Home

Jeff crept into the hallway, "Mom? Dad?"

Bruce immediately responded, "What?"

"Something is in my room," Jeff said to his parents, with fear obvious on his face.

Bruce flicked on the bedside lamp and looked at his son with both eyes squinted.

"What do you mean there's something in your room?"

"There's just something there, I swear."

He walked with Jeff to his room and sat in the desk chair, questioning his own flesh and blood. William was gone for the night, staying at his friend's house just down the street. Jeff went into a tale that left Bruce awestruck. Jeff had been sound asleep when he awoke suddenly for an unknown reason. Now awake, he lay silent and disturbed, but he could not identify the source of his awkward arousal. Around his bed, he heard creaking; something was circling slowly, shuffling across the floorboards. Then Jeff claimed that his pillow was tugged from underneath his head. He remained frozen for fear that this thing might hurt him. With his heart nearly pounding out of his chest, he made a run for it.

Bruce knew that his son was not one to tell fibs and truly believed his son. He, of course, believed his son, but it was still so strange to him. However, he could not deny all of the strange occurrences lately. He let Jeff sleep on the floor in his bedroom after gathering his pillow and comforter. Jeff seemed to handle it pretty well for a young boy, but the aggravation and constant fear were beginning to take a toll on him.

The next morning was the baptism of Erica, and the family arose to the smell of bacon and eggs. Rosemary prepared a feast for the clan before their departure for the church where their sister and daughter would be washed of sin. Out on the deck stood the raven yet again. He had been missing for about three days, but was back again. Jeff tried to ignore the raven, but his father brought it to his attention.

"I don't know what's with that thing," Bruce blurted.

Jeff did not reply. After breakfast they continued getting ready and went to the baptism. After mass, they had a few of their friends and relatives over for coffee. Father Gregory could not attend due to prior engagements. Rosemary acted as if everything was perfect, but in the back of her mind, the thought of what happened the previous night to Jeff remained. Was it all going to start over again? Was it an isolated incident? Maybe things would get worse? She pondered the possibilities, deeply afraid of what the future held for them.

Over the next few days, activity began to escalate. Jeff seemed to be the direct target. He spent most of his nights on the floor in his parents' room, and as a result of his fear, barely slept a wink. The tappings became more and more incessant, as did Erica's stories about something passing through her room. William claimed he was touched on two occasions—once while coming up the basement stairs and once when he was doing his homework in his bedroom alone. Rosemary and Bruce continued to hear heavy footsteps, usually coming up the cellar stairs, but now also emanating from the attic above their bedroom. All through these occurrences, the raven continued to be by Jeff's side. It continued to perch itself near the home and continued to follow him to school. Even the day of the baptism, the raven followed Jeff to a friend's home later in the day. Rosemary continued to remain in contact with not only John, but Father Gregory as well.

A high mass was scheduled to take place in the home the following week. John hoped that this would do the trick to help the family, but nothing is more unpredictable than the supernatural. John sat with Rosemary and Bruce. The children spent the day at their grandparents' home fifty miles away, so as not to be exposed to the goings on that day. Father Gregory showed up on time and within a few minutes after being introduced to John, he had begun his prayer. An hour or so passed and the mass was completed. Father Gregory, John, Rosemary, and Bruce had coffee together and made small talk. Would the mass serve to expel the force? Once again, only time would tell.

An Exorcism Scheduled to Free the Family

The high mass did seem to bring peace in the household. Just over a week went by with no real evidence of anything occurring, until Jeff was once again frightened by objects moving themselves in his room. His bed appeared to shake and the shadows he encountered only a few times were passing by in his peripheral vision on a daily basis. After days with no sleep, it was decided that Jeff, being the target, would be removed from the house and would stay at his grandparents' house nearby. Rosemary continued to hear the footsteps, but now they only occurred when she was in the home by herself. Bruce experienced nothing except seeing these strange shadowy images which at first, he thought were fanciful extensions of the mind. Jeff, although removed from the home, saw the raven at his grandparents' house.

The telephone rang in Connecticut, "John, it's Rosemary," a panic-stricken voice blurted.

"Hello, Rosemary. What can I do for you?"

"Nothing is changing at all. Bruce decided that Jeff should be removed and put in the care of his grandparents permanently. The poor kid has had just about no sleep at all lately. Erica seems virtually unscathed, thank God. William has been experiencing some phenomena, but is doing just fine. Whatever is here decided not to leave. What should I do?"

John stated he would call Father Gregory and speak with him about the matter. After his call to the rectory, another priest was scheduled to visit the home. His name was Father Graves. This time, however, the Rituale Romanum would be conducted. An exorcism was seemingly the only solution which could probably end the fear in the house. He scheduled it for the end of the week to allow all of those involved to prepare. Although no one was possessed, the oppression was intensifying, especially for Jeff, who received most of the torment from the spirit.

The day of the exorcism, John headed to the home early to meet with Rosemary and Bruce before Father Graves' arrival.

Bruce asked John his professional opinion of the situation. "John, do you think this will stop everything? I mean, we've had the blessing and the high mass, but things seem to progress and even get worse. What happens if this doesn't work?"

John's answer was not short-winded. "Bruce, if there is one thing I can stress to you and Rosemary, it would be to not give up hope. This force wants you to give up hope more than anything else. Keep your spirits up. Will the exorcism eliminate this entity from your home? I don't know. No one does. The point is that you need to continue to fight and fight really hard. Losing hope is only fueling it to continue. Don't give up."

John continued to explain other cases and some of the basic concepts of demonology to both of them. He stressed that it is an intense battle, a matter of faith that must be fought from deep within.

Father Graves arrived and introduced himself. He was an older man in his early seventies, coarse gray hair sporadically strewn on his head. He was very tall and stood up straight like a soldier standing at attention. He sat down and discussed what he would be doing and asked if Rosemary and Bruce wanted to remain at the house during the ritual. They agreed to stay on site and he prepared by blessing all present and blessing them with holy oil.

Father Graves who conducted the rite with confidence and a deep reverence for God moved the group. It was not a secular confidence, but one that was obviously inspired by his faith and love in the Holy Spirit. He carried on without even a hint of becoming tired or short breathed. After about forty-five minutes, he blessed all present again, asking God to protect them from all evil forces that reside on this earthly plane.

"After an exorcism," John explains, "there is often a lull, a calm period. It may take days or weeks before it is known whether the disturbance has been eradicated."

Early the next morning, Bruce picked up the kids at his mother and father's house. After arriving home, Rosemary prepared lunch for everyone. Jeff looked at his parents and revealed something that shocked them.

"He's gone," Jeff stated.

Bruce questioned him. "Who's gone?"

"The raven. He's gone and we won't see him again."

Jeff was right. They never saw that mysterious raven again. Jeff would not be followed to school again by it, nor would it appear on the porch again. It totally disappeared from their household. From this point on, the haunting was either completely eliminated or retreated to a dormant state. The exorcism was a success, expelling the cause of this family's torment.

Reflecting on the Case

"This case was very intricate and in depth," John reveals. "What caused the phenomena in the home to start? We don't really know. There were too many factors involved to identify one particular cause for the disturbance. The one aspect I can definitely see as a success was the family's determination to resolve the issue at hand. They went back to church, they sought out the clergy, and they had their youngest child baptized. Many people experience these disturbances and want someone else to rid them of their problems, when in actuality, they need to stand up and fight it through faith. Blessings and exorcisms will help most of the time, but it is up to the family involved to take a stand to ensure that the presence does not gain reentry or a strong foothold after its extermination. Rosemary was determined to get rid of the entity and Bruce was very motivated to do the same. They recognized what was going on, got help, and worked in conjunction with professionals to bring the case to a close."

"One interesting facet was the raven. Why was it around and why was it attracted to Jeff? There are many theories as to what it was doing. You have to remember that the family is partially Native American, and their belief system certainly encompasses the possibility of the existence of animal spirit. You could look at it as negative, but I truly feel that the raven was positive, acting like a protector. When it left, there were no more occurrences to report. Was it part of the problem or did it leave because it no longer had to keep watch or protect the boy and his family? It is another fascinating aspect to the case that really can't be proven either way, but is unique because it was a completely physical experience. The raven remained through the duration of the haunting and disappeared after its ending. The photos of this raven were phenomenal. This creature was absolutely huge and was quite intimidating. When I first saw the pictures and how personal this raven was, I just couldn't believe it. To this day, there has not been a relapse and all appears to be calm for the family. I still stay in touch with Rosemary and can see the direct effect it had on her life to endure such a fight."

The Banishment of an Oppressive Force

The Banishment of an Oppressive Force

The following is the dramatic recollection of true events that occurred to a young researcher by the name of Mary. Mary resides in Maine where she is engaged to her long-time boyfriend, Michael. Her struggle lasted for over six months and the possibility of repercussions will always be a threat to her. Her struggle to regain control of her life was not a short one, but instead a lengthy process that continues even today. Occasionally, residual effects occur, as the entity which plagued her tries to regain entry, but as of the writing of this book, no major repercussions have occurred due to her deliverance by the Catholic Church.

John sat at the dinner table one evening with his wife and his son, recalling their days at school and work as millions of other families do every evening. When the phone rang, John answered it just as he did every night after six o'clock, a time where his phone seems to be flooded with calls from all over the region and even the country. Calls from the clergy, calls from other researchers, and calls from those in need are quite common.

This call, however, was one that was expected sometime tonight. Mary, a young woman in her twenties, had an ongoing struggle for a few months now and was fighting to rid her life of the presence that had taken away her innocence. She had been participating in local haunts in her native state, hooking up with many of the researchers in her region of New England. She had the mild traces of a gift, the ability to discern, to pick up on what is around in a given area by opening herself up—an ability that can work to a person's benefit, but also can negatively impact him or her. For instance, the ability to discern may help to identify what is around causing the disturbance on a particular case, but doing so might also cause a person to allow access to that spirit into their lives, into their very being.

John asked Mary to hold on and went down into his office where he continued the phone call from the troubled woman.

"When I met Mary for the first time, it was actually over the telephone. Another researcher I am a good friend with was handling her case and referred her to me for advice. I knew there was more to the case and that it was a credible situation, because I've known the researcher involved for well over a decade. He's the first to debunk a case if it is psychological in nature or a complete hoax. This, however, was a very real case and he knew it. His main goal in referring her to me was to help teach her what was going on in her life and try to ease some of the burden she faced by helping her get the direction she needed. In many of the cases that I am involved in, that is exactly what I do. I try to piece together and identify what is occurring in the person's life and help to assemble the puzzle bit by bit. With most of the cases that are demonic in nature, I can provide the essential tools and understanding to combat the force. The only problem lies in the fact that it is up to the individual to utilize these tools to their advantage. In many cases, they do not and the situation intensifies greatly to the point where their lives are in absolute shambles. I do not deliver or exorcise people from spiritual forces. This is the job of certain devout clergy whom I trust and respect greatly. I, however, give suggestions, depending on the needs of the client and the intensity of the situation. Throughout thousands of investigations and years of learning many of the key aspects that pertain to diabolical forces, I have noticed many common threads where cases may be very similar and the way to fight back and take control is very similar as well.

"People need to realize that much of the turmoil is fueled by themselves. People have the ability to avoid most confrontations with the supernatural, but careless dabbling or a disregard for the true reality of its existence can cause some real issues. People poke at the very idea that the supernatural can excite their lives or give them an edge. After a spark of interest, their desire slowly fades in many instances, and they dismiss the entire notion of the supernatural. The problem then lies in the fact that they have already knocked at the door and upon retreating, left it open just enough. I must reiterate that most people do not have problems on this level, but week—by week, the cases come in to myself and others in the work who try to reassemble the lives of those afflicted with supernatural problems.

"After speaking with the researcher, then with her, I knew that eventually the clergy would have to become involved directly. She worked on a case in her area where there was a very old barn that was abandoned. It was being converted into a home and the construction team began work on the building. The day they began construction, the workers complained about being touched and pushed and also tools would move themselves around the barn. Well, the owner who was having the barn converted contacted a local paranormal research team to go in and figure out what was happening. His building crew had basically fled the scene, many leaving their equipment behind.

"Mary went in with the group and was trying to figure out what was occurring and opened herself up quite innocently. Further research that night led the group to the back part of the building, where upon moving some hay out of the way, they found many wax emblems, candles, and other paraphernalia associated with negative occult-based practices. The group wrapped up the investigation that night and headed home.

"One thing people must realize is that researchers are vulnerable in the same way as anybody else is to the negative repercussions of the paranormal world. Probably even more because they are exposed to the realm that few get actual exposure to. Sure, you are trying to help others around you, but the fact is you could fall victim as well and need to constantly watch your back. One can never let their guard down when dealing with the paranormal world. Getting cocky or too confident is dangerous because your guard may drop, allowing something to gain a foothold that could cause some real serious problems in the long run. These 'things' seek revenge or punishment for any positive intervention that may be offered. They have a specific assignment or a goal. By intervening, you, as a researcher, are interrupting their mission.

"With areas that are used for practices, the group will often call on particular demons or deities to watch and protect the site. This is my theory to what happened to Mary. She, by getting involved in the case, unknowingly and unwillingly had something attach to her. By attach, I mean that a spirit was by her at all times trying to gain entry. When she opened herself up, she had innocently and inadvertently allowed the entity to enter her body. It was not apparent at the timeframe of the investigation, but her experiences began to take hold within a week of the investigation at the old barn.

"It was a few days after the case, and Mary noticed that the lights would go on and off by themselves. Cold spots would appear in the home and vanish within a few seconds. What was most disturbing is how the force gradually yet persistently forced its way into her life to the point where she would have outbursts and she would actually have her body movements controlled by something other than herself. A few minutes later, not able to recall what happened, Mary could only rely on what her boyfriend told her about that particular timeframe. Her fiancé, Michael, described it as something that he could not fully comprehend, but realized that it was definitely not Mary initiating the attacks. This small-framed woman would almost be frozen, would not blink, and would violently attack him while screaming profanity and what would be considered blasphemous religious comments. These attacks occurred about ten times over her bout with the demonic. At the time of the attacks, her awareness and consciousness seemed to be controlled by the dark entities and temporarily suspended while they did their work.

"Michael defiantly claimed that he did not believe these events were spiritually related because he never believed in the spiritual side of existence. He would simply turn the other cheek when Mary would go out on her investigations with local ghost hunting groups. He respected it and even tagged along on a few instances, but never truly believed until now.

"She claimed that there was more to this, too. Mary was very down-to-earth and seemed genuinely frightened and sincere about wanting to get rid of this force that had a grip on her. She told me about an incident that few have experienced: an attack so vile and degrading that it leaves a permanent scar on the victim. Mary had been sexually attacked by this being to the point where penetration had actually taken place on multiple occasions. The demonic spirit was assigned a duty and adapts to fulfill that command which it was given.

"As the nightmares persisted, the physical appearances, the touching sensations, and the fits of unrecollected rage went on, she was becoming tangled in a web of complete despondency. I knew that between what she reported and the things the researcher told me through the investigation process that this poor girl had some real problems. I spoke with a Catholic exorcist and scheduled an exorcism. Not only would an exorcism be needed, but intense counseling to help her cope with her victimization in this situation. The counseling would be needed to help accept that the struggle was real, a difficult concept to grasp, even for skeptical clergy and researchers.

"The day of the exorcism was very intense. I can only explain it as a heavy feeling hanging around in the atmosphere. You can sense the confrontation and you have a tightening in the very pit of your stomach. A few days before the exorcism as well as a few days after the exorcism, I am always on high alert. These entities are so powerful and hateful that you never quite know what is going to happen. They are so enraged with any intercession to try to help those victimized that even if it takes a lifetime, they will try to avenge your willful action to take part in releasing a fellow human from the bondage of evil.

"The couple drove down from Maine and came to my home. I had the day off from work and sat with them for quite some time, discussing the situation. You could see it in her face, the nervousness, and the reflection of every emotion affixed to her face. Mary just wanted it all to end. Her plight had been long and was a daily struggle. Her main concern was the possibility of failure. What if the exorcism didn't work? Would this continue forever? Would the attacks and fits get worse and more frequent? She did not know what to think or expect. She really was willing to do anything to be released from the forces that lurked just on the other side of our direct awareness. Those who occasionally cross into our physical realm can interact, influence, and affect us in many ways.

"Michael and Mary followed myself and another researcher later that day out of state to a church where the exorcism was to take place. I can remember it as clearly as yesterday, walking up those steps into the church. The feeling was truly foreboding. I knew the case was real and could only pray that the struggle would end that day. I am never comfortable at an exorcism, even after attending and assisting in so many. The unpredictability of what will occur is rather unsettling. They can be rather tame or absolute mayhem may erupt without any real warning signs. Within a matter of seconds, the possession could take place or the possessing spirit or spirits might remain dormant. As an investigator, one cannot predict what the demonic will do or how it will respond. It will fight to the very end to win in most cases, but will use trickery and deceit to do so. Persistency is key to eliminating these foreign entities.

"Within ten minutes or so of arriving at the church, the rite began. Overall, the first fifteen minutes or so were calm. There were some noises emanating from the back corners of the church. The noises sounded like cracking and breaking. However, about twenty minutes into the ceremony, all hell broke loose. Mary did not blink for several minutes, and her gaze as well as her demeanor was starting to change. She had this blank stare and turned very, very pale. She looked sickly, like a hospital patient. She dry heaved frequently during the reading of prayers and sweated abundantly. Such physical occurrences usually occur to those oppressed or possessed. Within a few seconds, she was filled with rage and began to strangle her boyfriend while cursing profusely.

"Mary's strength was immense. It was almost impossible to restrain her. Even though she was not an overly large woman, it took three full-sized people to control her during these outbursts.

"While her attack was taking place, the cracking noises in the back of the church became much louder and the sounds of fluttering occurred. By fluttering, I mean a noise often associated with the lower level of the demonic realm that occurs when activity actually takes place. It sounds like a rustling, like if you took several pieces of paper or plastic bags and crinkled them together rapidly. This noise can usually be heard before something physical takes place, before some type of manifestation occurs.

"During all of this, a loud boom occurred behind the altar in the sacristy as well as the onset of an extremely cold breeze that filled the immediate area surrounding Mary and the exorcist. During this deliberate distraction, all of the researchers restraining Mary let go of her, giving her the ability to strike the exorcist if the possessing entity so desired. Luckily, he was not assaulted, but all were several feet away from her confused, frightened, and misled by the external phenomena. The outburst, noises, and temperature change were real and concrete, nothing that anyone who was there could deny.

"That is what is so fascinating about an exorcism. There are often external occurrences that center around the possessed person, which can be downright frightening. These tactics are part of the plan by the demonic to interrupt or disturb what is being done. The possessing demon or demons do not want to be defeated and will throw anything in your way to break up or disturb the exorcism. It is absolutely crucial to keep one's composure during an exorcism. Remaining focused is not an easy task, but is essential, especially on the part of the exorcist.

"Another interesting aspect and a key component to the exorcism is the revelation of the name of the entity. A name may come through, which is considered a sign of the entity weakening. Remaining nameless and secretive is the demonic spirit's best strength. Once identified, it is easier to expel the oppressor. Names associated with the demonic are something I tend not to repeat. I prefer not to give any type of recognition to such a negative and oppressive power. Mentioning its name could certainly give it power, simply due to the fact that you are giving it energy by thinking of it. There was a name that emanated and came across during the rite, one that has been traced down and identified. Several months after the exorcism, one of the researchers present at the exorcism deciphered the name and was giving me the information he had obtained from religious-based textbooks. Right in my kitchen above our heads, the light flickered and something touched the back of my head. Right then and there, I knew he had either identified the demon or at least partially deciphered its identity.

"This is a precise example of what I refer to as recognition. Mentioning or dwelling on a particular spirit essentially brings it to your side. This is not the case every time a name is mentioned, but has been known to actually occur.

"After the exorcism was completed, the exorcist wanted to go over the ritual once more to ensure that what was there was not simply hiding. With this case, it seemed that there was a possibility that a curse was put on Mary. Mary came forth with information that was projected to her that both the exorcist and I interpreted through our experience and knowledge to be reflective of a curse, more specifically, of a generational curse. The second attempt went without interruption, and the end was marked by Mary stating that she felt what she could only describe as electrical impulses on the top of her head when a religious item was placed on her. In my experience, this is a good sign and signifies that the entity has departed. The problem is ensuring that it or other entities do not wean their way back into the lives of the individual. To ensure the best possible protection, I encouraged Mary and Michael to use prayers and holy water in every room of their home, starting with the lowest level of the home and working their way up to the top. You can never be too careful when it comes to the demonic. They will do anything to deceive or hurt a human being. They take pleasure in the demise of man, and in a case of possession, will try to have the possessed broken to the point that they are bestial. They want the ruin of man to come about and will do anything to accomplish this mission. Once a person has fallen to the demonic, willingly or unwillingly, you always run the risk of the problem reoccurring. It might not happen right away, but the possibility for a second fall always exists. This threat will exist all the days of the victim's life. This is the demon's job. It does not have to sleep or eat. It will hang around and plot for a lifetime or more if it has to. Once it has access or is assigned a duty, it will wait until the time is right to strike again.

"Another interesting point that fascinates many who have been in the work for a substantial amount of time is what I just mentioned about the demonic plotting and continuing for years. For example, a generational haunting, where a curse has surfaced after many years, is a prime example. A curse could be placed on a person's grandfather, for instance, and might affect your father, and then affect you as well where you might experience phenomena. In this case, the demonic has kept its assigned duty fully functional throughout the years and without hesitation.

"In Mary's case, we had what we refer to as transient possession. This means that the possessing entity or entities had the ability to come and go as they pleased, using Mary as their instrument. Today, Mary has not had a relapse, although she did have some residual effects for a few weeks after the rite. Today, she lives day by day, hopefully avoiding that which had their hands wrapped around her.

"One of Mary's mistakes, in my opinion, was not going through the home focused, praying in the name of God with holy water as I suggested. Anything around at that point was not being commanded to leave and still could have been lingering in the wings.

"I remain in contact with her and she really has come a long way. The work also encompasses the aspect of counseling in which only a few people support these individuals. These people obviously cannot reveal their dilemma to many for fear of being ridiculed or labeled as mentally unstable. Mary continues to rebuild the pieces of her life."

Poltergeists

Poltergeists

Poltergeist is a term that has been associated with the world of occult studies for a long time. Some claim that any paranormal disturbance is poltergeist activity, while others attribute it to outward manifestations of energy that reflect an intelligence working in the background. Others tend to believe that such phenomena are strictly related to manifestations from within an individual in which energy is directed outside the body by a mechanism which, at this point, has not been conclusively determined. The term has been widely overused and spread very thin in recent times, and the phrase continues to turn heads and spark curiosity while still dividing different schools of thought.

"The word poltergeist," John states, "is very loosely used today. Every noise, every paranormal occurrence in a home is deemed to be indicative of a poltergeist. I tend to use this term only for cases which reflect the traditional association of the word.

"Usually, a genuine poltergeist case will reflect phenomena which seems to directly surround a child going through puberty, and outward physical phenomena which in some way is linked to that adolescent. Objects will move on their own, extreme destruction will take place in the home without a known cause, and phenomena will tend to occur only in the presence of the child who is going through the natural changes associated with puberty. Don't get me wrong, there are other cases which reflect many of the same attributes of the poltergeist experience, but the extremely rare nature of poltergeist cases seems to surround young teens and preteens. People today use the term "poltergeist" to describe any phenomena associated with the ghost syndrome, but in my professional opinion, this is inaccurate. A case of residual haunting, a disembodied voice, true possession, and other psychic phenomena tend to encompass many of the same attributes, but are different in their nature and intent.

"I have only encountered maybe about ten or so actual cases that I would deem as a poltergeist case in the last few decades. The phenomena in these instances really speaks for itself. The most amazing elements of a poltergeist case are the outward experiences. In these cases, you actually experience the physical phenomena. Furniture will move, windows will break, the child will be thrown around, bangings will occur, and other strange situations as well will occur in the immediate vicinity of the child. It is common for people in the home as well as researchers and others involved with such a case to experience physical activity, while with other cases, only certain people will witness phenomenon.

"Sometimes, tables will move around the room, clocks will go backwards, objects will be systematically broken, all right in front of your eyes. Also, this destruction may not always take place directly in front of you, but will occur literally in the blink of an eye. You can turn your back for a moment and turn around to find objects relocated, holes in walls, and virtually anything else that could possibly happen. I've been witness to this firsthand. Honestly, it blows your mind—the fact that with absolute silence and precision, with no one in that area, such destruction could take place. It drives you to the point where it is hard to accept that these things are possible. There is seemingly no logical explanation for these occurrences, and the root of the actions not usually fully determined.

"With cases of the demonic and cases pertaining to human spirit, there are often warning signs that something is going to occur. Often, there is a drastic drop or rise in the temperature or an unexplainable odor in the room. With poltergeist cases, there are usually no warning signals, no way of knowing that something is about to happen. Things of a large magnitude will occur without any cause or explanation.

"One particular case that stands out for me involved a young boy, twelve years old, who resided in Massachusetts with his mother and father, one older brother, and a younger sister. The case came to the attention of the Warrens and remains one the more remarkable cases I had the chance to work on.

"I can recall one night the boy was sitting at the kitchen table working on his schoolwork. I was there with a few other researchers and the Warrens. When this boy was concentrating on his homework, his chair would pull out from the table, leaving him a few feet from the heavy piece of furniture. It happened a few other times before his mother stepped in. She could see the worry on her son's face, and the angrier the boy got, the more frequent the chair would move. She stood against the back of his chair so it would not pull back away from the table. I remember looking at Ed and we made eye contact, not interacting verbally whatsoever. There was not much to say in such a situation. The phenomena were so outrageous that it was almost impossible to comprehend what was occurring at that particular moment. Well, as the mother stood there blocking the chair, the phenomena took an interesting twist. As the mother held down the chair, the table slid forward, several feet away from the boy. After a few moments, the activity ceased and all was left normal. However, it took some time for the event to sink into our minds.

"With poltergeist phenomena, it plays some serious games. It is a 'now you see it, now you don't' type of situation. Activity can reach outrageous proportions, then dissipate in a matter of seconds. Spontaneity is the key component of poltergeist phenomena. You never know when or for how long the activity will occur. Unfortunately, this is the very reason why, unless you have the whole house under surveillance, you could miss recording some of the unusual events of a poltergeist case. It can happen at anytime, anywhere, and for varying amounts of time.

"Many have asked in my experience if an exorcism will help in a genuine poltergeist case that revolves around a child. The answer is no, but there is a remarkable direction a poltergeist case may take. Not all poltergeist cases can be explained solely as poltergeists or the result of energy deriving from puberty. Some poltergeists are unique opportunities for the demonic to tie in and work just below the surface in the shadow of the phenomena. Some of the same types of phenomena occur in demonic cases, but one must be very decisive when judging what type of case is at hand and what directly ties in. The outward manifestations are an effective diversion for the demonic. They can hide out unrecognized due to the distraction caused by moving furniture and the like.

"Personally, when I have worked on poltergeist cases and I have looked into the eyes of that child as the phenomena goes on, I see that gaze, that stare that I have seen too many times when dealing with the demonic. I know that there is usually more tied in with the case. I know that it is just not the transition in which energy conveyed by the child is stirring up chaos, but instead, an intelligence operating with the child as a conduit or puppet. It becomes quite obvious to me that there is another intelligence involved with many poltergeist cases—a force with a particular mission and a motive to work unrecognized. The demonic is a tricky power that will do anything to deceive. I know that when a child seems to not be there that there is that cunning force who deceives working within that person.

"For a child to read your thoughts and to know information that is not accessible to them, for a child to know about private matters, or to change their personality quickly, is completely unnatural. This reflects many of the cases I have worked on in which the demonic was an integral part of the problem, either oppressing or possessing individuals. Poltergeist cases are just that, a poltergeist case. Something preternatural is altogether different.

"Another interesting point with the boy and his family in this particular case was the cuckoo clock in the living room. As phenomena occurred, it would go off and the hands of the clock would go in the opposite direction from what they normally do. It was a given that when activity would take place, this clock would take on a life of its own.

"This case had many objects which would be systematically moved around. I remember how trophies would move around, relocating themselves to other areas where they had not been. In one bedroom, there were a few dolls and stuffed animals that would move from corner to corner in that room, as if they were on a merry-go-round. Windows were punched inward and holes carefully carved into walls. It seemed that every time someone stepped into that house, that phenomenon would begin to occur. Another interesting aspect was the spontaneous fires that lit without any visible cause. Fires would actually break out throughout the house with no known cause.

"Another really bizarre case I worked on occurred quite a few years ago in New York State. It was my only experience with what we refer to as the Water Poltergeist. It actually rained within the home, but not rain like torrential downpours, but droplets that fell throughout every room in the house. At times, we had ten researchers up at the home, all of whom experienced the phenomena. The case had the normal poltergeist activity, but this twist was one I had never seen and have not seen since. This location also faced destruction, resembling that of a typical poltergeist outbreak. Coffee pots were broken, flowerpots and dishes were thrown around, and furniture moved violently around the room, as if pushed by unseen hands.

"Poltergeist cases are nothing new to the world of psychic research. Many documented cases by credible individuals are documented. Even in my region, we have record of a phenomenal poltergeist case. In Stratford, Connecticut in the mid-1800s, a minister by the name of Eliakim Phelps had many unexplained phenomena occur in his home. His case, however, could stem from a number of sources. It was rumored that he held communication sessions in an attempt to contact spirits on the other side. Therefore, he had a good chance of attracting just about any kind of spirit. Children lived in the home, but it might have been because of his spirit communication sessions that something entered their lives, but this cannot be stated conclusively.

"Mentioning the word *apport*, often turns heads when one speaks of a genuine poltergeist case. An *apport* is the appearance of an object from an alternate location. The demonic also has this ability to perform what is called substance transference. Usually in a poltergeist case, objects will systematically and often relocate themselves from other areas of the home. In cases of demonic outbreaks, something completely foreign to the location might appear. Vomit, rocks, blood, and just about anything imaginable might materialize from an unknown place.

"Although many disagree about the cause of poltergeist, there is no doubt that the resolution is both usually unexplainable and unpredictable. Poltergeist activity usually cannot be remedied by an exorcism or minor religious rite. A communication session will also usually yield no results. Things are usually left to run their course. Poltergeist cases vary, but the initial outbreak of intensified phenomena will usually occur for a duration of weeks or months before it ceases completely. Oftentimes when the child reaches the end of the first stage of puberty, the outward manifestations often die down until almost extinct. Of course, there is no hard-and-fast definition of a genuine poltergeist explosion, but a concurrent paper trail documenting cases from hundreds of years ago until this modern day have shown a striking similarity. Cases from different eras, locations, countries, and socioeconomic backgrounds turn up strikingly similar situations."

The religious person brings his or her faith, the scientist brings the tools of science, the unbeliever, skepticism. All leave with a different perspective on the matter, a different experience under their belt. One brings religious tradition which is often unable to give meaning to the phenomena, the scientist witnesses events which cannot be explained empirically, and the skeptic has a hard time discounting the validity of the occurrences. Each person leaves with many questions left unanswered. How does this happen and how can we explain it in the future?

Moving into Unthinkable Devastation

Moving into Unthinkable Devastation

"Joe, we got it, we got the house! It is finally ours, the lawyers closed on it today."

Joe was speechless. The phone call from his wife, Rachel, was long overdue. The two, along with their three children, had been searching for a home for about five months. The acquisition of the colonial they landed was a long and tedious two-month struggle. The previous family pulled out of the deal last minute, stating that they no longer wanted to sell the home even though a down payment was given a few days earlier. After the lawyers stepped in and everything was cleared up, the previous family agreed to move out. After a seemingly endless struggle, they could now move into the luxurious home and begin the next chapter of their lives.

"Great," Joe exclaimed with relief in his voice. "When can we move in?"

"Anytime we want," Rachel exclaimed with excitement still evident in her voice.

The two agreed to start moving in right away. The very next day they would start some preliminary work on the house. Basic cleaning and some painting touch-ups were needed, but the house appeared to be cosmetically sound, with no visible defects on the outside of the house. Joe and Rachel saw almost every part of the house on their first walkthrough. There was an upstairs bedroom, which belonged to the previous family's son who kept the door locked at the showing. There was also a basement bathroom which was receiving plumbing work. As soon as they drove up, Joe and Rachel knew it was the right home for them. They felt drawn to the home, as if it was fate that brought them to the home. Their discovery of the home seemed to come just at the right time. They had three children in addition to themselves which quickly filled up the four bedrooms in the home. This home was a step up from their previous ranch, which had three bedrooms. Peter and Phil, two of their sons, had to share a bedroom, which caused many quarrels between the two brothers. The house was also situated on two acres of land and had an aboveground pool—both characteristics that appealed instantly to the entire family.

Within minutes of their tour, Joe and Rachel knew that this was the home they dreamed of for their entire lives. They had plenty of money to put a down payment on the home and eagerly awaited the day they could be settled in their dream home.

A few weeks before, the news came that the closing on the house might have hit a snag. The previous family wanted to stay after their eldest son of nineteen years refused to leave and swore he would not leave the home as long as he was alive. The son threatened to burn the house down if they sold it and discarded many of the legal documents that his parents obtained from the real estate agents. This young man said that he would stay in the house at all costs. He even threatened his father's life at one point if his father was to sell the house. The few weeks before the closing took place, the son installed a deadbolt lock on his bedroom door so that even if the family signed the house over, he would be able to barricade himself in the room. After a run-in with the police and much coercion, the teen left with his family. Now that the conflict was over, the family packed up their belongings and moved themselves out of the house rather quickly.

The next morning, Joe was fully rested and proceeded to wake up his children and wife. After breakfast and a walk with the dog, they headed over to their new home.

Rachel inserted the key into the lock, releasing it. The children ran in hurriedly to stake their claims on their bedrooms. Joe and Rachel looked at each other and thought how they hoped to live in this house for the rest of their lives.

Within a half hour, the clan had filled mop buckets and cut up old towels into dust rags. Today would mark their first day in the home and tomorrow they would move all of their belongings in. First, a cleaning was needed to ensure that the home met Rachel's high standards of cleanliness.

"I often get very intrigued when a family in a case which I am involved with states that they were drawn to a home," states Zaffis. "This is not to say that all homes which we feel compelled to reside in are haunted, as this would be a completely ridiculous theory. However, in many of the cases I have worked on or have studied, this has proven to often be a direct factor. Oftentimes when we look back on a case that is demonic in nature, we see trends that at the time are unidentifiable until all the facts are examined more closely. A family may enter a home and have good intentions and may be completely unaware of the fact that a new chapter is about to be started in their lives—a road so few go down, but nonetheless some encounter."

Joe hustled up the stairs to take a look at the rest of the home again. It was weeks since he had last been in the home and was eager to refresh his memory of the layout of the house. Joe walked from room to room, opening each of the doors and windows of the rooms to air them out. He entered the bedroom down at the end of the corridor and stopped dead in his tracks.

"What is all this?" Joe thought to himself. He continued to think of how bizarre it all was. Joe was confused, but more angry than anything. The walls of the room were covered in black writing. The far wall displayed words that were of unknown origin. The wall was covered with symbols and markings of every sort.

The wall to his left displayed the phrase, "Fuck whoever moves into this site and all who succeed them. I curse you all and curse this ground."

Joe looked at all the graffiti and was irritated to the point of speechlessness. Upon further inspection, he noticed the back of the door had been smeared with paint and had blasphemies scribbled from top to bottom. He questioned why was this place so special to the boy. He must have really been attached to the home.

"Rachel, get in here!"

Rachel put down her mop and headed upstairs. Flinging the door open, she could not speak. She looked at her husband, "What is all this shit?"

"I don't know. I was hoping you knew."

Rachel was puzzled. "This is the room we couldn't see when we came here before because it was locked, remember?"

"You're right, Joe. I remember it exactly as it happened. Remember when the realtor said he kept his door locked all the time? He found it quite odd,too, when the parents told him this."

Rachel looked at Joe and assured him after a paint job and some cleanup that the room would be as good as new. Anyway, their daughter was only two and a half and would have no idea about the vulgarity that had been written on her soon-to-be bedroom walls. Joe nodded and agreed, the two carrying on while Joe went to work immediately on the room.

Joe knelt back, looking at the negative inscription, wondering what must have been going through the mind of the room's previous owner. Joe knew nothing about the young man except that he was late in his teen years and delayed the closing on the house. Joe cracked open a can of paint and tried to put these thoughts into the back of his mind. After an hour or so of painting, the room would look much better and he planned to put another coat on the next day.

Peter cleaned all the baseboards on the first floor while his brother washed the windows on the second floor. They had a long day ahead of them, but did not seem to mind the work. They were eager to have their own bedrooms. The two brothers got along well, but private space had been desired by each of the boys since a young age. The thought of having their own rooms was an exciting prospect.

"Dad!" Phil screamed louder. "Get in here now!"

"What's wrong?" Joe began running to the bathroom to see why his son was calling him.

"Look at the toilet and the sink."

Both the toilet and the sink were completely backed up, as if it was clogged by debris.

"Joe, you better come down here," called Rachel from the kitchen.

Joe ran downstairs to find his wife standing directly in front of the kitchen sink. It was clogged, backed up, just inches from overflowing.

Joe looked at her and smiled, "No big deal, I'll just run to the hardware store and get something to unclog the sinks."

The family continued to clean, Rachel heading downstairs to the finished basement. She smelled something burning, as if someone lit off fireworks. She entered the boiler room hesitantly. There was smoke lingering, but no fire could be seen. She walked around, looking for the source of the smell. The furnace blew out, causing smoke to float around the room.

"Joe, you better get down here."

Joe ran down the basement stairs to the boiler room.

"What?"

"Look at the furnace. Something happened to it."

Joe's blood thickened, "What is happening around this shit hole? I thought the home inspector gave the thumbs up on everything. Call the furnace company; they're open all the time."

Rachel went upstairs and dialed the operator. She had to hold back the tears that were welling up. Their dream home was turning out to be a nightmare. She prayed to herself that this was the last of their problems, assuring herself all would be fixed today. Joe remained downstairs, deciding to check everything out, taking a closer look at every nook and cranny. His patience was worn thin.

"Oh, come on," he said to an empty room. He knelt down sticking his hand under the oil tank. Beneath the oil tank laid a darkened puddle of oil that expanded slowly by a constant drip in the front of the tank.

Joe sat with his back leaning on the tank. The day turned out to be the complete opposite of what Joe expected. First, a room was vandalized with complete filth, then the plumbing backed up. The furnace was on the fritz and now the oil tank was leaking. The first thing that crossed his mind was that the home inspector must have missed a lot of faults within the home. Joe did not realize that these problems were nothing that could have been determined by a home inspector.

Hours passed, and Joe gathered the family, "Let's go pick up your little sister and get something to eat," he said to Phil.

They left their daughter, Kate, with Rachel's mother while they prepared the house. The group left to pick up Kate, then scope out the neighborhood, hoping to locate all of the local hot spots. Although they live only a few towns over from their previous residence, they had not seen most of the town.

A few hours later, they returned to finish up the rest of the cleaning before calling it a night. They wanted to begin moving in some of their belongings the following day and hopefully be settled by the end of the week.

Joe opened the door, wishing he never had done so. No one moved out of the foyer. Gazing into the dining room, shards of glass and crystal were scattered around the room, only wires poked through the ceiling. The chandelier crashed to the ground while they were out having dinner. Everyone stood motionless as Rachel approached what was left of the brass fixture. Even the boys, who seldom were quiet, remained silent. After cleaning up the mess, they shut the lights off and headed back to their other home that would soon be abandoned by them, wondering just what their new life had in store. The first day did not go as planned, causing headache after headache.

"One thing that stands out with oppression is the systematic approach the demonic takes to break an individual or an entire family down," states John. "Obviously in such a situation as moving into a new home, there is already a great deal of stress. The onset of such destruction in the home over such a short period of time can cause complete discord. Here, we have a normal family just getting started in a home, and the phenomena already started as soon as they stepped foot in the door. The demonic will destroy material possessions or meaningful items because it triggers a direct response from the people it tries to affect. In this case, the emotion was anger and pure angst. Obviously at this moment, it seemed like a bout of bad luck, but as time went on, the plan unfolded and this strategic precision by the demonic proved to only be a small part of the larger picture.

"Many homes that go through the initial stages of infestation and oppression start off fairly subtle, then snowball into an intense outbreak over time. There was an intelligence here, it's clear-cut exactitude unknown at this point."

Rachel called her sister, Diane, hoping to find some comfort. Diane agreed to meet them at the house early in the morning to finish the cleaning and help move all of the boxes. Her husband, David, would come to lend an extra helping hand.

The next morning could not come quick enough. Joe and Rachel wanted to get everything into the house. Of course, it would be a few days before everything would be in and settled, but if they worked hard, they could certainly get most of their belongings moved in. Once again, they left Kate with Rachel's mother, allowing all of their energy to be focused on the move. Between all of them there would be four adults and two able-bodied children. The first load was already packed on the rental truck and Joe's brother-in-law followed in his pickup with an additional load.

At the house, Diane spoke with Rachel about what her sister revealed the night before to her on the telephone. She said that she should have someone take a look at all of the insignias and assess the situation. Maybe everything that was going wrong had some external cause; perhaps it all was not overlooked problems by the home inspector. Maybe there was a different origin of the problems. Rachel did not think it was a bad idea, but still thought that the idea that the house had a mind of its own was a ridiculous theory.

Rachel had called her parish priest at this point and told him about the writing and thought a blessing of the home would ultimately ease the situation. Her priest agreed to come over that afternoon to bless the house.

John further explains. "At this point, the thought of supernatural, or specifically in this case, the preternatural, was not an option. Most people do not believe or tend to doubt the idea that the spirit world can interact with the physical world. Even those who had had mild experiences or those who attend church and say that they believe in spirits really do not when it comes down to it. Here, we have an innocent type of situation where it seems preposterous that the preternatural could be involved. The family never practiced any type of magic or dabbled in any way with the occult. The idea was the farthest thing from their minds at the time."

"Get the door, Joe," Rachel yelled from upstairs.

At the door stood Father Mahoney. Mahoney had been a priest for thirty-two years and had been noted in the area for his work with the mentally ill. His visits to the psychiatric ward at the nearby hospital were regular and his compassion strong. He often spent hours sitting and speaking with those who were mentally ill. Now standing at the doorstep, he wondered what events lead up to the call to him for a blessing. Father Mahoney knew the human mind very well and dealt with people, from his parishioners and other clergy to those who were mentally ill. He sensed on the phone a bit of anxiety in Rachel's voice. Perhaps he was letting his imagination run wild, but a piece of him could not help but wonder if there was something spiritual in nature rooted here, something that could be determined upon closer examination.

The history of the house was fairly normal, but it had been brought to Father Mahoney's attention by neighbors and an adolescent in this parish that the eldest boy of the previous family who resided there heavily used drugs, alcohol, and even the stranger practice of animal mutilation. Father Mahoney once spoke with the boy who had had been forced to attend a summertime confirmation class and felt he was troubled. Father Mahoney's natural curiosity was at a peak when thinking about the room Rachel had described.

"Hello Father," Joe said with a smile from ear to ear. Joe really liked the priest. This was the priest who had not only confirmed him, but who married Joe and Rachel and baptized all of their children. Joe not only considered him the parish priest, but a friend.

"Hello Joseph," Father Mahoney stated firmly. "I haven't seen you in my church in awhile. I hope to see you soon."

Joe's smile continued, "Yes Father."

Rachel came down to greet him. She was happy that he could make it and she put on a pot of coffee. She sat with him and told him of the plans to move in immediately. After all, they were going to take a little more time, perhaps a few more days, to settle everything with the physical damage that the appliances in the home sustained. After speaking with her sister, it seemed more realistic that the end of the week would better suit the finalization of the move.

Father walked around and blessed the house as requested. While reading specialized prayers and sprinkling holy water, he put forth his best effort to fill the home with love from above. Before departing, he wished the family luck and went on his way.

"After getting involved with the case and speaking with Father Mahoney," states John, "I realized that the house always had an aura of disaster. The four previous families who lived there over the past twenty years or so had all ended their marriages in divorce. The previous family, who had just moved out, was on the verge of splitting up, and their son was very heavily involved in Satanism. After talking with some of the neighbors after subsequent investigations at the house, I was revealed some information that turned out to be crucial. The night before Joe and Rachel started moving their things in, the neighbors across the street called the police. At the home were several people who were never really identified. They had a fire in the backyard and were quite loud. It seems that the eldest son hung around a little longer than expected and had a few friends with him. This would later become a heavy aspect because of what Joe found in the backyard fire pit."

After a busy day of moving, many of their belongings were moved in and much of the cleaning was done. The repairmen came and things seemed to be a little better as far as the stress involved with the move. Joe volunteered to stay at the house and would come home later. Joe put in for some time off at work to complete the move and was full of ambition. Saying goodbye to everyone, he headed straight to the dining room to hang up the new chandelier that Rachel and her sister had picked up at the store earlier that day.

Knock-Knock-Knock!

"Come on in!"

Joe paused, but there was no response.

"I'm up on the ladder, come on in," he stated.

Joe stepped down from the ladder and headed to the door. Upon opening the door, he found nothing but the chirp of crickets and the sound of a car passing by the house. He shut the door and headed back to the dining room. Joe did not think much of it, but was a bit confused. The same knocks occurred the previous night when he walked right by the door. Upon answering it, he found the same empty porch he found on this night.

After an hour or so, he came down from his perch and looked up at the chandelier. It was really beautiful. The cut glass and gold trim really made the room look finished. Joe went to the kitchen to wash his hands. To his surprise, the sink was backed up again. He headed upstairs to try another sink. As he approached the bathroom, he heard the sound of running water. Turning the corner, he found both faucets on full blast. After washing his hands, he turned off the faucets and headed back downstairs. Step by step, he got closer to the bottom, but he could not help but wonder what the cause of these events was. He knew that the kids did not leave the water on. He walked by the bathroom at least once since they left. He shook his head and continued painting.

The next day, Joe once again worked by himself, finishing the painting and basic work needed on the house. For a third night, the knocking began to occur after nightfall. As he had the previous two nights, Joe went to the front door and opened it up quickly, as if to catch a prankster running away. He stepped out onto the porch, but again, there was no one on the front porch. His night was cut short, however, by all the electricity turning off completely in the home.

The following day, the family moved in and brought the last batch of boxes. This would mark their first night in the house. Although there was still more work to do, the house was not in a livable condition.

After another exhausting day, the family went to bed fairly early, not knowing that their slumber would be interrupted in the middle of the night.

"Mommy!" Kate began screaming frantically. "Monsters, monsters!"

Rachel and Joe entered the room followed by the two boys. They listened to Kate as she described men that wandered around in her room, visible with the dim lighting cast by a nearby night-light. After several minutes, the boys and Joe went back to bed. Rachel stayed in the room until Kate fell asleep.

Rachel could not help but wonder. Maybe Kate truly witnessed the men in her room, but the idea seemed illogical to Rachel. After Kate was deep in sleep, Rachel tiptoed away, back to bed.

The next day was marked by two surges that killed all power to the house. One outage occurred when the boys powered on the television, and the other occurring after Rachel unplugged the hair dryer. The circuit breakers appeared to be working fine and the power went on some time later.

Things were a little tense on this day. Rain crashed down heavily on the roof. The newscaster predicted a substantial storm that would end by the following morning.

"Mom, get up here!"

Rachel headed upstairs to find Peter staring at the floor. Water was absolutely everywhere. Throughout the second level, water leaked in random areas of the house. The exact origin of the leaks was unknown, but the water was clearly visible. Panicking, she grabbed all of the towels she could find, and even a few blankets, trying to absorb as much of the water as she could. The battle would resume for several hours until the storm stopped. Strangely, a few days later it rained heavily, and not one leak was apparent and no water backed up into the house.

Rachel sat in the recliner. It was four o'clock in the morning and she was up for an hour. For the third night in a row, Kate woke up screaming at three o'clock in the morning. She was in bed with her father now, but somehow Rachel could not fall back to sleep.

Why was everything going wrong with the house? Why was Kate so frightened and awakened every night? There was no clear answer. She knew that first thing in the morning, she would call Father Mahoney and have him come back to see if just maybe there was something going on that was unnatural.

"At this point," stresses John, "the presence is starting to make itself known. The physical breaking of items could have been passed off as bad luck, but now an intelligence started to become apparent. The three knocks on the door for three nights are all too common a sign that the demonic is taking hold. The electrical problems, the sinks backing up, these were much more than mere coincidences. A home is usually the biggest financial investment a person will make in his or her life. By systematically wreaking havoc in the house, it starts to cause disturbances and turmoil among family members. Financially, a person may become a wreck. Next, the stress causes problems getting along with others in the family. On top of this, the sleep patterns are altered and the children become terrified. This is the point where infestation transforms into oppression and a full-scale war is about to begin."

"This family never believed in the spirit world, but received a harsh lesson that became clearer over time as the demonic tightened its hold. A family will often reject the notion that something spiritual in nature is occurring because they do not receive any feedback from the other members of the family. The strange thing is that most of the family had some type of experience, but did not want to admit it for fear of being mocked. When dealing with cases and interviewing families, many times information or experiences will come forth in which the other members of the family had no idea ever happened."

After Rachel explained to Father Mahoney about her growing concern, he suggested a mass be performed in the home. He also suggested that she give someone a call who might be of help to her. That person was John Zaffis.

John knew Father Mahoney because of a case from the mid-1980s where a deliverance from an oppressive force was required. The case was originally referred to the Warrens and John was handling it as their chief investigator. Ever since, the two remained in touch on a fairly regular basis.

Trying To Make Sense Of The Misfortune

"Hello, John, it's Rachel. Father Mahoney told me to give you a call."

"Oh yes, I just got off the line with him. He told me you would be calling."

"So you're a demonol…or something, right?"

A chuckle came from John on the opposite end of the line, "Kind of. I'm a psychic researcher and have worked with Father Mahoney's parishioners in the past. When would you like me to come over?"

"What about tomorrow?"

"That would be fine."

John and Father Mahoney met over at the house around noon. A mass was performed without any interference. After the mass, Father Mahoney packed up and left, wishing the family luck for a second time.

John sat at the kitchen table talking with Joe. Joe gave John the lowdown on what had been occurring. Joe thought the idea that the supernatural was at play was completely ridiculous, but nonetheless, he wanted to adhere to his wife's wishes. Joe mentioned that he heard the stories and had read about it, but never wanted to believe that any of it was true. Joe showed some concern because of his daughter's constant complaints of the "monsters" that came out every night and woke her. Telling John to hold on one minute, he went to the kitchen drawer and pulled out a developed roll of film.

"Here are some pictures I took before we moved in. Toward the back, you'll notice the ones that have all the writing on the walls. That's Kate's room. When we got here, there were all types of symbols and profanities on the wall. I painted over them, all except the ones on the back of the door. I didn't have time to get rid of those yet. When I pulled up the area rug, there were pentagrams and some more writing on the floor. I got it all up with a scraper."

John took off his glasses and placed then on the kitchen table and looked at the photos. He could not believe the amount of satanic graffiti and vulgar language that was evident on every wall and on the floor.

Joe offered to show him around and the two went off around the house from top to bottom. In the basement, John went into the room leading to the garage, which had a door opening up to the backyard. In the far corner were some boxes that were left by the old owners and some old newspapers. John caught a glimpse of something thrown over the boxes. Picking it up, he noticed that it was a robe. A long, black garment, which lay as if were taken off in a hurry and thrown.

With flashlight in hand, both Joe and John went into the backyard toward the fire pit. John sifted his hand through the ash as dusk was setting in and found something hard. He pulled out what looked like a bone from the dust. Further looking brought about four other pieces of bone. John kept in the back of his mind what Father Mahoney had told him about the previous owner's teen son who was involved with Satanism.

The two headed back to the kitchen for another cup of coffee.

John looked at Joe seriously, "I don't know what to tell you. You definitely have the potential for something going on here, there is no doubt about it. I know that you do not want to believe it, but remember that you have a daughter, and she is complaining all the time. Why don't you try moving her to another room and see if her nightmares end?"

Joe agreed that it was worth a try. After John left, he switched his daughter's room with Peter's, who agreed to his father's wishes.

"Rachel," Joe said, "do you think something is really going on here? I mean I guess its ridiculous, but what about all the stuff we found, like the bones and the wax symbols? I just don't buy it. John seems sincere, but if this stuff exists, why would it mess around with us? We never did anything to it."

Rachel agreed, but her attitude changed very quickly. While John was in the backyard with Joe, she questioned Kate thoroughly about what she saw in her room. Kate had described things of different heights that would appear in her room. Her stories were very detailed and she was sincere in her fear. Although just a little girl, it was evident that Kate was being honest with her mother. As bizarre as it seemed, there was still something even more strange tied in.

Kate told her mother how her visitors had appeared to her on another occasion and offered her candy, reaching out to her. Kate, of course, screamed for her parents. This idea of something pestering her daughter was so frightening because if it was real, it had gone virtually unrecognized by the rest of the family for an unknown length of time.

"As far as these entities being different heights," John specifies, "this tells me in regards to classification that these deities would most likely represent different levels. The demonic realm can be thought of as being hierarchical, like an army. The devils are higher in rank, and the demonic are the soldiers. The demonic will bring about the phenomena and only occasionally will a devil step in, usually only when a desired outcome is not met."

It was three o'clock in the morning. The clock next to Rachel ticked steadily, each second going by as the previous one had. Darkness hung in the house and all were out cold. It seemed to be peaceful, tranquil, a night of rest. After lying down at about eleven o'clock, Rachel passed right out.

"Mommy! Help me!"

Rachel jumped out of bed, slamming into the doorway. Rachel ran to Kate's room and turned on the light immediately.

"What! What honey?"

Kate was curled up in a ball wrapped in a blanket on the floor. Rachel picked her up off of the floor. Kate was shaking violently. Rachel began to sob lightly. What was going on with her daughter? Why did she awake almost every night at the same time and complain of men in her room?

Rachel picked up the phone the next morning and called John. She hoped to catch him before he went to work. The phone rang until the answering machine picked up. She left a lengthy message for him about the previous night's events.

Later that day, the phone rang. John called her back to find out how everything was. Rachel told him of the previous night and also stated today that the faucets in both the kitchen and the master bathroom had been turned on. Rachel had also noticed that no matter how many times she turned off the basement light, that it would always be turned back on the next time she checked.

John said he would get back to her after he contacted Father Mahoney.

"At this point the phenomena began to intensify," stesses John. "Even occurring in the daylight hours. Not only were there physical occurrences, but both Rachel and Joe were constantly arguing. Looking back, they don't know why they would have fought over such small occurrences. It was not normal for them to fight like this. Pitting family members against one another is another tactic of the demonic: the divide or conquer approach. Rachel began to realize what was occurring and began to have her guard go up, while Joe still didn't really buy any of it."

A high mass was set up for the next day. Once again, Father Mahoney and John met at the home. The high mass was said and not even the slightest occurrence took place. John hoped that this might ease the burden of what was going on. Only time would tell what would occur within the walls of the home. With the mass, there was a good possibility the phenomena would come to an abrupt halt. There was also the possibility of a dormant stage occurring, followed by the inception of more actions by the demonic. The other option is one the researcher, the clergy, and more importantly the family feared would happen: a direct assault and the intensifying of the condition. Instead, the mass provoked the spirits instead of deterring them.

Activity began to peak a few days later. Lights were going on and off constantly and objects would move themselves from one room to another. After a two-day lull, Kate began to wake up again after her visitors made themselves known. Joe and Rachel were at each other's throats, and Peter was beginning to complain about the basement. When Peter was in the basement putting his bike away in the garage, a door opened, then slammed on its own. After speaking with John, an exorcism of the home was scheduled for the following Monday. Kate, however, seemed to be the target of most of the activity, perhaps because of her innocence or young age, leaving her vulnerable to more attacks. Rachel had taken her daughter to the grocery store at dusk one evening. No one was home to watch Kate while her mother ran to the store, so both bundled up in their winter coats and entered the car. Kate began to complain that the entities were with her in the backseat. Rachel looked in her mirror and quickly looked at the backseat, trying to glimpse the intruder to prove that her daughter was telling the truth. She saw nothing. Kate sat behind the passenger seat and began crying, facing the window and closing her eyes. Rachel tried to comfort her, but her attention was quickly drawn away from her daughter. Heavy thumps, like feet kicking or hands punching, struck the back of her seat. Kate's wails intensified. There was nothing visible in the back of the car, but the pushing continued and intensified. After two or three minutes, it stopped completely.

Both Peter and Phil were sent to their grandmother's house on the day of the exorcism. Joe, Rachel and Kate remained in the home, along with John and Father Mahoney.

Father Mahoney went straight into the ritual within moments of entering the home. About ten minutes into the exorcism, there was a dramatic turn. Kate, although not quite three yet, began to mumble words in a foreign language. Father Mahoney looked at John and continued without even a second thought until the exorcism was complete. When he finished, Father Mahoney quickly said several prayers over Kate and blessed the young girl.

John reflects on the incident. "In regards to the little girl, at the time I had no idea exactly what she was saying. It was a language that I did not recognize. After, when speaking outside with Father, he told me that what the child had actually said was a few names in Latin. At the time, I knew it was all too real, but had a hard time comprehending what just happened. This little girl's speech was similar to that of any three year old. The fact that she had spoken Latin was very strange."

"What was somewhat soothing was that at the end of the exorcism, the smell of roses was very overpowering. This in most cases is a positive sign that occurs at the end of many exorcisms. I knew that some progress had been made, but was unsure if things would continue to escalate or die down completely."

Father Mahoney left and told John he would be in touch if the struggle continued.

"Thank you, Father," Joe said.

"Take care, son," Father Mahoney said with confidence. Father prayed that what was residing in their home had been cast out. The fact that the little girl had spoken Latin during the ritual was more than enough for him to believe the demonic had its clutches on the home and was directing its hate toward the family.

John explains the aftermath of the situation, "After an exorcism, it is usually hard to know what to expect. Will there be peace and tranquility? Will it taper off or will the oppressors be expelled immediately? Only time will tell, and through follow-ups, it will be determined what measures, if any, will be needed. I've been on so many exorcisms over the years, but there has never been an exorcism that is predictable.

"I stayed in contact with the family. As far as phenomena, all has ceased. I am, however, sad to say that Rachel and Joe have divorced, following in the footsteps of the home's previous owners. Overall, I feel this case reflects an innocent family that fell into a scenario they did not mean to take part in. The chain of events was real to them and to this day, both Joe and Rachel look back knowing that what was at play was something they were trained not to believe, but in reality actually existed."

Mirror Magic: Conjuring the Spirits of Lust

Mirror Magic: Conjuring the Spirits of Lust

The modern movements stemming from an interest in the unknown give rise to many different techniques for self-empowerment. People of all cultures will go to great lengths to attain this power, an advantage of some sort in their everyday lives. Others are curious about the different belief systems and sample pieces of different practices out of curiosity. There are so many different beliefs and practices that it can often be intriguing to probe these worlds, which in itself appears harmless, but one does not quite know what they will come up against. Many will experience nothing while another will encounter many negative experiences. Each experience is unlike another's own experiences, making each occasion and case unique—the severity shifting up and down on the scale of anguish. Dabbling is just like rolling the dice; what comes up is entirely unpredictable.

It is not uncommon for John to be sought out for aid pertaining to those who have dabbled with occult who did not expect anything bad to happen. They were most likely experimenting with the world of the unknown for verification of its existence. Perhaps they wanted to test the limits of their mental powers. Others gave up on traditionalized practices and sought the aid of more unconventional methods of belief. Regardless of the reason, several cases of this nature are submitted to John's organization each month.

The following case dates back only a few years and was taken from John's case log. It exemplifies the types of problems people might run into when fooling around with negative invocation methods.

While staring into an old mirror, Alan stood completely still, invoking what he thought would be powers to help him obtain his main goal, which was to achieve dominance over women. Growing up, Alan had very few girlfriends. He lusted after women who he saw, but upon getting involved never achieved the sexual dominance he so desired. Alan, a tall, dark-haired man in his early thirties, knew that he was slipping from his prime. Girls he met at the bar were interested in younger men. With no other place to turn, he tried the world of dark magic.

Alan remembered one of his short-lived girlfriends who was heavily involved in witchcraft and claimed to obtain much of what she desired by implementing ritualistic practices she mastered throughout her earlier years. He thought it was probably nothing more than the power of suggestion, but he still had an underlying hope that an external agent was at work that could possibly bring about the attainment of a desired outcome for him. Perhaps her desires fueled her to obtain what she wanted by changing her view and approach, but he still was not quite sure. He believed that the spirit realm most likely existed, but still remained skeptical due to a lack of experience with the world of the occult.

A month before his first experiment with the mirror, Alan began researching many textbooks that embraced matters of magic, the existence of demons, and the hierarchy of hell, as well as the summoning spirits to one's side. Alan really was quite unknowledgeable and dove in immediately to achieve instant gratification. It would only be a matter of a few short weeks before Alan began to notice a change within his life reflective of his brushing up against the preternatural underworld.

"Ultimately what Alan was trying to do was invoke the spirit world to obtain desires based on his selfishness and sexual perversity by means of crystallomancy," states John. "Crystallomancy is a process that often uses a bowl of water, a mirror, or anything that may be transparent or cast a reflection. In this case, a mirror was used to invoke assistance and to gain influence and power over women so Alan could have sexual relations with a multitude of females."

Alan started to notice that his experimentation was not working and tried the invocation process a few more times. He tried lighting incense that he read about in a magic handbook and purchased the root at a local herbal store. He was more determined and serious in his endeavors than ever before. His process of experimentation went to a mindset of complete determination. Alan's intent was now very serious and he repeated the perverse prayers boldly, staring into the well-polished mirror.

After two weeks, Alan was becoming obsessed with the mirror. When he was not actually invoking, he cleaned the mirror as if it were a prized possession. Cleaning it anywhere from five to ten times a day, Alan was determined to make sure the surface was nothing short of perfect.

On a Thursday night after work, Alan headed to the bar downtown for a drink. Across from him sat many women. Alan sat, lusting after them, imagining himself involved intimately with the women. He did not want to hear their aspirations or their backgrounds. He did not care what they thought on any subject, nor did he wish to hear anything about them. Instead, he wanted to dominate them, penetrate them, and absolutely violate them any way he could.

That night his wish came true. He was approached by a young women in her mid-twenties who caught him staring at her with his burning eyes. After an hour of dialogue, Alan invited her to his house. He eventually consummated the ephemeral affiliation and asked her to leave the next morning after getting ready for work. She left her number, but Alan knew that he would never call the woman, and discarded her number within a few minutes after her departure.

Alan almost immediately desired another woman. His first taste sparked an ever-growing desire to get as many women as he could. He began to use the mirror more and more until his invitations to specific deities became the focus of his madness.

"Alan had gone from experimentation to regular involvement, to obsession, then reached all out direct communication," explains John. "I remember speaking with him on the phone for the first time, listening to his story, realizing that he was treating this mirror like a living and breathing person. He consulted the mirror and treated it like a god. Most of his actions revolved around the mirror, treating the object like it was a mentor. He really thought that it was the mirror giving him his luck with women. Alan, however, began to notice more and more that something was not right in his life. His obsession gave way to a force that made itself known physically on more than one occasion.

"The first time Alan was attacked, it was late one night after one of his female guests left following their having sex. This is when Alan began to realize that there was more than the power of suggestion at work. He then knew that what helped him achieve his perverse desires was not a figment of the deepest part of his fantasies, but instead a real entity that would seek out Alan's very own destruction after several months of appearances."

Alan lay in his bed trying to sleep, but was not able to do so. He felt as if eyes were staring at him, yet there was no visible presence in the room. He rolled over, ignoring the deep feeling that radiated throughout his entire body. Whatever the reason for the uncomfortable feeling, Alan had no desire to acknowledge the sentiment.

Alan started to drift off into twilight of sleep when he felt something on the bed of substantial weight. After a few moments of being held down, he flew out of bed to the other side of the room. Covered in sweat, the hot feeling that encompassed him was gone. He felt as if he were being smothered by a large blanket of electricity. Alan sat in the corner thinking about what happened. All of the invocations he performed had taken their toll. He read the books, said the words, and hoped for some type of action. Well, that was just what he got.

John discusses Alan's behavior. "Alan never thought that anything bad would happen as a result of the incantations. At first he didn't even think they were going to be effective. When results became apparent, he began to delve deeper into the bizarre rituals. That is when I believe the presence moved in. It waited for him to basically give himself up and waited for his guard to be completely down. At that moment there couldn't have been a better time to strike.

"When I got to know Alan, I saw a person who was quite friendly and ultimately harmless. Sure, he wanted women, but he never really experienced a woman sexually, this curiosity being the catalyst for his strong compulsions. He claimed that he used the rituals to acquire women because he did not want to pay for sex or forcibly rape anyone. His bizarre intentions became real and caused a struggle that goes on to this very day.

"I arranged for Alan to rid his home of the mirror and to have him come up to Connecticut for a Roman Catholic exorcism, but the plans fell through. A few days before the rite when speaking with him on the phone, he claimed he could not give up what he had. At this point, he was usually having sex between two and five times a day with different women. He knew and admitted it was not right, but could not bring himself to give up what he craved.

"I have not spoken with him in quite some time. The exorcism never happened and he continued on with his form of worship. I can only hope things have not intensified for this confused man. When I stopped communicating with Alan, he had been bitten and scratched on several occasions and had reoccurring nightmares. He often saw a dark shadow in the room with him that would seem to stare at him and then disappear. There is no doubt in my mind that his struggle carries on. Unless he renounces his involvement in such practices and performs a complete turnaround, his suffering may never end.

"Alan's study of the occult stemmed from his influence from the literature from one of modern day's perverse occult forefathers, Aleister Crowley. Crowley was born in the latter part of the 19th century in England and eventually came to this country. His ideas were rooted in his experiences under another occult-based man, Eliphas Levi. His study in the Temple and the Hermetic Order of the Golden Dawn sparked Crowley's initial interest and developed his beliefs and practices. Many people view Crowley as the forefather of many negative New Age movements. Crowley's experiments into the unknown were indicative of Satanism. He had renounced his Christian upbringing and often referred to himself as "666" or "the Beast." Alan felt a strong connection with Levi.

"The problem is just that; people get very easily influenced. They may simply pick up a book and feel that magic will work for them. Most would-be practitioners are not well versed in the occult, but instead experiment, merely dabbling with a few rituals before leaving the practices in their past. This is sometimes when whatever they summon comes back to them. Others experience the effects and crave more power, delving deeper and deeper into practice until they reach a point where they are completely consumed by what they see, hear, and experience. Perversity becomes their god, their very actions and thoughts on this level of wickedness. It is quite common to run into those who seek help, but when push comes to shove, they often cannot give up or renounce whatever it is that is around them. They are consumed, obsessed, and give it the recognition it needs to carry on its assigned duty. Getting people to break away from such practices, even when they are seeking the help for themselves, is often nearly impossible."

An Encounter with a Specter

An Encounter with a Specter

Throughout the ages, people have reported physical visitations and eyewitness accounts of unworldly beings in every culture no matter what religion, age, class, or political view they may subscribe to. Ghostly manifestations have not limited themselves to one or a few particular groups. Looking deep into one's immediate geographical area or studying scripts from distant lands will turn up the fact that encounters with specters of the night are part of a large scale phenomenon which have been reported since the beginning of recorded history. Rooted in the very depths of popular tradition is a belief that spirits have the ability to communicate with the living world.

Biblical references cite spiritual beings as well as tales passed on by oral tradition from non-Christian denominations. No single background embraces spirit phenomena. Instead, a multitude of traditions embrace the notion of spiritual subsistence. The encounters are often reported by multiple witnesses who describe an exact being even though the two individuals were not present during the time of the event. Modern day thought has accepted many of these impasse visitations as fact, while others have labeled them as folklore or the product of an overactive imagination. It is said that most human beings at some time in their life brush up against the supernatural world on this plane of existence. Many have had brushes with the world that lies next to ours, seemingly a coherent world which crosses into our conscious surroundings on a more frequent basis than we think. Spirituality, although not limited to the confines of culture or age demographic, has one main clear and concise issue which hovers over the whole notion of spirit manifestation. That issue is belief. Many accept without a doubt the fact that spiritual forces do interact on several occasions with humanity. Others who have not had an encounter with a specter may never believe and with an acceptable reason. In a culture that treads into many areas of study, breaking down barriers, and uncovering the ins and outs laced with purely scientific thought, the lore of the "ghost" remains an ever-popular mystery that has been explored by many, but is viewed as a myth by most people. The old saying 'seeing is believing' is what many need to validate that there is a spiritual realm. Without these first-hand encounters, some remain skeptical while others continue to support their experiences with the fact that they have encountered something supernatural in nature in their lives, something that is all too real to them and those who dive into the world of the supernatural acceptance.

"On cases, it is rare to encounter a full-formed being," states John. "Many have encountered figures that represent another time period, others have caught a direct glimpse of a departed loved one, and still others have witnessed beings that can only be described as demonic in nature. Although the physical specter is a rarity, it still occurs. Encounters are often brief and occur with the blink of an eye. Others, however, bear witness to imprints on the environment in which a point in time is replayed. This is what we refer to as the residual affect of the haunting. Others might encounter a being that has intelligence and is dabbling in our realm and knows full well what it is doing. This is not an example of a residual playback, but instead suggests intelligence. Each situation really is unique, but nonetheless represents a supernatural encounter."

Union Cemetery lies in southwestern Connecticut. It is most known for its White Lady apparition, which has appeared in many situations to unwary passersby. Reports have surfaced over the years of other occurrences, but the White Lady remains as one of the top reported ghosts in the area.

"I can recall coming home with Ed and Lorraine late one night, probably about three-thirty in the morning. The case was grueling and we exited the highway to drive back to get some rest. I distinctively remember starting to doze off when my aunt yelled, "Ed, pull over, pull over!"

My uncle, nervous at her outburst, nearly jumped out of his skin.

"What Lorraine? What is it?"

"At that point, I woke up from all the commotion. Lorraine indicated that 'it' was forming. That 'it' being what she felt was the White Lady of Union Graveyard."

"We pulled over and got out of the car right next to the cemetery. In about the middle of the burial ground on the dirt path that cuts through the front and exits out the back, a form was taking on a life of its own."

"'John, take a picture,' Ed said. I did nothing, mouth gaping wide in utter amazement."

"John, take a picture," Ed said again persistently.

The figure was elongating and was displaying a torso-shaped essence.

"Yet again, I failed to move. After a few seconds, the encounter was over. Ed looked at me and signaled to get back in the car and did not say too much. I was so intrigued and taken by this encounter that I did not even have the chance to comprehend that I should've taken a picture.

"To this day, I can remember how vividly the form came to life. It was a full-fledged encounter with something that came and went very quickly. I always thought there was a lot of truth to all the hype at this location and got all the proof I needed right there in that moment, that there was more than just overactive imaginations of people who went to the graveyard. The notion that a ghost had manifested right before my eyes didn't really sink in for quite some time. Encounters of this nature rarely occur and I had a unique opportunity to experience the manifestation.

"Are some people more susceptible to this type of viewing? I think so. Many have had encounters since the time they were children. Some catch a quick glimpse at some time within their lifetime of something they consider to be unexplainable by logical means. Each person has their own inborn degree of sensitivity. Others may encounter nothing spiritual in nature during their lives. It has often been said that each of us is given some degree of an alternate sense, a sixth sense, if that is what you want to refer to it as. I feel some have access to this sense which we are all born with. Some have developed this sense while others keep it hidden within them. For instance, children are more likely to experience a haunting because they are naturally open to anything and perceive things as they occur. They have not yet been trained that ghosts and the like are a myth or an impossibility, as is often thought by mainstream society. They sense it because it is there and they are open-minded to anything that occurs within their environment. Entities will often gravitate to the most sensitive individual that is around for countless reasons. This may be the direct result of psychic sensitivity and even perhaps an emotional parallel the energy finds within that particular person.

"Also, women and animals are usually more prone to experience phenomena than men. People often report how strange animals act, looking at something that is not apparent with the basic sense of human sight. Animals seem to pick up on activity first before the people of the home pick up on something hanging around. Next, it is usually the women and children and if the phenomenon is strong enough, the men will witness what is going on in the home, too.

"There is still a mysterious aspect regarding why some pick up on these images while others remain psychically dead. As we progress, perhaps we can unlock these powers of the mind.

"The question has often been asked of me," continues John, "how exactly does the demonic manifest and what does it look like? Usually in my experience and through dealing with clients whose encounters are demonic, there is usually a warning before this entity manifests. Often, there is an extreme drop or rise in temperature as well as a sulfur-like smell or some other stomach-turning odor. Often, the form is purely black, so dark that you cannot see through it. Other times it will be fast-moving black or gray shadows that will dart about the room concealing itself. This particular encounter is often experienced in one's peripheral vision. At this point, it is merely playing a game, concealing itself, letting you know it is there and tightening the grip, but still causing doubt in the witnesses' mind because the person usually does not get a good look at the entity. Others have seen full figures that appear to be wearing full-length robes like that of a monk. This, of course, is extremely rare.

"More common threads of psychic experiences vary from the normal thought that all encounters with a ghost are strictly visual. Actually, you are more likely to experience the odors, temperature changes, flickering of lights, sense of being watched, the movement of small objects and the like. Visual encounters are atypical. I've been on thousands of cases and have had images appear, but they are atypical.

"Another strange occurrence where I came across a full-figured image was on a case a few years ago. The case was pretty heavy-duty and I anticipated that there could be some activity when both myself and the other investigators arrived. Sometimes, you just have that feeling that something is going to occur. Usually, it is best to keep yourself on red alert if you feel there is more to the case than has already been revealed to you beforehand. The problem is you really don't know exactly what the logistics of a case entail until you go to the home, meet the family, and attempt to piece together what is taking place.

"We were driving up the side road to the residence slowly. It was dusk and darkness was just setting in. As we drove up closer, the house was in plain view. It was an older home, dimly lit with a sinister feeling around it. Within a few hundred feet of the house, I saw a specter, dark and tall in stature, pass right in front of my vehicle from right to left, and then it just disappeared. I stopped the car and got out, the rest of the researchers confused about what was occurring. I looked in the immediate vicinity, but didn't see a thing. The phantom disappeared as quickly as it had appeared.

"Why exactly did this phantom appear? I really couldn't tell you. The case did end up to be of a demonic nature, so my guess is it was some type of diversion to perhaps scare me off or perhaps give me a warning to back off. I can't say for sure, but I'll never forget that image. It didn't surprise me that no one else saw it either. Some might think that the others in the car were perhaps looking elsewhere, their vision focused on some other part of the landscape. This is a possibility, but I'm more inclined to say that the image was projected to me as a personal assault on the senses. Instead, it chose to show itself to me by means of telepathic hypnosis. The intelligence made a mental connection with me to relay a specific message. This is actually quite common in many situations. Two or more people might be present, but only one of those individuals will experience the image because they were systematically selected to have the experience.

"Other examples of such encounters are perceptible in any area. One particular popularized area where such visuals are often seen is Gettysburg, Pennsylvania. This place is noted for its rich history, but for the seekers of the mystical, the area has been viewed as very spiritually active. The appearance of full-formed apparitions is not rare in this old world town. Many reports have indicated that phantom soldiers have been seen on the battlefields and even in the local township. By most reports, these experiences tend to be residual, the apparition not really having any idea that they are seen by the person. For the witness, it serves as a glimpse into the past, the apparition going about its business, but seemingly unaware of what surrounds it.

"I had a chance to work on a case in that area last year, and it was quite fascinating to hear of the experiences by some of the locals who lived and worked in the heart of Gettysburg. Reenactors, innkeepers, tour guides, and people from all walks of life have often experienced something outside the realm of the physical world.

"Seeing is believing. Those who have experienced specters from the past or intelligent beings are left branded with an experience that will remain in their memory. Some are more susceptible to having these experiences, but the possibility of witnessing such a vision is something that each human has the capability to do."

The Doll with a Past

The Doll with a Past

"Honey, look what I bought," Samantha called to her husband, Kevin.

He came down the stairs and approached her, "Not bad, but what about the face?"

"It's fine," she replied. "I'll be able fix it without any problems. I'm sure of it." Samantha had a fixation with restoring antique dolls. Her collection now numbered in excess of seventy-five vintage dolls, representing many of the time periods in American history. Her interest began when she was in high school when her grandmother taught her how to restore worn and tattered antiques. It was then that her passion for old dolls began, regardless of their condition.

She placed the doll in her and her husband's bedroom, placing it on the chest by the foot of the bed. After work the following day, she planned on trying to refurbish the once pale, white face that the doll had prior to being burned. Overall, its condition was mint, except for the slight burn marks on the face.

Samantha saw her husband approach the kitchen. "Where did you get that doll?"

"Over on Singleton road at a tag sale. Tomorrow I think I'll take a look at her and see what I can do. The face isn't so bad. I should be able to repair it to its original condition."

The two went about their business as normal and later that night crawled into bed. Both slept heavily until the next morning in complete darkness. Kevin woke up the next morning only to find his wife visibly confused and troubled.

"What's wrong, Sam?"

"I don't know," she replied. "Look at my legs, they are all scratched up."

Kevin examined her ankles and noticed long gashes with dried traces of blood from her ankles to about a foot up her leg. The scratches were pretty severe and Samantha was visibly shaken.

Kevin was puzzled. "How did you get them?"

"I don't know."

"Do you have a rash or anything on your legs?"

She told her husband that she did not have a rash and they both got out of bed. Kevin was thinking to himself how strange it was for so many gashes to appear all over his wife's lower extremities as they had. They did not have any animals, and he had not awoken because of her intensely scratching herself and she would have surely remembered inflicting such deep contusions. Nevertheless, Sam knew that the cuts would heal and she did her best to forget about the disturbing episode.

At work, Samantha was quite unsure how the cuts occurred. She soon forgot about the incident and absorbed herself in her daily routine. Later that day, she left work and headed home, eager to get to work on the doll. She spent over an hour on the doll and set it back on the chest by the foot of the bed to dry.

Kevin came home and opened the door. "Samantha? Are you home?"

"I'm in here," she replied to her husband. "I'm just working on the doll. I just set it down to dry."

"That's nice," he replied. "Get you purse, we're meeting my brother and his wife for dinner. They're meeting us at seven."

"Ok, give me a minute."

They shut the door behind them as they walked out to the car. Kevin turned the key in the ignition and backed out of the driveway. Inside, the doll continued to dry, sitting still.

The Second Night

Samantha slipped into her bathrobe and walked into the bathroom. She locked the door and turned the shower on, letting the water warm up. Her husband was already asleep, tired after putting in overtime at work most of the week. She untied the cloth belt and hung the robe next to the shower. Putting one foot in the shower, her attention was pulled to the scratches on her leg. The scratches were still there, but less in number. They were beginning to heal. She bathed and began to think of logical explanations for this, but was unable to do so.

She turned the water off and dried her chilled body. Slipping on the robe again, she headed into the bedroom and turned on the small desk lamp.

"Are you coming to bed, Sam?"

Samantha gasped. "I thought you were asleep. You startled me. Just give me a minute."

Samantha finished dressing herself and turned toward the bed. She caught a glimpse of the doll and how beautiful it looked. It was not quite dry yet, but would be this time tomorrow. She picked it up one last time that evening, examining her work and the exact precision it took to restore the attractive glow of the original features. She turned off the lamp and crawled into bed.

"Kevin! Get up! We're late for work!"

Kevin groggily turned over, squinting in the sunlight, which crept into the room.

Sam already jumped out of bed. "We lost power during the night. The alarm never went off."

Kevin rolled out of bed as his wife frantically laid out her clothes.

"Sam, look at your legs."

She peered down toward the floor. There were more cuts and scrapes, new gashes fresh with some traces of dried blood. There was no doubt that there were fresh cuts. "How the hell did this happen?"

Kevin was speechless. Why were his wife's legs covered with scrapes again? The two obviously did not have time to discuss this unsettling occurrence because they were already late. After getting dressed, Samantha ran out the door. Her drive to work was filled with thoughts about the scrapes on her legs. They were not sore or bruised in any way at this point, but how did this happen for the second night in a row? She continued to think, but still could not identify a cause of the wounds.

After work, Kevin came into the kitchen where he found Samantha reading the paper. The smell of a sizzling roast filled the entire house.

"Smells good," he said.

"Hey Kevin, how was work?"

"Not bad. Can we talk?"

The immediate urgency caught Samantha's attention, her face coming into view from behind the paper. "Sure, why?"

"These scratches," Kevin said. "Well, I was thinking and they have only happened over the last two nights, right?"

"Yeah," she replied, seemingly confused. "Why does that matter?"

"It sounds stupid, but you've only had the doll for a few days, and maybe that's part of the problem."

"What!" This theory did not make any sense to Samantha.

"I mean, well it's just weird that you had such marks and the only thing I could come up with is that they started as soon as you got that doll."

"That's true," she said, "but why would the doll have anything to do with it anyway? I mean it's cloth, plastic, and porcelain. It's an inanimate object!"

"I don't know," he said.

The two discussed the possibility, but it still did not sit well with either of them. It did not make any sense, but there were no other viable explanations at this point. The only change that took place in the home was the inception of the doll. Samantha did not really feel comfortable blaming the doll, but Kevin was adamant that the doll was a factor in the scratching incidents. After the whole discussion, Kevin suggested moving the doll to another room away from the both of them, specifically Samantha. Maybe if it were relocated further away from Samantha, the attack would stop. She agreed and the doll was left on the kitchen counter in between the refrigerator and the stove.

That night, both Samantha and Kevin were unable to sleep soundly. Samantha dozed off at about ten o'clock, while Kevin woke up frequently throughout he night. Kevin was petrified that his wife might be scratched during the night and he feared for her safety.

Kevin awoke before his wife and immediately examined her legs. There was nothing there. The scratches from the past were still fading and there were no fresh scratches apparent. There was no dried blood or any indication that new scratches were inflicted. He woke up Samantha and pointed out the fact that there were no new abrasions.

Samantha and Kevin talked again. This time, Samantha seemed more open to the idea that the doll was responsible for the lashes, but she struggled to logically explain how this could be. The idea did not make any logical sense.

Samantha got up and headed for the kitchen. She put on a pot of coffee for herself. Kevin was heading out the door to meet up with his father for their routine Saturday breakfast. Looking at Samantha, he could tell that she was bothered by the whole situation, "Are you alright?"

"Yeah, I'm fine. Just confused. Maybe you're right, Kevin."

"Do you want me to stay, hun?"

"No, I'll be fine. Go with your father."

She found what little comfort she could in her cup of coffee. She gazed at the doll as it sat completely still on the counter where she had left it the night before. She thought that there was only one way to find out if the doll was responsible. That night, she would put it back in the room. If more scratches appeared in the morning, Samantha could assume that the doll was connected to the scratching episodes.

Later that evening, Kevin watched television in the living room. Samantha walked by with the doll.

"What are you doing with that thing?"

"I'm putting it back in the room tonight," she said with a serious tone and face to match.

"What! Are you serious?"

"Yes, I am. It's the only way to know for sure."

"You're nuts," he replied. "I guess we'll know for sure after that, but is it really worth it?"

"Probably not, but what if it has nothing to do with the doll and it happens again? We should try to know why this happened. I can't believe I'm doing this either, but I have to know."

She hastily put the doll on the cedar chest. It looked at her with an ominous glare. It really was a beautiful doll, but was its appealing façade merely masking a more sinister energy?

"Goodnight," Samantha said to Kevin.

He replied in the same fashion, leaning over her to kiss her. The darkened room was still, dead night reigned within the room, no sounds conveyed. Just dead silence accompanied Kevin, Samantha, and the doll.

The next morning Samantha awoke to the sound of the telephone ringing throughout the house.

"Hello," she said.

A low, creaky voice whispered, "Hi, Sam. We still on for lunch?"

"Hi, Claire. Yes, I'll pick you up at noon."

Samantha hung up the phone and thought, what about her experiment? She threw back the covers, exposing her legs.

"What?" There were new scratches, this time higher up. Now her thighs had scratches as well. She woke up Kevin, who was shocked to see the fresh cuts on his wife's thighs and calf. After sitting in silence, they agreed to call their minister.

Samantha found the phone book to look for the number.

The phone rang. "Is Reverend Miller there, please?"

"Hold on, one moment please," a sweet voice said. "I think he's outside."

"Thank you," Samantha replied. She waited nervously, hoping that Reverend Miller would know what to do. Hopefully, he was there so she could end this chaos.

"Hello, this is Reverend Miller, what can I do for you?"

"Hello, this is Samantha, Samantha Peterson. I need some input on a…well a rather strange matter."

"Oh," he replied to her. "What type of matter?"

Samantha let it all out, making sure that she told him everything. After a few minutes, Samantha was sure that he would not be able to help her and would probably tell her to forget about it.

"I'm not really familiar with this stuff," he stated. "There are, however, others that have gone through bizarre occurrences as well. One of my parishioners came to me after having doors slam on their own, furniture moving, and terrible odors that appeared from seemingly out of nowhere. When I spoke with them, I really was unsure of what to do, so I did a little research. Not too far from here, there are actually a few organizations that investigate such matters. Hold on, let me see if I kept any of the phone numbers in my book."

"Thank you, Reverend Miller." She waited on hold, silence on the other end. She could hear him stirring around, trying to locate the number.

"Here it is," he seemed relieved to have found the number. "Give this guy a call. His name is John Zaffis and he runs the Paranormal Research Society of New England. If you need anything else, feel free to call me. God bless."

She jotted down the number on an envelope, thanked him, and hung up the phone. She immediately called John.

"Is John Zaffis there, please?"

"No, he's not," the voice said. "Can I take a message? He's on his way over to the library in Ansonia to give a lecture at one in the afternoon."

"Alright," Samantha said with disappointment in her voice. She provided the friendly voice with her contact information and said her goodbyes.

"I know where that is," she thought. "Maybe I'll go to check it out and see if he can help me."

She got ready and took the keys to her car. She drove to the library and parked the car immediately. She was twenty minutes late after getting lost. She walked into the library, remaining quiet as not to draw any attention toward herself.

She looked up by the projector and saw the man giving the lecture. He was not at all what she expected. He had a striped sweater on and dark blue jeans. He was very engaging, letting the audience interact with questions. "He looks so normal," she thought to herself.

"This is picture of the destruction that a poltergeist may inflict on a family," John said while pointing up on to a large screen. The picture depicted large holes in the walls of a bedroom. People looked on with awe, each one conjuring up their own mental image of the situation that must have occurred in the home.

The lecture went on for about another hour. When it was over, John started to pack up his belongings. Samantha approached him slowly, nervous about asking him about what she should do.

"John?"

"Hi, what can I do for you?"

"Can I ask you a question about something?"

"Sure, go ahead."

"My name is Samantha Peterson." She told him about everything that had been occurring, incorporating every possible detail she felt was relevant. When she was done relaying her tale, he agreed to call her and set up a time to meet for the following day. After going home and clearing his schedule, he agreed to come over at two the following afternoon.

After arriving at the house and being given a tour of the home and a look at the doll, he sat down and turned on a tape recorder. He asked several questions that might pertain to the trouble at hand. They spoke for about an hour about the doll, her past, her beliefs, and other relevant information. He also spoke with Kevin.

J: Did all of the scratches occur after you received the doll or were there any type of experiences before you bought it? Also, where did you get the doll?

S: I got it over at a tag sale not far from here. I saw a bunch of items outside and figured I'd stop to see what they had. When I saw the doll, I had to have it. It was so unique. I've collected rare dolls for years and had never obtained one that looked like this one. It was only six dollars because of the burn marks. The family was cleaning out their attic and found the doll a few weeks previous to my buying the doll. Evidently it was there when they moved into the house. They decided to try to sell it with all the other old items from the attic as well as some of their personal belongings.

I paid the woman and brought the doll home and put it in my room so I could try restoring it the following day. That night, I was evidently scratched several times even though I didn't recall any of it. When I woke up the following morning, the scratches were there. Just ask my husband.

J: You saw these scratches, Kevin?

K: Yes John, I did. I thought that they were peculiar. There were just so many scratches on the lower part of her legs and ankles, and I never heard her scratch the previous night or felt any commotion in the bed. If she was scratching that much, I'm sure I would've noticed. Also, we have no animals except for fish, so there is no way a cat or even a dog caused the scratches.

J: This doll, was it kept in your room all night, Samantha?

S: Yes. I placed it on the cedar chest at the end of our bed. I left it there the entire first night. The next day, I started to restore the doll and placed it on the desk about four or five feet from the chest. It actually never left the room until the third night when I placed it on the kitchen counter. That night when the doll wasn't in the room, no new scratches appeared. The following night, the doll was put back in the room. When I awoke the next morning, I was shocked to find more scratches. That's when I decided to put it in the garage, away from the house.

J: Personally, I think we should try another experiment.

S: There's no way I'm putting that doll back in my room, no way.

J: No. Don't worry about that. I think you should bring it back to the original owners and inquire about it. Maybe they had experiences with it or at least can tell you some type of history pertaining to it. If they haven't had any experiences, maybe they'll take it back.

K: That's a great idea, John.

J: I don't think the doll is scratching you at all, Samantha. Usually with objects, there's something attached to it, something that identifies with it. The doll isn't rising during the night and scratching you, it is some type of spirit that is attached for reasons you and I both don't know.

John and the frightened couple agreed that this was the best option—to find out the doll's past.

After John left, Kevin and Samantha drove over to the home with the doll and rang the doorbell.

An older woman opened the door. "Can I help you?"

"My name is Samantha and this is my husband, Kevin. I bought a doll from you not that long ago."

"I remember you. Is something wrong?"

Samantha smiled at the woman, "You have no idea." She once again relayed the events, this time to the woman. The woman was shocked. It sounded so far-fetched, but at the same time, she could see the sincerity of these grown adults.

"We got the doll out of the attic while we were cleaning it out," the old woman told the both of them. "It was up in the rafters by itself. We removed it and put it in a box with the rest of some of the items we were going to sell. It wasn't mine nor was it my son's. It has probably been here a long time."

"Do you know anything about it or anything that might relate to it?" The woman went into elaborate detail about the house when Samantha was struck by something. She said, "Did you say that there was a fire here?"

"Yes, why?"

"Well, the doll had a burnt face. Did anything bad happen concerning the fire?"

"I know a little girl was severely burned and ended up passing on."

That was all that Samantha needed to hear. It seemed possible that the doll belonged to a girl, perhaps the girl who perished in the fire. The doll was burnt when she obtained it.

Kevin knew what his wife was thinking and intervened. "Mrs. Garvey, do you think we could put the doll back in the rafters?"

"Sure, I don't see the harm in that."

The two went upstairs with the old woman, who directed them to the area where the doll had been found. They placed it up in a cubbyhole and descended back down to the lower level of the home. They thanked her and left.

That was the last time they saw Mrs. Garvey and more importantly, the last time they saw the doll. That night and every night since, there were no more problems. Samantha called John after about a week and revealed that the plan worked, giving him all the information Mrs. Garvey had revealed to her and Kevin. John never heard back from Samantha, a good sign in the Work, usually meaning things are calm.

The Haunted Homestead

The Haunted Homestead

The town of Stratford, Connecticut, houses a tract of land with a deep, rich history. The Boothe Homestead, now entitled "Boothe Memorial Park," encompasses a full thirty-two acres filled with a unique landscape, inimitable architecture, and an even more irreplaceable history. Stratford was originally organized in 1639 and is the easternmost town in Fairfield County.

When one thinks of a historical homestead, thoughts of a farm with a large house and a barn often flood the imaginative mind. Boothe Memorial Park, however, takes the imagination to another level.

The original home dates back to 1663 and was built by Richard Boothe. Boothe was the first in his family to settle in Stratford and historical records suggest that Boothe was one of the first forty founding families of the township. The original foundation was built over in 1820 where the house stands today. Today, the upstairs of the house is a museum that is open to the public. The home, however, is not what makes the property a place for the deepest imagination to run untamed.

Many innovative structures were erected and maintained by both Steven and David Boothe. The brothers were often referred to as eccentrics and were not afraid to express their opinions in regards to town politics. They often criticized local township authorities for their ways, which they viewed as corrupt and unjust.

A clock tower set atop the old carriage house oversees the property from a bird's eye view. In the past, the clock displayed the incorrect time—because the Boothe's, in their own eyes, were unfairly taxed for the exquisite timepiece.

A cathedral was erected in 1933 and dedicated to the Great Depression. It was aptly entitled the "technocratic cathedral." The bizarre structure stands tall and is made of redwood, its flat timbers representing a style unusual in such a community.

Three large crosses stand on the lawn, steeping the onlooker with confusion. The brothers, David and Steven, were said to be heavily involved with different types of spiritual thought, and embraced and sampled many of the religions the world had to offer. They seemed to be intrigued by different schools of thought, specifically related to religion. For instance, the brothers hosted Easter sunrise services for quite some time. It is recorded that thousands of people from many different backgrounds, religious sects, and age groups attended the early morning event on the celebration of Jesus' resurrection, the essential truth of Christianity.

After criticism from many religious fanatics, the Boothe brothers decided to terminate the event with its last gathering in 1938.

A miniature lighthouse was also built on the property, even though the ocean is not within viewing distance. A tollbooth stands as a reminder of the old style stalls, reflective of major roadways in the state, mainly the Merrit Parkway. A diminutive windmill as well as a rose garden and blacksmith shop adds character to the premises.

One area that really stands out for visitors is the rock garden. After descending down a few steps, one ends up on a grassy plain, which houses a stone circle in the middle of the terrain. Around this circle are cement seating arrangements which stir the imagination into a state of clamor and curiosity. No one can really specify what the area was used for, but there are many theories. At the end of this area stands a large stone podium. It overlooks the basilica, bringing back the thought of sermons and preaching. At the foot of the podium are two large, thick steel hoops, presumably used to restrain living creatures, possibly humans.

"Today, Boothe Memorial Park serves as a place families can go to picnic and visit to view the wide array of buildings on this beautiful piece of property," John says. The large expanse of the park attracts many visitors. Sometimes when you go up there, it is impossible to find a parking space. Boothe Park is a unique tourist attraction for visitors and locals.

John discusses aspects of Boothe Park. "I've been up there several times over the years to visit the location. What really makes Boothe unique to me is my involvement with the psychic groups that met up in the main house on the property for a number of years. Initially, I thought it would be interesting to see what types of beliefs were out there and what types of individuals experienced these other territories of thinking. I was on several cases at this point, and knew that there was more out there in the world than what the eye could see and what falls into the realm of basic perception. I wanted to see if there were really those out there who were channeling, reading others, communicating with spirit guides, and experiencing things outside the basic human intellectual capacity. Well, after attending the classes at Boothe, I realized that there was a reality to many so-called psychic experiences. Even though all of this took place about fifteen years ago, I vividly recall the moving experiences I had at Boothe."

Bonnie Turmel is one of the individuals who took part in the psychic classes up at Boothe. She has a striking ability to pick up on spirit and spirit guides, and has a special connection to the supernatural realm. She spent many of her evenings at the site, experiencing much of what Boothe Memorial Park had to offer, not necessarily just physical or mental impressions Boothe leaves on visitors, but psychic impressions and experiences.

"Boothe is, to say the least, very interesting," states Bonnie. "There is so much in regards to spirit energy that resides there. I can remember many of my experiences up there when we would meet for the psychic meetings. As far as experiences with previous residents, I have experienced some of the phantoms that continue to occur. While I was outside gazing up into the home, I was a bit startled. I could definitely see the silhouette of a woman peering out of the attic down at everyone. She appeared to be keeping tabs on the goings on and was present, as visible as you or I. There was also the appearance or impression of an amber color light in the same window.

"Another interesting impression I can distinctly recall is the presence of what I believe to be old man Boothe. He would appear most of the time in the bathroom. In one instance, he came out of the bathroom and walked by the doorway and up the stairs. Such occurrences are certainly uncomfortable and really make you think deeply about your experiences. There was one man who refused to use the bathroom because he was so afraid of what was in there.

"When meditation practices were used I often had the feeling that we were not supposed to be there. I definitely had the desire to 'get out' on more than one occasion. Also, during the meetings, there would be frequent blackouts, bangings heard by all, and no matter how high the heat was turned up, it would always be cold in there. Our energy must have been used for the bangings and other occurrences to happen up there at Boothe. It really is a strange place where I do not really feel comfortable. There are so many mixed emotions tied in with Boothe. One night, the room would be used for a church function and the next for a psychic class. There were so many mixed practices and emotions in that place which must add to what is occurring there.

"Even to this day years later, I do not feel the need to go back there. If I have to pass by the property for any reason, I instinctively protect myself. I usually get severe headaches from the area, so I always envision myself in a white light when passing by Boothe. To me, the area is uncomfortable and has always been that way for me ever since I spent so much time up there.

"One of the situations that really stands out for me is when the teacher up there who conducted the meetings would actually take the spirit out of body. This is not really recommended because spirit lingering around could seize the opportunity to enter. This, however, was fascinating. One individual was up on the table and that particular person could actually astrally project themselves. I noticed that they were not breathing and let out a yell. She was immediately brought back. Seeing the breathing process stop really frightened me, plus in the back of my mind, I couldn't help but think that there was an ample opportunity for something else to use this chance to enter her."

"By astrally projecting, this woman would actually leave her body, her conscious state elsewhere," states John. "The teacher would help willing individuals leave their physical body behind, while removing their consciousness. Another aspect that was also very interesting to watch was a process called transfiguration. The person who volunteered was placed under a red light and basically channeled in spirit. I could never take part in this procedure, but I watched. This really is scary because spirit is allowed to be channeled into the person. When this actually worked in several instances, you could see the people actually change, their physical formations morphing into that spirit which was channeled in. I never really heard of such a thing until I observed it up at Boothe."

"I never," John continues, "saw a physical apparition during these meetings, but certainly experienced many other actions of the spirits that were around. As Bonnie mentioned before in regards to the heat, it didn't matter if it was hot or cold outside, or if the heat was turned on in the building. During the meetings, it was always cold. Heat can be used as a mechanism to create or manifestation, and I'm sure that was part of the issue up there at Boothe."

"Another strange occurrence," John continues, "was the ring of an old antique phone that was not in service. Many old-fashioned items are located on the premises because there is a museum on-site. During one of the sessions, this inoperable phone started to ring uncontrollably. It blew my mind that this could even happen. Also, the old grandfather clock would chime although that was also inoperable."

Joanne Mekdeci also attended these classes at the former home of Richard Boothe. Joanne's abilities are undeniable in regards to psychometry and other aspects of an alternate ability many do not have or do not know how to use.

Psychometry is an ability to read individuals, their ambiance, the very state of their lives, and those around them in the form of spirit, based on the impression conveyed by an item that the medium is holding. Often, vivid pictures, emotions, colors, and various other psychic impressions will emanate as a result of holding an object closely related to the subject being read. Many times, a watch or other personal item will be used.

During the interview for this chapter, I had a chance to meet with Joanne in her home. She was showing me how psychometry actually works. She held my wallet and spoke of what she felt. It was during this interview that I received my first spirit voice on tape, commonly referred to as electronic voice phenomenon

(EVP). When I was going over the tapes, I heard it clearly. There was no one else present in the room besides Joanne, John, and myself.

"My time spent at Boothe Park was very informative," states Joanne. "It was probably the better part of fifteen years ago that I attended the psychic classes. I remember seeing the image of a girl and that of a grown man peering out of the main house on the property. I was never really frightened at Boothe Park, even when I saw such apparitions. The girl was probably about four-foot-eight inches tall, maybe between eight and ten years old. I had the impression that her hair had been arranged in long ringlets and she was dressed in clothing from an older time period. She seemed to like the company and watched many of the meetings that took place in the home.

"In regards to the spirit leaving the body, I was never really too scared. Most of what was around the Boothe Homestead was pretty benign, leaving me comfortable in the large billiard room where the classes were held. I did not feel that there would be any antagonistic interference by anything in the home.

"During meditation sessions, bangings and clicking would frequently occur. After I got deep enough into my meditation, these noises would be lost, almost foreign to me.

"At the point where transfiguration would take place, there would be an interesting change over those who took part in this elaborate process. Sitting under that red light, individuals allowed spirit to move in and out, something that is very interesting. I was never uncomfortable because of the nature of Boothe. This process is different from mediumship, which allows spirit to totally take over the human body. That can be extremely dangerous."

"The psychic aspects are very elaborate in how they come about," says John. "Extrasensory perception (ESP) encompasses a broad range of terms. Telepathy, or thought transference, is just part of the way the human perception is expanded. I truly believe some people really have this ability to pick up on and receive messages from the spirit world.

"Those who are psychically gifted do not always necessarily sit down and talk with spirits, so to speak. Instead, through thought transference, they are given images, colors, emotions, and the like to interpret what the message actually is. They are contacted by an alternate sense which they have as a gift or which they have developed. I have seen it with many individuals and cannot doubt its existence. Sometimes, these individuals have information that they could not know unless fed this information. Many ask that since spirit attracts spirit, could some of these messages be on a demonic level? Absolutely. Those with the ability often have encountered such beings. Often, they are in touch with spirit and can discern the nature of the spirit. Psychics need to be careful because they can run the risk of coming across such energies. A great deal of the time, they do not even have to try to communicate with any type of spirit; they can simply pick up on it when it is around, usually identifying its nature.

"Another ability on this level is sensing the human aura. I was able to learn a great deal about this over the years by working with those who can psychically see these energy zones. The aura appears as colors that emanate from the human body. Sometimes, it is large, encompassing the entire head, while other times it might be just a small tinge apparent in a particular area. Different colors represent the current state or emotional state which is emanating from a particular person. Those who are psychically gifted can often tell who is and isn't sensitive to the spirit world simply by analyzing their aura. The hues, spikes, and appearance of colors can help determine the mindset, spiritual strength, and physical condition of an individual.

"As far as psychokinesis goes, this is most notably the movement of objects and the like. This can be caused by mental concentration by those who have extended abilities, but in my experience, most of the time, an outside force moves the objects. The mental movement of objects usually encompasses the movement of very small objects. Demonic entities can move larger materials, and the higher up on the scale, the heavier the object that can be moved.

"One question that I have been asked frequently is whether or not out-of-body experiences (OBE) exist. I feel that they can and do occur. Is every reported case indicative of an out-of-body experience? Definitely not. I feel that some I have encountered have, however, had a moving experience where they were actually separated from the vehicle of the human body. Usually, those who have such an experience become deeply religious or have a whole new outlook on life. I have never had such an experience, but there are too many credible reports to dismiss out-of-body experiences as a myth.

"The psychic experience is one that puzzles many, brings up thoughts which question conservative thinking, and completely turns heads around. Many have had a psychic experience and many law enforcement agencies and universities use or fund such aspects of human perception. This other sense is present in many who have been given this indispensable and unique gift."

This text is by no means written as an entertainment piece, nor is it meant to declare a sound doctrine. Instead it is a justification, an explanation of the fact that supernatural and preternatural activity, no matter what its origin, undoubtedly exists. Whether a product of the mind, a parallel existence, or a source that lies beneath our tangible senses, no one can dispute that these "things" do not exist. The problem that lies is in the context of the "source" or in "origin" of the paranormal existence.

Different schools recognize different means for the existence of the supernatural. I do not necessarily take a strict scientific view, a strict religious, or even a strict psychological viewpoint. Evidence will lead to the cause and therefore the method or approach needed for coping with the situation at hand. Instead, I tend to incorporate various schools of thought which directly apply to the specific case.

One circumstance may be linked to depression, posttraumatic stress, repressed memories, or any relevant psychiatric diagnosis. Such cases are referred to the proper mental health specialists. If there are no psychic phenomena, then cases are referred to the correct bodies of study which may help the individual or family such as the mainstream medical field. The same is true of natural, environmental phenomena or causations. These reports are weeded out so the clients can rest assured that the problem is not supernatural or preternatural.

Another may warrant checking into an intense psychic awareness in a particular client where they are simply "more attuned" than the average person. Others are full-on demonic assaults caused by inhuman, intelligent entities. These are not the pitchfork-bearing creations of mythical art, but instead a negative consciousness that afflicts some physical environments as well as individuals by either external sources or occasionally the internal mechanisms through possession or obsession. The demonic exists, but modern society has turned the idea of such energies into a sensational, Hollywood-style and incorrect notion.

You cannot categorize the supernatural or preternatural into one specific category. Each case is different and needs special attention based on the facts it puts forth. Each case is clearly unique and different approaches are taken to resolve or come to an understanding based on the facts presented through intense research.

For those who are looking for help, it is available and always has been by dedicated researchers and underground clergy who stand up for the truth.

Brian McIntyre

For further information and more case studies, contact John Zaffis at:

On the web: www.prsne.com or www.johnzaffis.com

Postal address:

John Zaffis
93 Emerson Drive 06614
Stratford, CT

Phone: (203) 375-6083

0-595-32509-2

CPSIA information can be obtained at www.ICGtesting.com
Printed in the USA
BVOW04s0558171014

371146BV00002B/5/P